DOES PUTIN HAVE TO DIE?

THE STORY OF HOW RUSSIA BECOMES A DEMOCRACY AFTER LOSING TO UKRAINE

ILYA PONOMAREV
MEMBER OF RUSSIAN PARLIAMENT, 2007–2016

with GREGG STEBBEN

FOREWORD:
VLADIMIR PUTIN'S BROKEN PROMISE OF DEMOCRACY

Skyhorse Publishing

Skyhorse Publishing books may be purchased in bulk at special discounts for sales promotion, corporate gifts, fund-raising, or educational purposes. Special editions can also be created to specifications. For details, contact the Special Sales Department, Skyhorse Publishing, 307 West 36th Street, 11th Floor, New York, NY 10018 or info@skyhorsepublishing.com.

Skyhorse® and Skyhorse Publishing® are registered trademarks of Skyhorse Publishing, Inc.®, a Delaware corporation.

Visit our website at www.skyhorsepublishing.com.

10 9 8 7 6 5 4 3 2 1

Library of Congress Cataloging-in-Publication Data is available on file.

Print ISBN: 978-1-5107-7590-9
eBook ISBN: 978-1-5107-7591-6

Cover design by Brian Peterson

Printed in the United States of America

Contents

Publisher's Note

The authors have made every effort to provide accurate information and rely on authoritative sources. However, as noted in the text, the special circumstances dictated by Putin's invasion of Ukraine required the authors to quickly translate large portions of this book from Russian into English; with some names, titles, and quotes affected by that rapid translation. The opinions expressed in the book are those of the authors and not necessarily those of the publisher. We believe strongly in the most robust dialogue and debate.

Foreword: Vladimir Putin's Broken Promise of Democracy

Author's note:
The following is the transcript of a speech that Vladimir Putin gave, in German, to members of the Bundestag of the Federal Republic of Germany on September 25, 2001 about his vision for a democratic Russia.

Once you read it, you are probably going to ask yourself, "Is the guy who gave this speech in 2001 really the same Vladimir Putin?"

And then you would be correct to next ask yourself, "If the guy who gave this speech just two weeks after 9/11 could turn into a dictator over the span of the next 20 years, is there anyone in Russia who is capable of turning the country into a democracy without turning into a tyrant or dictator, instead?"

Both are questions of the greatest importance; that's why, throughout this book, I address issues like these and many others that are closely related. And then, in the last chapter, which is an FAQ, I wrap things up by dissecting these two questions specifically.

Bundestag of the Federal Republic of Germany
September 25, 2001, Berlin
President Vladimir Putin

Distinguished Mr. President,

Distinguished ladies and gentlemen,

I am sincerely grateful for this opportunity to speak in the Bundestag. This is the first such opportunity for a Russian head of state in the entire history of Russian-German relations. And this honor granted to me today only reaffirms the mutual interest of Russia and Germany in dialogue.

I am moved by this chance to discuss Russian-German relations, the development of ties between my country and united Europe and international security problems here, in Berlin, a city with a difficult fate, a city which happened to become the focus of confrontation with almost the entire world on more than one occasion in the modern history of humanity, but also a city in which never, even in the darkest periods, did anyone succeed in stifling the spirit of freedom and humanism that had been nurtured way back by Wilhelm von Humboldt and Lessing.

Nor was that done in the grim years of Hitler tyranny. Our country deeply reveres the memory of heroic anti-Nazi fighters.

Russia has always had special sentiments for Germany, and regarded your country as one of the major centers of European culture—a culture, to the development of which Russia has also made a significant contribution, a culture which has known no borders and has always been our common asset and a factor of bringing peoples together.

That is why today I will take the liberty of delivering the main part of my message in the language of Goethe, Schiller, and Kant, in the German language.

(Follows translation from the German.)

Distinguished ladies and gentlemen,

I have just talked about the unity of European culture. However, in the past that unity did not prevent two horrible wars from being unleashed on the continent, two world wars within one century. Nor did it prevent the building of the Berlin Wall, the formidable symbol of the deep division of Europe.

The Berlin Wall is no longer. It was destroyed. And today it would be relevant to recall why that became possible.

It is my conviction that the dramatic change in the world, in Europe and on the expanses of the former Soviet Union would have been impossible without the main preconditions, namely, without the events that took place in Russia ten years ago. These events are important to understanding what precisely took place in our country and what could be expected from Russia in the future.

The answer is simple, as a matter of fact.

Under the impact of the laws governing the development of information society, Stalinist totalitarian ideology could no longer oppose the ideas of freedom and democracy. The spirit of these ideas was taking hold of the overwhelming majority of Russian citizens.

It was the political choice of the people of Russia that enabled the then leaders of the USSR to take decisions that eventually led to the razing of the Berlin Wall. It was that choice that infinitely broadened the boundaries of European humanism and that enables us to say that no one will ever be able to return Russia back into the past.

As for European integration, we not just support these processes, but we are looking to them with hope. We view them as a people who have learned the lesson of the Cold War and the peril of the ideology of occupation very well. But here, I think, it would be pertinent to add that Europe did not gain from that division either.

It is my firm conviction that in today's rapidly changing world, in a world witnessing truly dramatic demographic changes and an exceptionally high economic growth in some regions, Europe also has an immediate interest in promoting relations with Russia.

No one calls in question the great value of Europe's relations with the United States. I am just of the opinion that Europe will reinforce its reputation of a strong and truly independent center of world politics soundly and for a long time if it succeeds in bringing together its own potential and that of Russia, including its human, territorial and natural resources and its economic, cultural and defense potential.

Together we have already taken the first steps in that direction. The time has now come to think about what should be done to make sure that a united and secure Europe becomes the harbinger of a united and secure world.

Distinguished ladies and gentlemen,

We have done a great deal in the security sphere over the past few years. The security system that we have built over the previous decades has been improved. One of the achievements of the past decade is the unprecedentedly low concentration of armed forces and armaments in Central Europe and the Baltic. Russia is a friendly European nation. Stable peace on the continent is a paramount goal for our country, which lived through a century of military catastrophes.

As everyone knows, we have ratified the Comprehensive Nuclear Tests Ban Treaty, the Nuclear Non-proliferation Treaty, the Biological Weapons Convention, and also the START-2 Treaty. Regrettably, not all the NATO countries have followed our example.

But once we, distinguished ladies and gentlemen, have started to discuss security, we should first and foremost understand from whom we are to defend ourselves, and how. In this context I cannot but mention the catastrophe in the United States on September 11. People the world over keep asking how that could have happened and who is to blame. I will give you answers to these questions.

I think we all are to blame for what happened, and first and foremost we, politicians, to whom the ordinary citizens of our nations have entrusted their security. And this happens first and foremost because we have so far failed to recognize the changes that have happened in our world over the past ten years and continue to live in the old system of values:

We are talking about partnership, but in reality, we have not yet learned to trust each other.

In spite of a plethora of sweet words, we are still surreptitiously opposed to each other. Now we demand loyalty to NATO, now argue about the rationale behind its enlargement. And we are still unable to agree on the problems of a missile defense system.

Over long decades of the 20th century the world was indeed living under conditions of confrontation between the two systems, confrontation that pushed humanity to the brink of annihilation on more than one occasion.

That was so fearsome, and we grew so accustomed to live with that anticipation of catastrophe that we are still unable to understand and appreciate the changes taking place in today's world. We seem to be missing the fact that the world is no longer divided into two hostile camps.

The world has become far more complex, distinguished ladies and gentlemen.

We do not want or are unable to understand that the security structure built over the previous decades that was effective in neutralizing former threats is no longer able to cope with new threats of today. Too often we continue to argue over issues which we think are still important. They probably still are.

But at the same time, we do not recognize new real threats and turn out to be unable to foresee terrorist attacks—and so ruthless terrorist attacks at that!

Hundreds of innocent civilians died in the bombing of residential houses in Moscow and other large Russian cities. Religious fanatics, having captured power in Chechnya and having turned ordinary citizens into their hostages, mounted a brazen large-scale armed attack against the neighboring Republic of Dagestan. International terrorists have openly—quite openly—declared their intention to establish a fundamentalist state on the territory between the Black and the Caspian Sea—the so-called khalifate, or the United States of Islam.

I would like to stress right away that talking about any "war between civilizations" is inadmissible. It would be a mistake to put the equation mark between Moslems in general and religious fanatics. In our country, for example, the defeat of the aggressors in 1999 was predetermined by the courageous and tough rebuff of the residents of Dagestan, a Russian republic the population of which is virtually 100 percent Moslem.

Shortly before my departure for Berlin I met with the religious leaders of Russia's Moslems. They came up with the initiative of convening an international conference on "Islam Against Terrorism" in Moscow. I think we should support this initiative.

Today we are coming up against not so much the aggravation of the well-known international problems as the rise of new threats. Russia is taking practical steps to put up, together with some CIS nations, a real barrier in the way of the traffic of drugs, organized crime and fundamentalism from

Afghanistan via Central Asia and the Caucasus into Europe. Terrorism, national intolerance, separatism, and religious extremism everywhere have the same roots and bear the same poisonous fruit. That is why the methods of fighting these problems should be universal as well.

But first agreement needs to be reached on the fundamental matter: we should not be afraid of calling a spade a spade. And it is extremely important to understand that evil deeds cannot be used to achieve political objectives, however noble such objectives may seem.

Naturally, evil must be punished, and I agree with that. But we should also understand that no retaliatory strikes will replace comprehensive, purposeful, and well-coordinated struggle against terrorism. I absolutely agree with the US President on that.

I think our partners' readiness to joint efforts in countering real rather than illusory threats will demonstrate how serious and reliable they are as partners. These threats are quite capable of spilling over from the distant frontiers of our continent to the very heart of Europe. I talked about that on more than one occasion, but after what happened in the US there is no need to prove anything.

But what are we lacking today for cooperation to be efficient?

In spite of all the positive achievements of the past decades, we have not yet developed an efficient mechanism for working together.

The coordinating agencies set up so far do not offer Russia real opportunities for taking part in drafting and taking decision. Today decisions are often taken, in principle, without our participation, and we are only urged afterwards to support such decisions. After that they talk again about loyalty to NATO. They even say that such decisions cannot be implemented without Russia. Let us ask ourselves: is this normal? Is this true partnership?

Yes, the assertion of democratic principles in international relations, the ability to find a correct decision and readiness for compromise are a difficult thing. But then, it was the Europeans who were the first to understand how important it is to look for consensus over and above national egoism. We agree with that! All these are good ideas. However, the quality of decisions that are taken, their efficiency and, ultimately, European and international security in general depend on the extent to which we succeed today in translating these obvious principles into practical politics.

It seemed just recently that a truly common home would shortly rise on the continent, a home in which the Europeans would not be divided into eastern or western, northern or southern. However, these divides will remain, primarily because we have never fully shed many of the Cold War stereotypes and cliches.

Today we must say once and for all: the Cold War is done with! We have entered a new stage of development. We understand that without a modern, sound, and sustainable security architecture we will never be able to create an atmosphere of trust on the continent, and without that atmosphere of trust there can be no united Greater Europe!

Today we must say that we renounce our stereotypes and ambitions and from now on will jointly work for the security of the people of Europe and the world as a whole.

Dear friends,

Today, thank God, Russia is talked about in Europe not only in the context of oligarchs, corruption, and Mafia. However, there still is a substantial lack of objective information about Russia.

I can say with absolute confidence that the key goal of Russia's domestic policy is first and foremost to ensure democratic rights and freedoms, decent living standards and safety for the people of the country.

However, distinguished colleagues, let us look back at some events of the recent past. Russia took the painful road of reform. The scope of the tasks we had to address is without parallel in history. Naturally, mistakes were made. Not all the problems have been resolved, but today Russia is a quite dynamic part of the European continent. Moreover, it is dynamic not only politically, but also economically, which is especially encouraging. Political stability in Russia is ensured by a number of economic factors, not the least by one of the world's most liberal taxation systems. Our income tax is 13% and profit tax 24%, and this is real. Last year our economic growth was 8%. This year we expected to get just 4%, but most likely we will have about 6%—say, 5.5–5.7%. We will wait and see.

At the same time my conviction is that only large-scale and equal pan-European cooperation will make it possible to achieve qualitative progress in resolving such problems as unemployment, environmental pollution, and many others.

We are set on close trade and economic cooperation. In the nearest future we intend to join the World Trade Organization. We count on international and European organizations' support for our bid.

I would like to draw your attention to things which you as members of parliament will undoubtedly be able to appreciate better and which cannot be dismissed as propaganda. As a matter of fact, our nation has gone through a revision of priorities and values.

Spending on social needs tops the 2002 consolidated budget. And I would like to stress specifically that for the first time in Russia's history spending on education has exceeded defense expenditures.

Ladies and gentlemen,

There are different pages in our history, some of them rather painful, especially those relating to the 20th century. But in the past, we often acted as allies.

Today's Germany is Russia's leading economic partner, our most important creditor, one of the principal investors and a key interlocutor in discussing international politics.

I will give you one example: last year trade between our countries hit an all-time record of 41.5 billion marks. This compares with the Soviet Union's aggregate trade with both German states. Can we be happy with this and sit back and relax? I don't think so. Russian-German cooperation still has sufficient potentialities for development.

I am convinced that today we are turning over a new page in our bilateral relations, thereby making our joint contribution to building a common European home.

In conclusion I would like to say the words that were once used to characterize Germany and its capital. I would like to apply this idea to Russia and say: of course, we are at the beginning of the road to building a democratic society and a market economy. There are barriers and obstacles on that road that we are to surmount. However, if we leave aside objective problems and occasional ineptness of our own, we will see the beat of Russia's strong, live heart. And this heart is open to true cooperation and partnership.

Transcript source: http://en.kremlin.ru/events/president/transcripts/21340

Prologue

One

A few years ago, when I was in Warsaw, I went into a church to listen to some organ music, but the organ was silent.

Instead, I found a group of women from Russia.

The USSR no longer existed, but they seemed to have been preserved in "Soviet brine."

Standing in front of the priest, smoothing their chemically enhanced curls with handkerchiefs, they listened, reverently holding wax candles at their voluminous stomachs, as he listed the virtues a Christian can acquire.

"Moderation (temperantia), humility (humilitas), kindness (humanitas), prudence (prudentia) . . . " he called.

On the fifth virtue, the priest stumbled—perhaps he forgot the Russian word.

"Suffering! Suffering!" the ladies yelled at him, as if to punish him for his abject failure.

The priest, stunned at the reaction of the Russian women, exclaimed, "What is it with you Russians that you must always see suffering as a virtue?"

Two

If you ask the average American or European when the Russian war against Ukraine began, they will tell you it all started on February 24, 2022.

If you ask the same question of an average Ukrainian, they will tell you the war began in February 2014 when Russia invaded Crimea.

I started writing this book two years before the invasion of Crimea, in 2012. However, my war with the Russian system started a long time ago. I thought we had defeated it in 1991, but by 1993, I realized something was wrong. I hoped for some change in 2000 after Yeltsin was gone, but my illusions evaporated very quickly. So, my political fight began in 2002, and I have never stopped.

What you are holding in your hands now draws heavily from a seven-hundred-page book I originally wrote in Russian, for Russians. The original text was my attempt to convince my fellow Russians that we could put an end to many centuries of Russian suffering together. I attempted to convince my fellow Russians that we could, together, take control of the future of Russia and make it one that glorified us, the Russian people, instead of our human suffering.

Three

Obviously, the book you are holding in your hands is not seven hundred pages in length, and it is most certainly not written in Russian.

However, if you get the sense that what you are reading has a slight (or even strong) Russian accent in some parts of the book, you can understand why.

When we started work on this English-language text, we set our goal to find a balance between a) pushing to publish the book as quickly as possible because of Russia's 2022 invasion of Ukraine, and relying heavily on Google Translate to quickly facilitate condensing seven hundred pages in Russian to about three hundred pages in English, b) retaining my authentic native voice, and c) ensuring all the concepts contained here are made clear for you, an English-speaking reader in the West. My coauthor, Gregg Stebben, has jokingly (I think) said that part of his job has been to apply a process of de-Russification to some parts of my original book.

Anyone who knows me knows how much I love and admire the writing of John Steinbeck. In fact, much of my travel in the United States has been to try to locate sites that Steinbeck wrote about in his novels. I know all of California's Central Valley for this reason—here was the communist strike in *Of Mice and Men*, here in Monterey, you'll find echos of his *Cannery Row*, and here stood the used-car lots from *The Grapes of Wrath* . . .

By the way, did you know that just after the Iron Curtain came down on Eastern Europe, Steinbeck and acclaimed war photographer Robert Capa traveled to the Soviet Union (including visits to Kyiv and the rest of Ukraine) to report for the New York *Herald Tribune*? The 1948 book that followed is called *A Russian Journal*. I highly recommend it.

One passage that I find both particularly chilling and relevant today:

> *If the United States were completely destroyed from New York to Kansas, we would have about the area of destruction the Ukraine has. If six million people were killed, not counting soldiers, fifteen per cent of the population, you would have an idea of the casualties of the Ukraine. Counting soldiers, there would be many more, but six million out of forty-five million civilians have been killed. There are mines which never opened because the Germans threw thousands of bodies down into the shafts.*

One reason I bring up my hero Steinbeck here is that, in my heart of hearts, I would love for you to read my entire seven-hundred-page book someday after it has been painstakingly translated into English and perhaps respond to it by saying, "Ponomarev! It's like he's a Russian Steinbeck!"

I realize that's one hell of a tall order. Carefully crafted over ten years, my original work takes as much time as needed to celebrate language and ideas as Steinbeck celebrated in his books. The book in your hands is a different beast; it has been written and edited with urgency during a time of war. The ideas are important, but there's no time to finely craft the language. Could we have spent a few more months focusing on the translation from Russian to English? Of course, but now is not the time for that. Instead, my goal is to inspire you into action with the ideas and plan contained here, despite my sometimes imperfect command of the language. As we all know, in Ukraine and Russia, time is of the essence.

Another American writer I will invoke here is the Nobel Prize–winning physicist Richard Feynman. To be honest, he is so much more than a writer and even so much more than a recipient of the Nobel Prize. For instance, he was a fierce advocate for using the scientific method to separate fact from fiction, and by applying the scientific method he was the guy who figured out why the American Space Shuttle *Challenger* exploded. Then when he tried to reveal the truth about the shuttle as a member of the congressional committee tasked by President Ronald Reagan to determine the cause of the accident, other members of the committee tried to prevent him from exposing his findings. But on live TV, despite the efforts to stop him, he explained to the commission and the world why the *Challenger* disaster occurred.

Yes, on the one hand, he was a brilliant scientist. I knew of him, as a boy and then college student because, as you will learn here, I am a trained physicist myself. But unlike many scientists, he was also filled with curiosity about the world far beyond science and physics. He loved interacting with people, and he had an amazing sense of humor and energy. He was an artist (he loved to go to his local strip joint and draw nudes) and traveled the world performing as a drummer. And he was famous among his friends for his practical jokes.

Although I never met him, I imagine that spending a day with him would be more like spending a day with comedian Robin Williams, rather than Albert Einstein. Speaking of Einstein, the two physicists are often considered by others in the field as the two greatest of the twentieth century, with many putting Feynman at #1 and Einstein at #2.

Feynman's star power led to him being immortalized in an Apple "Think Different" ad, a one-man show starring actor Alan Alda as Feynman, and a film starring Matthew Broderick as Feynman. And just coincidentally, my coauthor here, Gregg Stebben, wrote and performed his own one-man show about Feynman many years before Alan Alda and Matthew Broderick discovered him.

But my point here is about Feynman's two autobiographies, called *Surely, You're Joking, Mr. Feynman* and *What Do You Care What Other People Think?* One of the first things you notice as you begin reading these books is that the way Feynman writes is . . . different. It's like he's talking to you, and he has a very strong accent from Queens, New York. His accent was so pronounced it's part of his Wikipedia entry:

As an adult he spoke with a New York accent strong enough to be perceived as an affectation or exaggeration, so much so that his friends Wolfgang Pauli and Hans Bethe once commented that Feynman spoke like a "bum."

I bring up Feynman here for two reasons: One is, the man has had a tremendous impact on my life, and I am excited to share him with you in case you've never heard of him. But I also bring him up because, when you read his two autobiographies, you have to allow yourself to become accustomed to his different way of speaking in the books. He had a strong accent, both when speaking and writing. So do I. And I hope you will look past that and look deeper at my message about this plan for democracy for Russia.

Much of what you'll read here was penned long before the 2022 Russian invasion of Ukraine. However, it's interesting to note how much of what I wrote before the invasion is even more relevant now.

My point is, just as Ukrainians understand that the Russian war against Ukraine began in 2014, you will want to continue reading with the understanding that Russia's problems did not start with Putin; they've just been deliberately magnified and exacerbated by him.

This may lead you to ask, "Does Putin have to die?"

Of course, what you are really asking is, "Is it possible for Russia to become a democracy while Putin is still alive?"

One of my jobs here is to make it possible for you to answer that for yourself by the time you get to the end of this book.

Four

I have written quite a few articles, blogs, and social media posts and given many interviews. In them, I always try to address those who are watching, listening, or reading as my family.

When I wrote my original seven-hundred-page book in Russian, I chose the title *For My Family* because at home, with your family, you don't strain, looking for the right words. Instead, you say things straight as they are. Or, as Jean-Jacques Rousseau said, "My job is to tell the truth, not to make you believe it."

Even with this shorter, English version of the book, I hope I can address you as my family because even though you are not part of my immediate Russian family, you still are my global relatives.

I worked in the oil and gas industry, building, among other things, automation and communication systems. Then I drove through Russia, through Western Siberia, and I realized, here they are, telecommunication towers that I played a role in helping to erect. I know that a number of Russian oil companies, pumping our common wealth from the bowels of the earth, are working on the fields that I developed and put into operation. The Internet resources that I helped to create are read by millions of people. The laws I wrote and collaborated on affect the lives of these individuals and millions of others. And here are the buildings and offices of several hundred Russian companies that stayed in Russia and did not leave for the West because I helped convince leaders to stay. However, this is not enough. I can do more. Others can do more. You can, or could, do more—if we arrange life differently.

Many people feel they could do better if their current circumstances didn't hinder them.

And then they ask me, accusatorily: "Why were you born in a good family? Why did you become the youngest vice president of the largest Russian industrial company? Why did you get elected to the State Duma? Why did you get all those advantages, but nothing you did ever changed our lives? You run to rallies, appear on television, call for something, want to lead somewhere, and they call you an oppositionist, but why do our lives keep getting worse? And now you've left the country altogether and live outside your homeland."

Yes, all of this is true. I have addressed every point many times without making a single excuse. I have often explained why I have said what I've said and done what I've done.

Five

When I was a child, I lived with my grandparents in Poland. It was there that my grandmother, Lyubov Nikitichna, taught me a lesson that I will remember forever.

Like many children, I loved to draw pictures of war: fascist tanks on fire, our planes with red stars, running soldiers firing machine guns at the Fritz.

But how can you draw an enemy tank without a swastika?

So, I drew it—a whole sheet filled with fascist "Tigers" and "Panthers" on fire.

Proudly, I showed my drawing to my grandmother, expecting praise, but I was in for a big surprise!

My grandmother did not praise me. On the contrary, she fiercely scolded me, which was a rare thing in our family:

"What are you doing?" She reacted sharply, looking astonished and alarmed, and even angry.

"What? What? What did I do?" I was stunned and frightened by her response.

"How dare you draw this?"

"Why? What?"

"You are the son of a Soviet scientist. Grandson of a diplomat of the USSR! We are at the forefront here, and you are the face of the country! You have no right to draw a swastika!"

I was just a little boy. I did not understand what the swastika meant, and why it was so upsetting for her to see drawings with it by my hand in her house. However, I realized the importance of being the face of my country, and I was proud of it, even at that young age.

For her, it was essential to explain to me that the Nazi swastika would symbolize the merciless enemy of our Motherland—fascism—forever.

Every year on May 9, our family met to celebrate Victory Day, the day we Russians declared victory over Nazism in World War II. Then, all my relatives gathered around the TV to participate in a national minute of silence. These sixty seconds of silence every year reminded me not just about the horror of war but about responsibility. As I grew up, this sense of responsibility to stand for our people's and country's future deepened within me—a future without wars and without the superiority of one human being over another, which is up to all of us.

Six

I am a Russian man. I was Deputy of the State Duma from Siberia from 2007 to 2016, in the era of "developed Putinism." Now I live in Kyiv, outside my Russian homeland. Yet even from Ukraine, I still participate in Russian politics.

I am usually called an oppositionist, although I hate this word. An oppositionist is someone who is always *against* something. I'm not *against* something; I'm *for* something else. However, I'm not *for* the little benefits—and not-so-little pleasures—that those who call themselves the "elite" are for. I am for the development of the new, not for mere redistribution of the old. I am for something that has never been, and still is not.

You will hear much more about this as you read on, including what I call "the *new class* of Russians" that will make a new post-Putin Russia achievable, vibrant, and prosperous for all who participate. It's time to re-create our country and reclaim it for the people. We must make it a country where we want to live and where we can thrive, instead of a country from where so many suffer and so many flee.

Seven

Once, while I was being interviewed on the radio, I was asked, "Have you met happy people? And if so, where are these people, and why are they happy?"

Although I was on live radio at the time, I really had to think about that. Have I met *happy* people? What are the hallmarks of *happy* people?

Of course, we've all met people making careers, raising kids, making money, going to the beach or the mountains on the weekends, and having good dinners during the week.

But are they *happy*?

Then I realized:

Yes, I have seen happy people whose eyes burn with some goal or idea.

It's not easy to have a goal. Most people live without a purpose. They get used to their circumstances, whatever they may be, and just try to minimize the pain.

But is the avoidance of suffering the same as being *happy*?

That's when I realized the importance of having purpose in life. Especially one for which you would even sacrifice your life. To find that purpose is the most interesting quest you may ever have.

In search of my purpose, I set smaller milestones at different stages. I don't know if those small goals will eventually lead me to my main goal or not, but as I achieved them, the main goal has taken shape more and more clearly.

So, here is my main goal in life—and for this book:

I want to implement the Big Project: build a team that, like the U.S. founding fathers, will redesign Russia for all Russians. We will inspire the nation with the Idea and lead the passionate ones who can implement it.

I already know many who can and want to do it, and soon I will get to know many more.

The war in Ukraine is awakening the most capable circles of Russian society, who have been mere observers for way too long. This book is addressed to them—my future comrades-in-arms, in Russia and worldwide. Maybe you will become one of them?

Part One: Some Personal History

CHAPTER ONE

Putin and Me

One

Imagine Putin's death.

It doesn't matter from what: coronavirus, a brick falls on his head, or now, during his unsuccessful war in Ukraine, he takes a bullet in the head from an insider. Perhaps there's a rope involved.

In Russia, this death immediately causes a huge imperious backlash—*emptiness*.

This instantly leads to a conflict between rival power clans. Names are not so important now, Sechin, Kovalchuk, Chemezov, or others.

After so many years of stagnation in Russia, many ambitious, influential, and wealthy people gave up on the possibility of changing things and now just go with the flow. However, they still have sharp teeth and a lot to lose. So when they see real danger for their lives and properties, they will immediately dive in with their best political game.

Regionalization of clans is possible, leading to the disintegration of the country. Other scenarios are possible. In any case, there would be several competing centers of power. Each will need their own radicals, an infantry, to fight each other.

There is a point of view that if there were several such centers of power in Russia with approximately equal resources, there would automatically be a democracy with fair elections, rotation of power, freedom of the press and speech, and an independent court.

But there is another opinion, this time from Putinists, that this situation is fraught only with blood, chaos, and collapse.

I cannot more strongly disagree with the last two points in particular. The former means the reinstatement of oligarchy, literally the return to the Yeltsin era. I am sure it will inspire no one in Russia. (Well, almost no one.)

The latter is the outcome that may become the reality: when the new leadership would not know where to go and could not lead. Will have no vision, no ideas, no inner strength.

This book contains a third vision held by myself and my comrades. Our transparency is the guarantee that chaos will not erupt. Instead, bloodshed could be largely limited to Putin and his minions, who, like horror movie vampires, have been sucking the very lifeblood from ordinary Russians since 1991. They should be terminated with an aspen stake through their hearts. Or a silver bullet. Or a rope.

Two

I must admit it: When it was time to pull the trigger, my finger shook.

I did not know at the time, of course, that I would be the only member of the State Duma to vote against Putin's annexation of Crimea in 2014.

I didn't know that it would be a moment that would cause tremendous change and upheaval both in my life and in the world. At that moment, my shaking finger was firing just the first bullet into the regime, not knowing what the future would bring but still fully aware that we would have to fire far, far more bullets in the upcoming war—including that final silver one, which is yet to come.

It was Putin himself who convinced me to do it.

It happened just a few days earlier. There had been a big assembly in the Kremlin for members of Parliament like myself and the governors, with Putin giving a famous speech about Russia's successful annexation of Crimea that was full of terms like "national traitors" and "fifth column."

As you probably know, the first person to introduce the phrase "national traitors" into the political vocabulary was Adolf Hilter in *Mein Kampf.*

Putin's words were, apparently, quite stirring for everyone (except me) in the St. George Hall of the Grand Kremlin Palace, because everyone (except me) jumped to their feet cheering, and chanting, "Hail to the Chief."

I remained seated. As I looked about the rest of the erupting crowd, I thought to myself, "Somebody needs to be against this."

Then there was a personal escalation fired directly at me. While I remained in my seat, some of Putin's propaganda people photographed me in my chair and released the photo to the media the next day with the shameful and damning (and untrue) claim that I had refused to rise during the national anthem. Later, they put some giant banners on the streets of Russian cities with my picture on them, along with Boris Nemtsov, Alexei Navalny, and others. "National Traitors"—that's what they said. Some went beyond it: "Aliens among us," featuring the monster from the famous movie of the same name.

Here I am, on the lower right, with Boris Nemtsov (center), Alexei Navalny (upper right), and musicians Yuri Shevchuk (upper left) and Andrei Makarevitch (lower left). The banner reads, "Fifth column. There are aliens among us." *(Photo credit: Ilya Ponomarev)*

This, of course, was not true. We were not aliens. They were. It does not matter, however. This was what they did, and it was what they said, and for me it was the last straw.

Three

So, who was I to oppose Vladimir Putin? And why did I do it?

As you know from the cover of this book, my name is Ilya Vladimirovich Ponomarev. I was a member of the Russian State Duma from 2007 to 2016. And as you now know, I was the only member of the Russian Parliament to vote against the annexation of Crimea in 2014.

It was my vote against the annexation of Crimea that led to me being forced into exile from my own country while I was a sitting member of Parliament.

Now, in 2022, looking back on my lone vote on Crimea in 2014, it becomes easier to understand why I had become such a threat to Vladimir Putin because:

**At the time of the annexation of Crimea,
I predicted it would lead to a full-scale military conflict between
Ukraine and Russia.**

I also vowed at the time of the annexation that if Putin would invade, I would fight alongside Ukrainians against his troops. That's what I am doing now, not only by publishing this book but also by creating, in collaboration with Ukraine's Territorial Defence Forces, an uncensored, on-demand news channel in Russian for Russians called "February Morning," with a team of 100 people who broadcast live from the heart of Kyiv and even (underground) from inside Russia, giving Russians a way to get news about their country unfiltered by Putin's propaganda machine. And finally, and most importantly, by mounting up resistance in Russia, committed to fighting until Putinism is destroyed, along with its leaders and lackeys.

And what the hell, here are a few other facts from my life:

I was born in Moscow. My first job, at age fourteen, was with the Institute for Nuclear Safety at the Russian Academy of Sciences; this is where my father worked. I started my first successful tech start-up while in high school, at age sixteen.

At age twenty-one, I was working as a director of business

development in the CIS (or Commonwealth of Independent States) countries for Schlumberger, the world's largest provider of technology and services for the oil and gas industry.

At age twenty-four, I was the Vice President of Technologies at Yukos E&P, the leader of the Russian oil and gas industry.

At age twenty-seven, I left Yukos and got involved with several new entrepreneurial ventures, including a company called Arrava that offered interactive TV. Ted Turner from CNN was flying to Moscow in his jet to become our main investor at Arrava when Putin began his final crackdown on Russia's NTV in 2001. Ted volunteered to mediate in resolving the crisis, was rejected, and went home without making an investment. At that very moment, I swore that I would do everything I could to prevent the state from interfering again in my affairs or anyone else's, and my career in politics was born.

At age thirty-one, I became the Director of Russia's High Technology Parks Task Force for the Ministry of Information Technology and Telecommunications. We successfully covered Russia with a network of technology parks aimed at fostering innovation, bringing our most talented entrepreneurs back home, and supporting an emerging economy.

At age thirty-two, I was elected to the State Duma and became the chairman of the Innovation and Venture Capital Subcommittee of the Committee for Economic Development and Entrepreneurship—the leading technology policymaker for the Russian state.

I was thirty-nine when I voted against the annexation of Crimea.

Four

You may be asking yourself, "If his vote on the annexation of Crimea in 2014 was so life-altering, how did he manage to remain part of the State Duma until 2016?"

This is a very good question. What you have to understand is, from 2014, shortly after the vote on Crimea, and until I was removed from the State Duma in 2016 against my will—you should know that they had to pass a special law for removing me, a law that directly violates the Constitution—I was fulfilling my duties as a member of the Russian Parliament in exile. I was acting from outside the borders of my country because I was not allowed to cross the Russian border and go home.

To make it possible to continue voting as a Deputy, I worked with friends to smuggle my voting card back into Russia, and my friend and fellow parliamentarian Dmitry Gudkov was pulling the trigger to vote for me, while I was communicating to my constituents in Siberia via social media.

Of course, my vote on Crimea was not the first time that I opposed Putin. I was already a well-known radical, a Putin oppositionist. In fact, I was very much part of Russia's opposition movement from 2001, after the Russian president decided openly to destroy freedom of speech in my country. Since then, I have been a leader at the center of most protest activities where left-wing activists took part (and leftists were always way more active and more radical than other opposition groups).

It was not the first time a member of my family opposed Russian leadership, either. In 1981, my grandfather Nikolai Ponomarev was serving as the Russian ambassador to Poland, and he is credited with conspiring with the Solidarność movement and Polish leadership to ensure that the Kremlin did not invade the country, which is what happened in Czechoslovakia in 1968. This was a move that ultimately cost my grandfather his career.

My mother, Larisa Ponomareva, was a member of the Federation Council, or Russia's Senate—the upper house of Parliament—until she opposed Putin twice, first by casting the lone vote in the upper house against the new oppressive anti-opposition laws in 2012 (we, with the same Dmitry Gudkov who helped me vote while in exile, organized a filibuster in the Duma at that time, which is still the only such case in Russia's parliamentary history). Later my mother stood in the upper house against the Dima Yakovlev Law, which is also called the Anti-Magnitsky Act, while I was the lone vote against it at the first reading of the law in the lower house. By the time of the final reading of the law, seven other deputies of the lower house joined me in opposition.

If you are not familiar with the Magnitsky Act, which is now a global movement that started in the United States, or with Russia's retaliatory Anti-Magnitsky Act, I recommend my friend Bill Browder's best-selling books *Red Notice* and *Freezing Order* for follow-up reading; they are definitely worth your time.

The Magnitsky Act is named after Sergei Magnitsky, a Russian lawyer and accountant who worked for Browder (ironically, grandson of one of the founders of the United States's Communist Party). Magnitsky was tortured and murdered in a Moscow prison after he discovered and brought attention to a $230 million dollar theft from the Russian government that was carried out and covered up by government officials.

Yes, you read that right: Sergei Magnitsky was tortured and murdered by Russian law enforcement officers in a Russian state prison for being a whistleblower and calling attention to a $230 million dollars heist *from* the Russian government that was pulled off *by* Russian officials.

I hope this helps you begin to better understand how things often work inside Vladimir Putin's Russia.

Five

The U.S. Magnitsky Act sanctions foreign government officials worldwide who are deemed to be human rights offenders and freezes their assets. It also bans them from entering the United States and other nations that have now made the Magnitsky Act law, including Canada, Australia, the United Kingdom, and the European Union.

For Vladimir Putin, the U.S. and global Magnitsky Acts have been devastating.

Not, however, because the laws exposed the brutality and lack of justice within his regime.

No, the laws are devastating because of their impact on the invincibility of dirty Russian elites—and, therefore, the wealth of Vladimir Putin.

And when you hurt Vladimir Putin, or anyone inside his web of power and corruption, they're going to hurt you back.

Six

Putin's Anti-Magnitsky Act was at first designed to counter the initial U.S. Magnitsky Act; in other words, it would freeze the Russian assets and investments of any U.S. citizen charged with "violations of the human rights and freedoms of Russian citizens," and ban them from entry into Russia.

Of course, the number of Americans with assets and investments in Russia is very, very small (vs. the number of Russians with assets and investments in the United States), so to ensure the bill would inflict more pain on U.S. citizens, it also banned them from adopting Russian children. The adoption ban impacted, in particular, Russian children with major medical needs, as they were the children most commonly adopted by American families. When the law passed, there were reportedly at least two hundred Russian children who knew they were to be adopted by American families who were immediately affected, with another 1,500 adoptions in the works.

The Anti-Magnitsky Act is also known as the "Dima Yakovlev Law."

Dima Yakovlev was a twenty-one-month-old Russian boy who had been adopted by a U.S. family in Virginia three months earlier. Dima's American father strapped the boy into his car seat one day and drove to work, forgetting to drop his son off at day care on the way. Nine hours later, Dima was found dead in the backseat of the car.

There I was, about to be the lone vote against the Anti-Magnitsky Act, or Dima Yakovlev Law. The law was not popular with many Russians, who understood it was absurd to punish the United States by punishing sick, vulnerable Russian children. For this reason, the law was also known among ordinary people as the "Law of Scoundrels."

I, however, was not willing to be a scoundrel. And just as an aside, I believe my lone vote against the Dima Yakovlev Law on the first reading helped to prepare me to vote alone again on the annexation of Crimea.

Seven

It was on December 14, 2012—the day of the Dima Yakovlev Law vote —for the first time since I took my seat in Duma, that I asked myself this question:

"Will I be the only one voting 'no,' or will there be at least one other person among the 449 other deputies who can support me?"

At that moment, I recognized the opportunity both as a politician and as a member of Parliament. For me, it was important and right to go against every other deputy alone, if necessary.

Politicians are waiting for such moments to declare their irreconcilability in the struggle for an ideal, their readiness to go to the end, their loyalty to principles. Such moments in life are defining, but don't happen often.

As a deputy, I understood: if I go alone, my cause will lose. Yes, I would benefit from the public's attention. However, my strategic goals will become even less achievable, as I will become even more toxic for my peers.

The amendment banning foreigners from adopting Russian children would still be accepted, and 1,500 children standing in line for adoption by Americans will remain orphans.

I didn't know what to do. Go against everyone? Quarrel with faction friends, many of whom will vote like everyone else? Stand alone? There is nothing worse than holding a perimeter of defense against the whole world. However, I also knew that there should be no compromises on certain issues, such as issues that involve taking care of children.

My three good friends and fellow members of the A Just Russia party—Dmitry Gudkov, Valery Zubov, and Sergei Petrov—who usually voted alongside me were not in the Duma that day and did not realize the significance of the Kremlin's counterattack. However, I was sure that later, in the second reading, they would figure it out and then join me.

Meanwhile, I decided to talk to other colleagues. I approached them in the meeting room and quietly asked, persuaded, and appealed to their conscience. I saw that everything was meaningless. Many of them already knew that I was right. It took me some time to realize that an almost Shakespearean drama was being played out, except its heroes knew what they were doing. They switched to the dark side deliberately. That's how this tragedy was born.

The victims of the tragedy were not only orphans left without a family, but also my fellow deputies, who sold their souls that moment to the evils of Putinism and accepted their new positions as scoundrels.

Eight

As soon as I took the floor that day, a mountain of loneliness fell upon me.

Outside the walls of the Duma, thousands of protestors were waiting for a decision. Many were following me on the OpenDuma website, which I created with my friend and political partner Alena Popova to provide people for the first time with a live stream from the parliamentary sessions.

Yet the thing is, when you speak inside the House, you are cut off from the world. Hundreds of eyes are looking at you, but you cannot feel their energy, their excitement, their anticipation . . . or their disappointment or grief.

If I had seen some emotion—at least disbelief or doubt in their eyes—maybe I could have used that to ardently work even harder to dissuade, prove, explain why this amendment should not be accepted.

All the other deputies already knew they must vote for the law, even if they knew it was wrong. They also knew that the Duma and the Senate collectively would pass it, regardless of what they said against it or how they voted.

For most of them, the most important thing they could do was to survive another day by voting as they were told. Yes, they were cowards.

Nine

Of course, there were deputies who heard me when I spoke, and who were on my side.

However, overwhelmingly that day, all of them voted as they were instructed. They were not just cowards, but treacherous cowards! Actually, they were even worse than that. I can sometimes tolerate ignorant professional political whores, but I can't stand those who know the consequences and can raise their voice, but fail to do so. Such people dominate the present government of Russia, and their cowardice is the main driver that enables Putinism.

Anyway, then in 2012, in the first reading of the Dima Yakovlev Law, I stood alone as its opponent. In the second reading of the law, there were four of us. In the third reading of the law, there were eight of us. I am proud of every one of them.

I alone voted "against" in all readings.

And I knew that I had morally won and not become another scoundrel.

CHAPTER TWO

Putin Sucks in Crimea, Throws Me Out

One

I am often asked by foreign journalists, "If you knew that you would not be able to return home, would you still vote against the annexation of Crimea?"

I answer, "Yes, of course. That was my job."

I never cease to be surprised by the question.

And then, every time, I also explain: "I never intended to leave my country. I was preparing to go undercover, but stay."

In fact, long before the vote on Crimea, I was urged by my colleagues to leave many times. There were many opportunities, of course.

Before going into politics, I had worked for a very large transnational company, managed a venture fund, and advised the governments of several countries.

In fact, in my faction in the Duma, I was sometimes teased as being "the deputy for the Boston constituency" because of my connections with U.S. tech companies, particularly those in Massachusetts.

Two

Today, many cite my lone vote in 2014 against Russia's annexation of Crimea as an example of courage.

However, I did not, and do not, consider this a courageous act.

By the way, my vote on Crimea not only caused a great deal of change in my life, but also in the lives of almost half of my State Duma staff. As you may know, each deputy has a staff of forty-five, and twenty-two members of my staff from that time have been forced to leave the country or have been imprisoned. From my side, my vote was a meaningful and rational political action, just diligent work as a representative of the voters of the Novosibirsk region. Of course, it was not devoid of emotions—we are all people, and sometimes passion, hatred, and contempt for triumphant stupidity and injustice live in us.

I also had common sense. That's why I consider my decision in 2002 to leave my job at Yukos, the largest oil and gas company in Russia, and enter politics to have been a much more courageous one. The rest of the events that have followed are just consequences of that choice in my life.

I thought about the decision on how to vote on the Crimea issue for a long time; since the moment when the upper house, or Federation Council, allowed the use of the army at the suggestion of Vladimir Putin on March 1, 2014.

In fact, on that very day the Senate (formally responding to the request of Ukrainian President Viktor Yanukovych, who fled the country) allowed Putin to use troops on Ukrainian territory "to protect Russian citizens," and so started the war.

Addressing the senators, Putin asked to be given the right to use the armed forces on the territory of Ukraine "until the socio-political situation in this country normalizes."

The decision of the Federation Council was interpreted as Russia's preparation for a full-scale military operation against Ukraine. Voting at an extraordinary meeting of the upper chamber was open. All the senators that were reported as present—90 out of 166 members of the Federation Council—spoke in favor of satisfying Putin's appeal.

It is still not clear whether there was a quorum, because at the time of the vote, there were only eighty-five senators physically in the hall. Some of the names were somehow registered by the system, but never showed up. (Of course, it was just the usual miracle of telekinesis and teleportation in Putin's Russia; something some Western politicians envy. I heard

Mr. Berlusconi once commented that he would like to learn the trick from his friend.)

It is clear that the majority, fearing international sanctions, actually avoided participating in this shameful procedure. However, it did not change the outcome.

In Ukraine, for calling for the introduction of foreign troops into the territory of his country, former President Yanukovych was convicted of an act of treason. I spoke in the Ukrainian court as a key witness on this and helped the prosecutors to collect the evidence. Another former Russian parliamentarian, Denis Voronenkov, was assassinated in Kyiv just a hundred yards away from me, after he volunteered to deliver another statement on this matter in the same proceeding.

Three

Given everything I knew about Ukraine and Crimea, in that fateful March of 2014 I was choosing between two options: either abstain from voting at all, or vote "against."

You can bet that in Russia, voting "no" on important issues is always met with hostility. It has serious consequences. Those guys in the Kremlin still are in on the Soviet-era approach: "We, the people, like one man, have spoken."

Of course, in this situation, to abstain from the vote meant silently passing by while watching how bandits take away a bag of candy from a child—and not just a child, but a family member (Ukraine) who is in serious trouble.

However, for me, there was also another problem.

I was in the middle of a campaign to become Mayor of my city Novosibirsk, in Siberia, in which polls clearly suggested that the opposition could win. As you may know, Novosibirsk is the third-largest city in Russia, and it is considered to be Russia's Silicon Valley.

It was difficult to take such an unpopular step with voters—and with the very top voter in the Kremlin named Putin, who has nothing to do with Novosibirsk, but in real life could overrule all of its residents with the wave of one finger—just two weeks before this upcoming election. So, I decided to take an atypical step for a modern Russian politician: I asked my constituents, the voters of Novosibirsk, what they thought I should do about Crimea.

The issue of Crimea after the collapse of the Soviet Union has always been a subconscious buzz in the back of Russians' minds. In fact, this peninsula in the Black Sea has changed hands a lot over the course of history: Romans, Greeks, Skifs, Kievans, Tatars—an endless list of conquerors. For a couple of centuries, the development of the modern territory of Ukraine was determined in competition by three local superpowers: Russia, Poland/Lithuania, and Crimea. Eventually, Russia made an alliance with the best mercenaries in Europe—Ukrainian Zaporozhye Cossacks (which the latter considered a temporary union, but in fact lasted for almost 350 years) and destroyed both competitors. Crimea became Russian, and was consequently the location of several serious military confrontations with the Ottomans, British, French and even Italians. That made Russians call Sevastopol "a place of military glory"— which was reinforced during World War II.

In 1954, Nikita Khrushchev (himself a Soviet leader of Ukrainian background), in commemoration of the three hundredth anniversary of the Russian-Ukrainian union, transferred administrative control over Crimea to the Ukrainian Soviet Socialist Republic, or Ukrainian SSR. Nobody really cared too much at that time—it was just one country, at the end of the day. I think reassignment of Staten Island to New Jersey would have made a larger splash, although that's more or less what happened—the Crimean peninsula, with its deficit of water and electricity, and being connected to the mainland via Ukraine, looked way more natural inside Ukraine from a logistics point of view than it did in Russia.

Everything changed when the Soviet Union decided to split apart. In this situation, it was hard to comprehend why the ethnically Russian and Crimean Tatar peninsula stayed in Ukraine, and this question was immediately put on the table. However, Crimea turned out not to be the only point of conflict between Ukraine and Russia—the largest issue was the nuclear weapons that stayed in Ukraine, making it the third-largest nuclear power after Russia and the United States. The two superpowers definitely did not like that, and in 1994, a compromise deal was enforced on Ukrainians: they were to give up their arsenal in exchange for guarantees by the Americans, British, and Russians to safeguard Ukraine's territorial integrity.

Frankly, I was among critics of this agreement from the very first day. I would have preferred Ukraine staying nuclear (why should that really bother us Russians?) and Crimea being returned to Russia. That was the common position of many ordinary people, but it received very marginal support among the elites, who wanted good relations and economic assistance from the United States. So, the deal was made, and Ukraine kept its part of the bargain. To my mind, the case was closed: A deal is a deal, even if I disagree with it.

However, it was not a done deal for many Russians, and Putin could sense that—this guy really is connected to the pulse of the society, and he always uses it to his benefit.

I, too, understood this sentiment toward Crimea, and that's why I decided to appeal directly to my constituents to hear their thoughts.

The first time I started this discussion was at my next meeting with residents of Novosibirsk. Some forty to fifty people gathered on a snow-covered playground in a densely populated neighborhood, mostly older women.

I said, "One of these days, I will have to vote on Crimea in the State Duma, and I would like to know what you think—I am your deputy, I ask for your instructions on how to vote. Yes or no? For or against? On the one hand, Crimea could indeed be ours. On the other, the war . . ." I said and I then began enumerating the arguments for and against the annexation as neutrally as possible, avoiding showing my own position.

"There will be no war!" the assembled people murmured in unison.

"How will there not?" I said. "There would be popular mobilization in Ukraine. It also has troops in Crimea already. Kyiv has nowhere to go. No matter what happens now—Ukrainians will be pissed at us, they will fight, one day or another."

People began to think. One of the younger women spoke, inconsistently and with passion, about relatives from the city of Simferopol in Crimea, saying, "My family there, they are forced to learn Ukrainian, imagine that!"

The people hummed indignantly, "Crimea is ours!"

One woman cried out, "But the main thing is that there should be no war!"

Others applauded.

I asked, "So, you are telling me to vote against?"

"How is it 'against'?" they retaliated. "Crimea is ours!"

"But you say you are against war. And if Crimea is to be ours, then there will be war!"

The people were confused. Among the buzzing, the back rows began to move away from this unpleasant conversation.

"So," I asked, "Will we shoot at our Ukrainian brothers and sisters?"

One guy spat back, "So we will, if needed!" He was hushed by his wife.

"How about if we take a vote?" I suggested.

A sigh of relief passes through the ranks.

The result: twenty-seven to twenty-four, with a small majority against a war.

So we voted at every constituency meeting for almost two weeks.

And every time, the situation was about the same: the citizens of Novosibirsk, who came to the meetings, were pretty evenly divided on the issue of the annexation of Crimea. For me, this was a strong argument that the vote in the Duma should not be unanimous.

Four

Three other people convinced me that I was about to do the right thing. One was Vladimir Putin. The other was Winston Churchill. The third was Katya, my wife.

The first one, Putin, as I have already described, gathered all the important people in the Kremlin and addressed the Parliament two days before the memorable vote. I remember clearly:

Putin exclaimed: "Crimea is ours!"
And everyone jumped up and down, and praised him,
like during Stalinist Party Conventions.

I was disgusted. I didn't get up. And I was the only one still seated in the room.

That's also when I started thinking about my Novosibirsk mayoral campaign. Could I still possibly win that election if I voted against annexation?

This is where Sir Winston Churchill helped a lot, as I remembered he was the wise one who is rumored to have once said:

"The difference between a politician and a statesman is that a politician thinks about the next elections, while the statesman thinks about the next generation."

(Or maybe it's actually, as Google suggests, a quote from the American theologian and author James Freeman Clarke. The point is, at the time, the quote spoke volumes to me. And also at the time, I believed it was something that Churchill had said.)

Meanwhile, there was no ambiguity about my wife Katya's position on the vote.

She has always supported my most radical political actions, whatever they were, although they almost always meant new problems for the well-being of our family.

She clearly stated her position, serving breakfast that day: "If you don't vote against, you shouldn't bother coming back home."

I am still very grateful to her for this. This was the final moment of clarity I had been looking for, as the responsibility for the consequences for my family was lifted off my shoulders.

Five

It was a day and a vote that would change my life.

Yet for my colleagues, it was a rather routine procedure, for we all knew that no one in the hall could influence the decision that had already been made in the Kremlin.

Even my most radical comrades in the Duma, Dmitry Gudkov, Valery Zubov and Sergei Petrov, did not think I should dare to speak out "against."

To be honest, I doubted if I should myself.

Before the meeting, Gudkov approached me and announced that he, Zubov, and Petrov had discussed it and decided that they would not take part in the vote.

"Are you with us, as always?" he asked.

I answered evasively, "I am always with you guys, but I'll see how the discussion goes."

He was, of course, relieved to accept this as an agreement.

I had a glimmer of hope that, after everything, someone else might oppose it, and then I would be able to abstain whilst knowing annexation had not gone unopposed. That would make it possible for me to join my trio of friends, and to continue to compete in the upcoming elections to become the mayor of Novosibirsk.

So, while representatives of the government and Duma committees were speaking, explaining the legal side of the issue, I walked around the hall and discussed the situation with several other potential allies. Alas, everyone I spoke with just averted their eyes.

Six

A few words about my Novosibirsk campaign.

In this campaign, I had the blessing of a most unlikely person: Vladimir Putin himself.

The circumstances themselves are very interesting, because it was becoming almost common, even systemic, that oppositionists, like myself, were allowed to run in mayoral elections and even win.

Obviously, it was not our breakthrough, but a result of shuttle diplomacy, where I advocated that oppositionists would focus on local elections instead of federal campaigns, while the Kremlin would allow us to get elected instead of being arrested. When the agreement was reached, a clear signal needed to be sent to local authorities and law enforcement agencies that they should actually begin following the law in how they treated us, instead of manhandling and abusing us.

To send this message, it was decided that I and four other oppositionists would be invited to appear at the Valdai Forum, Putin's main presentation venue, where he usually invited experts from across the world to speak so that they could tell him how nice he was. This time, the president's staff wanted to use this nice opportunity to show the new "democratic face" of their boss. In doing this, the message would not only be heard in Russia, but also in the West, and they could kill two birds with just one stone.

I was asked to moderate a panel on local politics. Then, they said, Putin himself will come, and you can ask him a question so that he publicly confirms that this is the new deal.

I ran this panel, which was attended by many foreign and Russian journalists.

At one point during the panel, we asked for Putin's support for amnesty for political prisoners, and he agreed. As usual with Putin's promises, it was not carried out completely. Yet half of the arrested political activists were nevertheless released, including several of my friends and aides who had been thrown in prisons during the 2011–2013 protests.

Just securing his approval for amnesty as part of this political "dog-and-pony show" at Valdai made my appearance worthwhile, even if nothing else came of my time there. However, as it turns out, more did happen.

Seven

At one point during the panel, I stated, "I'm going to be the next mayor of Novosibirsk."

To which Putin responded before everyone in the room, "Good luck in the elections!"

Suddenly, I could feel everyone in the audience and even my fellow panelists beside me on the stage give a gasp.

It sounds cliche to say this, but for a few moments Putin's words hung in the air, and you could have heard a pin drop.

After the panel, a queue immediately lined up to speak with me: "You will be the next mayor of Novosibirsk! We got it! Putin himself told you to go be the mayor of Novosibirsk!"

Next, someone from the president's detail came up to me. "You once said you wanted to talk to Vladimir Vladimirovich?"

"I did," I said, although cautiously. By that time, what could I say to my archrival?

Of course, I would be thrilled to learn what was going on in his head, but that definitely would require a lengthy and relaxed conversation, not a quick chat. And the business issues I needed to have addressed— elections, the amnesty, the attack of his own people on our innovation economy and my beloved Skolkovo project, which I will tell you about a bit later—all this was pretty much resolved already. However, one should not refuse such offers.

"Okay, let's go."

And then, Putin and I were standing face-to-face on the sidelines of the Valdai Forum.

I could hear my heart pounding inside my chest. I was terrified that he could hear it, too.

"Hello," Putin said.

"Hello," I said, "I've been asking to meet you for quite some time."

"Yes," Putin said. "Well, what do you want?"

"Vladimir Vladimirovich," I tried to be polite, looking into his soul-less eyes, "actually, you have already said everything yourself. So, now I just wanted to thank you for closing the trumped-up Skolkovo criminal case."

"Well, yes," he nodded, "we figured it out."

"Without you," I continued, "this would not have happened. Thank you for making an objective decision and not starting a witch hunt. You know me. We will still be political opponents, but if I am elected mayor, I promise that the city will benefit."

"Okay . . ." he said.

"Thank you very much!"

"Is that all?" he asked.

Again, I heard my heart pounding, now twice as fast.

No doubt he was waiting for me to ask for something, some favor in connection with the elections, or with something else. So he could recruit me, as he had done numerous times in his KGB career.

But I said: "That's it. . . . We are still enemies, so I don't want to waste your time."

"Yeah." He responded with such an unclear intonation—either as a question, or a confirmation.

The conversation clearly went in a direction he did not expect. Everyone was always asking him for something. But I didn't.

Don't get me wrong, I was genuinely trying to use my charm on him, and not to fall into some trap. "I would, of course, be interested in talking with you in more detail. Not on your feet, here. If you want."

Putin, as a professional, was still reluctant to lose this recruitment attempt. (What else could I call it?) "For sure, it would be my pleasure! And please, be careful when you are working with some people in the government!" He started giving names of people I should avoid.

Man, that was an interesting twist.

"But it is you who appointed them, why should I be so careful?"

For the briefest moment after I spoke, his face contorted and it felt as if the balance of power had just turned.

I, of all people, an oppositionist who had just received his blessing to be mayor, had just spit in his face by questioning him. Questioning him! Vladimir Vladimirovich Putin.

Who was I to question him?

He stormed off. The meeting was over.

Eight

I bring up this meeting to make the point that both I and lots of other people had a lot invested in our relationship with Vladimir Putin. Was I really about to screw all that up?

Indeed, that was quite a concern for me. Politics is all about alliances and resources. Politicians usually are well balanced in the web of arrangements and agreements, which makes them predictable and allows sponsors and lobbyists to build long-term relationships with them.

Radical moves are not exactly appreciated by parliamentarians, as they jeopardize the predictable flow of business.

As Russian prisoners like to say: "An honest confession relieves your guilt, but inflates the sentence." An honest politician soon learns that a couple of bold moves feel nice once or twice. Soon, however, you are out of resources to make any more moves, and soon you will stop being in real politics.

You can bet that, to get elected to the State Duma, you need serious donors. To run for the mayor of the largest municipality in Russia, as I was, you need even more serious allies. And you can be certain that none of them would appreciate the idea of you challenging Vladimir Putin.

The very next day after my vote on Crimea, most of them asked me to forget their names at once and forever. That meant I picked them well— if they did not like me so much, they would have demanded that I return everything they ever donated, and could put some additional—and public, for the Kremlin to see—pressure on me to make sure it happened.

Some of my allies were just nice people who cared about their businesses and the people who worked for them, and being my friend would now put them all in danger. There were people who later called me to apologize for doing things like removing photos of us together from their social media and unfriending me there.

Still, it was worth it.

Nine

On that memorable day of the Crimea vote, the time had come for me to go up the plenary hall to reach my Duma seat for the final vote. As I climbed the stairs, I heard the Speaker say:

"From this rostrum, it has already been repeatedly remarked on today about a rare unanimity for our chamber."

This sounded particularly funny to me that day. Unanimity, or rather, unanimous submission, has long been one of the properties of this chamber.

Finally, it was time to vote.

Aleksey Mitrofanov, the deputy from Moscow, saw me reaching for the "against" button. He tried to grab my hand and stop me: "You're crazy! We'll all be shot here together with you!"

I quickly pressed the button with my other hand and pulled out the card so he could see that it was too late for me to change my vote. Another deputy, Igor Zotov, clutched his head in horror, "Are you serious?"

The final count was 445 deputies voting for the agreement, and my lone vote "against."

Valery Zubov, Sergei Petrov, and Dmitry Gudkov did not vote. One deputy chair was vacant.

As soon as the numbers appeared on the scoreboard, some dozen people immediately rushed to the side exit from the hall.

There, in a separate room, was a device that prints a list of voting results.

I knew that the deputies were running to find out the identity of the "renegade." Me.

I quickly left the room.

In the hall, I physically felt as if there was a vast, impenetrable emptiness around me.

Then, in the corridor, a nimble journalist was already waiting for me and asked in amazement, in a low voice, "Why?"

"I am for our peoples to be together—the peoples of Russia, Ukraine, Belarus," I responded. "But today's vote is a step in the opposite direction."

I had a car waiting outside. I fled to Sheremetyevo Airport and immediately flew home to the relative safety (so I hoped) of Novosibirsk.

Ten

This is a good time for me to remind you of my reputation as "the deputy for the Boston constituency."

In fact, long before the vote on the annexation of Crimea, a high-ranking Russian official once said to me, "If you, Ilya Vladimirovich, ever decide to leave, we will not persecute you. Think about it!"

Again, this was long before my lone vote on Crimea. I did think about it during those years beforehand. However, I did not leave.

Yet my country left me after the vote on Crimea by putting sanctions on my head a few months later, while I was traveling out of the country on official Novosibirsk business.

Eleven

I was in California, when a reporter from the Russian daily newspaper *Nezavisimaya Gazeta* woke me up by calling with an unexpected question. "Have you read the latest *Izvestia*?"

It was their rival publication, so the question puzzled me quite a bit.

"Nope," I replied. "I am in Silicon Valley, and I was asleep after a long meeting with a tech company about opening an office in Novosibirsk."

"Okay," he said. "Read it. Then call me back."

It was then that I saw I had missed about a hundred calls during the night.

My wife called, my kids called, my parents called, my friends and colleagues from the Duma called. Other reporters called. Also, at least one employee of the president's staff called, and insinuatingly asked "if I was going to an extraordinary session of parliament in Crimea on August 14?"

I quickly returned this call, even before I went online to read the latest *Izvestia*.

"This," they said, "is a big event. Will you go?"

"If everyone else goes," I said, "then, of course, I will go, too."

"So," they said, "that's why we called, just to confirm if you are going or not."

"If everyone else is going, then yes—I'm going."

"But, do you need to think about it? In the context of your vote . . ."

"Are you saying that I shouldn't go?" I asked.

"No, no, no, we're not saying that. But we just want to be sure you've thought this through and are comfortable with this."

There was nothing to think about. It was inappropriate for me as a deputy to succumb to such provocations.

"Okay. So, I just thought about it. And if everyone is going, then I will definitely be there, too."

Then there was a call from my party's Duma office. "Are you going to Crimea?"

"If everyone else is going, then I'll go, too. I'm a deputy. It can't be like that—a general meeting, and suddenly I'm not there!"

"And you," they said, "think it will be okay?"

"Gosh, if you genuinely believe Crimea is Russia, then what should be not okay here?"

To be honest, I did not want to visit the occupied territory. However, if something important was to happen there, and a new escalation with Ukraine was being planned, then it was worth going and trying to prevent it, wasn't it?

And then, yet another call from the Administration. "So, did you think about it?"

"Yes," I said. "Nothing has changed."

"Well, we've been thinking about it, too. We've been thinking about your safety in Crimea."

"So, you don't want me to go? Just say no. And I won't go."

"We can't say that."

"But you think it's not safe for me to go?"

"I didn't say that."

"Then I'm going."

During all of these conversations with my party, and the office of the president's staff, I was confused by one thing:

Why was everyone concerned about my safety if I went to Crimea? I just voted in support of the Ukrainians, so they should want to support me. Right?

What I didn't know yet was that, while I slept, several disturbing pieces of news about me had been reported, hence the wake-up call from the reporter about the latest issue of *Izvestia*.

Well, the first piece of news was that I was dead.

You see, once I finally got online, what I discovered was a story that claimed that some "angry Crimeans" had drowned me in the Kerch Strait when I tried to drive to the peninsula. There was a photo of my car going down in the waters of the Black Sea.

Of course, I knew I was still in California. And still very much alive. And my car, I believed, was still in my Novosibirsk garage. However, that's not what the Russian media said. Maybe they knew better? And who were these "angry Crimeans" who reportedly killed me for voting for them *not* to be invaded by another country?

Then there was the comment of the mobster whom the Kremlin installed as the leader of Crimea, Sergei Aksenov, "This so-called deputy Ponomarev wanted to come to us, but our people could not restrain themselves."

And yet another call from the Administration: "Are you still going?"

This was starting to get funny. "You know it's fake, right? You are talking to me. Clearly, I am not dead."

"We know," the caller said.

"So, you don't want me to go?"

"We didn't say that."

"Well, if you don't say it, then I am going. I'm not afraid of liars and I'm not afraid of looking into the face of danger. Moreover, I am not afraid of either the Russian or Ukrainian people, and I believe that I will always find a common language with them, unlike you!"

However, it turns out I was not going to that meeting in Crimea after all. Because while I was online reading about my own death, I discovered there were additional news stories—citing Federal bailiffs as their source—reporting that, even though I was dead, I also was forbidden to cross the state border back into my own country, Russia, and back to my district and my home.

Twelve

As all of this is quickly happening, I also had a sinking feeling in my stomach which only got worse after I fumbled through my pockets: I was now stranded 6,000 miles from home, and my total capital was twenty-one dollars and twenty-five cents.

Driven by the same sinking feeling, I raced to the nearest ATM. After inserting my Duma salary card, I immediately understood there would be no more money coming from there.

I had to immediately run back to my hotel, pack up, and leave. I had no money to pay for another night.

And then there I was, standing on a California street corner with $21 in my pocket, pulling a roller bag of clothes, with a computer in a backpack tossed over my shoulder, and desperately trying to work out some kind of plan for my family's safety while on the phone with my wife who was back in Russia with my kids.

And then, my official phone as a deputy of the Russian State Duma went dead.

CHAPTER THREE

Trapped in Silicon Valley,
I Discover Putin's Biggest Heist

One

Are you waiting to hear me say that I was really stuck, in a jam, really screwed by Putin while I stood there on that Silicon Valley street corner?

I cannot do that.

The truth is, once I knew that my family was safe, the air of freedom outside of Russia was intoxicating.

This is surely why there have been so many former Soviets outside of Russia (and often in Silicon Valley) who have sucked in this same rarefied air—and then been so inspired by it to create companies like Google, PayPal, Skype, WhatsApp, Evernote, and many others.

A sea of opportunities opens up in front of smart, educated, and entrepreneurial Russians when they begin living abroad. It is so much more spacious than in Russia that they quickly plunge into their own businesses and begin to bathe and revel in their success, protecting it from competitors, often former compatriots. It is not so different than Chinese or Indian diasporas.

No matter what, when you are outside of Russia, common Russian problems seem distant and foolish. It is as if a heavy weight pressing on your shoulders has been removed in an instant.

In contrast, Silicon Valley is liberating. Here, sometimes it seems that you can live without any state influence and coercion from outside. (Of course, as I write this, the U.S. Congress is holding hearings about "big tech" and Apple, Google, Amazon, and Facebook that violate that feeling of freedom—more on that later.)

It is here that dreamers of all sorts gather and invent the future. Even before getting stuck here in 2014, I had been coming to Silicon Valley several times a year since the late 1990s with the mission of attracting businesses and jobs to Novosibirsk, while updating my contacts in the venture capital world and recharging myself over and over again in this atmosphere of entrepreneurship and empowerment.

At the same time, it's true that most of my old Russian friends, even the wealthiest, chose to disappear into thin air when I called them from that California street corner, so as to not have to lend me any money. In such situations as being exiled, or being jailed, you quickly discover who your real friends are, and are not.

Yet some of my American friends (usually also of Russian or Ukrainian descent) immediately began asking me to help with their start-ups in a way that could be done for money without violating U.S. or Russian laws, given my status as a member of the Russian Parliament.

You read that right: even though I was now banished from my own country, I was still serving, from Silicon Valley, as an active and participating member of the State Duma.

I tried twice to get around the bailiff's orders and return to Russia. In April 2015, the Kremlin responded with my arrest in absentia and filing for Interpol's Red Notice, which is a request to law enforcement worldwide to locate and arrest you for pending extradition, surrender, or similar legal action. Thankfully, Russia's request was immediately turned down by Interpol. In May 2016, they passed a special law—one in total violation of Russian Constitution—in the Duma (which somebody nicknamed the Ponomarev Act) to strip me of my parliamentarian status for not being physically present at plenary sessions. It came as no surprise that they wanted to kick me out of the Duma for not showing up, since they also forbade me from going back to Russia so that I could show up. It's worth noting that they never asked the voters of Novosibirsk if they agreed with my removal as their deputy.

In June 2016, as soon as my powers as a Duma deputy were canceled according to the Ponomarev Act, I said, "Thank you, guys," and finally created my own company in the United States. It was called Trident Acquisitions, an oil and gas investments business aimed at bringing international capital and technologies into Ukraine—and pulling out Gazprom's poisoned teeth that sucked the blood out of the country and the whole European Union. In May 2018, we went public on NASDAQ, becoming the first publicly traded company from Ukraine in the United States.

Two
It was under these stressful but exhilarating circumstances that I realized Putin's main crime:

**Putin has stolen from all Russians much more than money.
He stole our future.**

It became even more obvious to me after he started the war in Ukraine in 2014. The invasion of Ukraine in February 2022 looked like the nail in the coffin, with the sudden global repulsion toward anything, or anyone, that even remotely appeared to be Russian. In Ukraine, we had a lot of discussions about whether this "cancel Russian culture" campaign is justified and productive. However, the truth is that Putin has "canceled" far more Russian artists, writers, musicians, directors, and actors, than Europeans—or even Ukranians—have ever done.

But the Russians in Silicon Valley?

They know what it's like to live in a system where there is no future, and this drives them to build their own damn futures, which they control, and which cannot be taken from them.

These futures must be returned home and invested in the creation of Russia without Putin; more precisely, Russia *after* Putin.

I felt this excitement and this value in a completely new way as I stood there breathing the thin and fragrant California Bay Area air. Suddenly, on that Palo Alto street corner, I experienced a touch of the very essence of true freedom for the very first time in my life. In that moment, I also became its most committed ambassador.

Three
You may guess everything that happened that morning was not completely unexpected.

Truthfully, I had been preparing for this moment for many years, except I always thought it would start while I was still in Russia, and then I would be forced to go underground.

This is a good time for me to introduce my friend, mentor and former boss, Mikhail Khodorkovsky.

At one time, as the CEO of Russia's largest oil and gas company, Yukos, he was the richest man in Russia. Then, in 2003, he was falsely accused of fraud and imprisoned for ten years in a remote prison next to a uranium mine. I had the idea to organize his escape with an evacuation to Mongolia. I scouted ways this might be possible, and found a risky but real opportunity to carry out the plan. Unfortunately, while I was working to put this plan into place, his second Yukos trial began, and he was transferred to Chita Detention Center in Siberia before I could execute it.

However, my reconnaissance for Khodorkovsky eight years earlier had given me a lot of valuable experience for planning for what I imagined would be my own escape someday.

Back in Russia, I had already been planning how I would go into hiding if necessary in a number of different cities. I was ready, on a moment's notice, to shuttle across the border to safety at a number of different border points.

I already had new passports and visas, so I could be on the move immediately without contacting any Russian or other government's agencies.

In short, I was ready for persecution and resistance, and I had been ready for a long, long time.

Four

A friend in Silicon Valley quickly provided me with a phone and some money.

The first thing I did was call my wife again.

We decided it is better for me not to try to return to Russia. According to our Constitution, no citizen of the country should be restrained from coming back home, so the decisions of the bailiffs were in direct contradiction to this. However, no judge in Russia ever cared about the Constitution—something we need to focus on when the changes in Russia we will speak of later finally arrive. Also, I was theoretically protected by parliamentary immunity. At the same time, it was clear that if

I was tried I would go to prison immediately, and I did not see the point in that.

I wanted to fight and not just observe others fighting and speaking for me while I remained locked in a cage, sending letters from some far-off prison. Russian lawyer Alexei Navalny made a different choice some seven years later and became a globally recognized hero, but his network all but disappeared within a couple of months, and he himself is no longer a player in Russian politics.

Another friend lent me a car. He didn't know it at the time, but I ended up sleeping in his car for a while—it did not seem wise to spend the very limited cash I could get on a hotel. Later, a Chinese guy from Apple—who knew firsthand what an authoritarian state was—gave me the use of an apartment in San Jose for free, and then eventually rented the apartment to me at a deep discount.

Thank God this situation occurred while I was in the States. If I were in Korea or Malaysia, where I had been headed within the next few days, things would have been much more complicated, even dire.

Five

I'd better explain how Putin's government justified closing the border to me.

There was no way, either legally or politically, that they could kick me out of the country for voting against the annexation of Crimea. Even to arrest me was not so easy, as I was protected by parliamentary immunity, and to remove it a certain procedure needed to be followed.

Instead, they fell back on an old and debunked accusation that I had embezzled money earmarked for the Skolkovo science and technology park project outside Moscow.

Actually, the accusation itself was absurd. I never was a Skolkovo officer, just the member of parliament who promoted the necessary legislation to fund Skolkovo, and I then traveled the world as an ambassador for the project.

We will talk more of Skolkovo later, but for now here's just a little bit of background:

The idea of Skolkovo was to create a Russian version of Silicon Valley. My crime, they said, was that I misappropriated 22 million rubles (about $750,000), and that among other things I paid myself loads of money in return for giving lectures on entrepreneurship at international business conferences that I also organized using the Skolkovo name.

But I didn't misappropriate the money. I couldn't even touch it, according to Russian law. It was Skolkovo itself which made the expenses I suggested, and all were approved in advance. It wasn't until after the vote on Crimea, when investigators were desperately seeking something they could use to smear me, that they invented these new Skolkovo charges.

And yes, this is the same Skolkovo project that was so important that it had been central to the conversation I'd had with Putin himself.

Once I left the country, these new Skolkovo accusations allowed federal bailiffs to issue a warrant to restrict me from crossing the national border, as if I was still inside Russia and was trying to run away with the stolen money, stolen money that I didn't have. Stolen money that I never had, because it was stolen money that had never been stolen.

Six

Now I was in Silicon Valley looking for a job.

So I did exactly what I was basically accused of doing in connection with the Skolkovo project: I got paid to mentor technology entrepreneurs, gave lectures in U.S. universities, and helped innovative companies raise money.

This is both sad and ironic, of course.

In Russia, they called me a criminal.

In Silicon Valley, they call me an entrepreneur.

Funnily enough, I was quickly asked to become an adviser to several Silicon Valley tech start-ups on government relations. In other words, I, still being a Russian parliamentarian, was advising American companies on how to build relationships with the American government. Given my status, it was perfectly legal, but it also made it really hard to figure out whose foreign agent I was at this moment!

Anyway, I have many contacts in Washington, and in Silicon Valley they don't know how to work with government bureaucracy at all. In Russia, of course, working with government bureaucracy is something we know too damn much about! It was easy to see that I could bring a lot of value to many companies.

Once I had clients, it became possible for me to start paying rent to that nice Chinese guy.

I was not planning to stay long, however. My plan was to go to Ukraine.

Why Ukraine?

There are many reasons, but the most important one for me is that if you show ordinary Russian citizens that as a result of the Ukrainian revolution (more on this later) the Ukrainian people live free and far better than Russians, this can inspire Russians to fight for change and a better life for themselves in their own country.

Seven

Meanwhile, it was essential for me to figure out how to continue to serve in the Russian State Duma, despite being banned from entering the country, a criminal case pending against me, and that I was now living almost six thousand miles away from Moscow.

For the next twenty months, I continued to vote on all bills in the Duma by proxy by the hand of my good friend, Dmitry Gudkov.

As we always did before, he and I constantly discussed the agenda and how to vote—until the Duma adopted that special law, the Ponomarev Act, that was explicitly drafted to remove me from office.

Eight

Emigration is different for everyone. You should not confuse it with tourism, because moving to a foreign country is very different from visiting.

For Russians, there are several types of behavior I have observed. The first is the choice of a few—the one that Russian novelist Aleksandr Solzhenitsyn made. This is when a person lives in exile but treats it as a minor temporary accident, an insignificant twist in life.

He or she wants to return, and has a clear plan of what to do in their homeland as soon as they return.

Such people do not integrate into the new society in which they live. For instance, Nobel prize laureate and author of *The Gulag Archipelago* Solzhenitsyn lived in Vermont as a recluse.

There is also an opposite position: "I don't give a damn about Russia. I am now an American/European/whatever," which is always followed up by a story about how bad Russia is. This helps people to somehow justify their departure. I see this also as a psychological defense against the usual Soviet claim that emigration is a betrayal. Such people deliberately cut themselves off from the country. Sometimes they even stop speaking Russian and don't teach the language to their kids.

The third group is mine.

Once in a different environment, we use its resources to build a bridge between this new place and Russia, Ukraine, and the entire post-Soviet space. We use this knowledge of another country as our competitive advantage, a way to earn money and fertilize our Motherland's politics and society with new ideas.

In the expert groups and task force teams of the West, I talk a lot about what is actually happening in Russia. After the USSR's collapse, the useful analytics level fell catastrophically. As a result, even the most sober-minded people in the West now live in boxes of stereotypes and prejudices about Russia. They take information from the mass media, and the media are fed back with what those people write or say, creating a vicious circle of misunderstanding.

Meanwhile, there are two groups in the West who do actually still care about Russian problems.

The first are the Russophobes. For them, Moscow is an eternal evil, an imminent aggressor and imperialist, so it should be either destroyed, or left alone and/or ignored.

The second are the "Putin-verstehers." This is from the German word "*verstehen*," meaning "to understand."

These are people who are either sympathetic to or apologetic for the policies of the Kremlin. They say, "Well, yeah, Russia makes mistakes, but the West is to blame. We provoked them ourselves." It's a crude analogy, but these are the same people who would blame a woman who is raped for wearing a miniskirt.

Both of these groups are equally harmful.

The truth is actually somewhere in between. Neither Russia nor the West is black and white. Both the West and Russia sometimes make mistakes, and sometimes they commit crimes. However, smart moves can be made that will reduce the likelihood of problems like these in the future and help transform Russia.

I always try to explain that the picture is full of halftones and much more colorful than it seems. My approach, along with everyone who shares it, is scolded by both sides—they hiss, "They are spies, damn it!" "They poison our minds." The pro-Russians call me an agent of the CIA and MI6, while the anti-Russians call me an agent of the Kremlin.

Who am I, really?

I'm just a guy who wants to bring the future back to my fellow Russians.

And if I can't go home, I'm convinced that Ukraine is the best place for me to be right now until I can make that happen.

CHAPTER FOUR

Why Ukraine Is More Important Than You Think

One

I can't say that I especially yearn for birch trees. Ukrainian, Canadian and American birches differ little from Russian ones.

However, it is extremely important for me to feel at home linguistically and culturally.

When I was in the States, I had no problem integrating into society. I speak English reasonably well. I understand the culture. I have valuable business and entrepreneurial experience. I have one of the best contact bases in the West of all Russian opposition figures.

But I feel like I'm in exile there. It is uncomfortable—there is no feeling for me of being home.

Everything around me is familiar, but still, it's not my native culture or language. They read other books there. Few people understand my jokes! I can joke in English, but it is entirely different.

That's why I wanted to go to Ukraine so much. It is a different country than Russia, with a different language, but it is close, and the people have a common cultural base with me. Therefore, there is no nostalgia.

In Ukraine, I am at home.

I am on TV on different channels almost daily—on average, three or four interviews per day. That may sound like a lot, but in Ukraine, there are a lot of different channels and media with news programming like talk shows.

As a rule, I do these interviews for Ukrainians in Russian.

Yes, I speak fluent Ukrainian; the first thing I did when I arrived there was to hire a teacher, and three months later, I began to speak the language.

Yes, there are broadcasts where I only speak Ukrainian, especially after February 24th, 2022. However, I am often asked to speak in Russian to deliver the message more accurately.

This works because in Ukraine, there is almost absolute bilingualism.

When speaking, I try to keep a pragmatic, balanced position in relation to all participants in the conflict—Ukraine, Russia, the States, the EU—everyone. It is not simple, even though people often expect political discussion on TV to be completely black and white. But things in real life are not ever black and white.

Many Ukrainians write to me on social media about these interviews, and people often come up to me on the streets of Kyiv to discuss Russia and Putin. So while the Russian media (including the opposition-leaning media) prefers to ignore me for being in Ukraine, I am well heard by Ukrainians.

Ukrainians also feel pain from the two nations drifting apart (although nobody admits it) and they hunger to hear the thoughts of a reasonable Russian person. I believe this will continue to be very important in the future of both countries.

Two

Even before the February 2022 invasion, Ukrainian TV channels were watched in Russia, both by ordinary people and the Kremlin; every harsh statement about Russia I make gets a reaction from the official think tanks and troll farms. On the other hand, these guys sometimes promote me well: for instance, until recently, the most-watched video on the Heritage Foundation's website was my speech in the United States that was discussed in the plenary session of the State Duma.

At what level do they monitor? I don't know. I don't know if this reaches those who make decisions or just remains at the level of those who control the social media bots.

Most Russian opposition folks treat pro-Kremlin media and activists as "untouchable."

"You should not shake hands with them," they say. I never shake hands with them, but I always speak to everyone. I think you should never give up on trying to bring people to your side. If people from Channel One, Rossiya TV, or NTV come up to me at the Free Russia Forum or elsewhere, I don't chase them away.

Instead, I say to these propagandists: "Guys, I'm talking to you if you don't misrepresent my words. I know you have a party line, you will put everything I do into a pile of shit anyway, but what I said should remain unedited, not distorted."

As long as they do not violate this simple principle, I will continue to communicate with them. I think that if even a few of my like-minded people or Novosibirsk voters hear my words in Russia, it's worth it.

Many of these propaganda people then call me and private message me on social media, telling me stories about how they are on my side, but they have families and mortgages to protect. Of course, I don't sympathize with this, but I keep a note of who can flip at the decisive moment. And when the invasion started, some already had.

I even created a special nongovernmental organization, or NGO, called Bravery Foundation, which protects such defectors from prosecution. We have exfiltrated some outside Russia; some were already arrested, and we provide them with a legal defense. There are even several cases of former high-ranking state employees who came to Ukraine to fight Putin with the Ukrainian military. We helped them with the travel and legal arrangements.

I will mention one high-profile defection in which we at the Bravery Foundation were involved. You may remember that, shortly after Russia invaded Ukraine, a Russian TV producer named Marina Ovsyannikova snuck in front of a live camera with an anti-war sign that read, "No War. Don't believe the propaganda. They're lying to you here."

Marina, for many years, had been part of the official Russian propaganda machine. But, believe me, her status in Russia changed the day she stood in front of a live TV news camera with her sign. After that, a lot of problems started happening in her life.

I did not care what her motives were and whether she converted to become a genuine oppositionist or not. What mattered to me is that she

(Source: Channel One)

paved the way for others, and we witnessed another twenty or so defections among the propagandists shortly after her move.

Media presence is a political tool. I use it to remain involved in Russian politics, albeit from a distance. So people watch and read me in Russia—and soon, when it's time for me to return to my country, I won't have to start a new conversation or create a new relationship or start at ground zero to build trust; I will be able to continue doing what I am doing now.

Kremlin guys actually understand this so much better than the opposition. That's why they made it a criminal offense to say anything about peace in Russian media as soon as the invasion started. They call it "discrediting the Russian Army."

Now, I don't get to explain anything to my Russian comrades on these channels where I am very well known. I hate being temporarily muted in Novosibirsk and elsewhere.

That's why I started my "February Morning" news channel in Russian, for Russians in Russia, about the invasion of Ukraine.

Three
Putin is obsessed with Ukraine for two fundamental reasons. The first one—and it is not funny at all—is Zbigniew Brzezinski's book, *The Grand Chessboard*, written in 1997. The new Kremlin leader read it at the beginning of the 2000s when it was translated into Russian.

According to Brzezinski, the former U.S. National Security Advisor for Jimmy Carter and father of MSNBC's Mika Brzezinski, Ukraine is an *"important space on the Eurasian chessboard,"* the state *"deserving America's strongest geopolitical support,"* the control of which is supposed to make a domination over the world possible.

It was a very strong signal for Putin, who is a devoted conspiracist.

The second reason was internal for Russia. Three tyrants shaped Moscow's political culture: Ivan the Terrible, Peter the Great, and Joseph Stalin, who ruled the hyper-centralized state with an iron fist. Admittedly, Putin's iron is a bit second class, but they are obviously the role models he follows and praises.

Ivan the Terrible, in the sixteenth century, was responsible for one crucial fork in Russia's history. Not many people know this, but Russians have a robust tradition of direct democracy that can be compared perhaps only to Ancient Athens, but without second-class, noncitizen enslaved people. Two main centers of such were medieval Novgorod (halfway between modern Moscow and Saint Petersburg) and Zaporizhzhia Cossacks (centered in present-day Southern Ukraine). Ivan the Terrible took care of the former, physically exterminating virtually every inhabitant of that ancient city, which was far more influential than Moscow at the time. Still, all democrats were pretty badly organized in the face of ruthless authoritarian invaders. By the way, they were fighting under the white-blue-white flag, which is currently adopted by the new Russian opposition as the flag of our future Free Russian Republic and is riding high in many antiwar protests today.

This flag, by the way, has an interesting story by itself. It was suggested a few days after the invasion of 2022 by designer Kai Katonina as a traditional Russian tricolor flag without the red color, i.e., without blood on it. Only later it was determined that this made it almost exactly the flag of ancient Novgorod. So, to my mind, for the new Russian Republic, which would emerge on the ruins of the Russian Federation, it is a perfect symbol, and I was the first to start using it as the official symbol of our "February Morning" media.

Cossacks resurfaced in the fifteenth and sixteenth centuries and were absorbed by Russia, but managed to preserve a lot of their self-governing practices. During the 1918–1920 Civil War, anarchists of Machno, which originated from the same Dnipro territories, helped the Red Army a lot, fighting against the monarchy—and were oppressed afterward by

Bolsheviks. After the collapse of the Soviet Union, the anarchic practices were again resurrected and became the foundation of the modern
Ukrainian state. The national anthem of Ukraine states it clearly:

> *As in Springtime melts the snow*
> *So shall melt away the foe,*
> *And we shall be masters*
> *Of our homes.*
> *Soul and body, yea, our all*
> *Offer we at freedom's call—*
> *We, whose sires were mighty*
> *Cossack braves.*

The embodiment of such political practice is called "Maidan." This
Turkish (and also Persian and Arabic) word literally means what is in
European tradition called the "Market Square." For Cossacks, it was the
place where important decisions were made.

Ukraine has experienced Maidan twice in the last twenty years.

The first, in 2004, was when Ukrainians peacefully overturned an
illegitimate election and an attempt to install a corrupt and authoritarian
president named Viktor Yanukovich. Birds of a feather flock together, so
he was heavily supported by Putin—and this support, which repulsed
many Ukrainians, was the first major blow to the Russian dominance
over the country. It was also the first major public humiliation for
Vladimir Putin.

In 2014, there was a second Maidan, also known as Euromaidan,
involving the removal of Yanukovich, who after a bitter defeat in 2005
still managed to legitimately became president in 2010. The success of
Ukraine's direct democracy practices was engraved in Putin's head as a
mortal danger, so much so that Maidan itself became his key enemy. The
2014 Euromaidan led to Putin's invasion of Crimea.

For the same reasons Maidan and Ukrainian self-organization
threaten Putin, they serve as examples for us to follow.

Four

Many supporters of Ukraine in the West today would like to understand better Ukraine's history, not just its recent history that includes

independence and the Orange Revolution, Euromaidan and the Revolution of Dignity, the annexation of Crimea, and the invasion of Ukraine. There is also a desire to understand the rich modern history of Ukraine that goes back hundreds of years.

Understanding this history gives valuable perspective on the current situation and how the relationship between Ukraine and Russia might change, for the better, in the future.

Everything I am telling you here is based on my own personal experience. I am a Russian guy, born in Russia and raised in Russia. I became a Russian politician. I am well-read and well-educated. However, it wasn't until I went to live in Ukraine and began learning the Ukrainian language that I also began to learn some fundamental truths about Russia.

When I arrived in Kyiv, I learned Ukrainian in the first months of my life there. Although, to be honest, I didn't need to do this—I've never had the need to speak Ukrainian while in Ukraine, but I did it on principle and to show respect for the country that became my home.

Let's be clear about this: no one in Ukraine has ever forced me to give up my Russian. Like many other Russians in Ukraine, I am living proof that the Kremlin propaganda's accusations that Ukrainians are all neo-Nazis and discriminate against Russians are entirely untrue. Even after the invasion of 2022 started, I never felt either danger or discomfort when speaking Russian. Not even in Western Ukraine. Not to the slightest degree.

Five

I made a lot of astounding discoveries about my Russian heritage as I went about mastering the Ukrainian language.

While studying the Kyiv churches, I came across the relics of Prince Volodymyr, the founder of the Ukrainian state. But wait—isn't he the same man we Russians celebrate as Prince Vladimir the Great, the man who converted Russia to Christianity? Where was he born? In Ukraine!

And then another shock: What is the famous Ukrainian trident? The sign of Petlyura and Bandera, Ukrainian nationalists? That's what I thought for a very long time. Yet, in Kyiv, I learned this is the seal of the same *Equal-to-the-Apostles* Prince Vladimir, who, to me, has always been a Russian prince and founder of the Russian state, revered not only by Orthodox but also by Catholics.

It was here I realized:

The true symbol of the Russian state
is a trident of Ukrainian origin,
not a two-headed eagle.

Soon I also learned that, in Ukraine, the Ukrainian language of the nineteenth century was called the Russian language ("rouskiy"), while Russian was (and still is in Ukrainian) called literally "the language of Russia" ("rossiyskiy").

Now, this may seem like it is splitting hairs. First, however, let me point out that this is akin to the people of "Bahhston," or "Minna-sow-ta," or those speaking with a "Cawk-nee" accent asserting that it is they who speak the mother language of English, instead of the other way around. But, of course, we all recognize that these are regional variations of the English language—just as you may be learning for the first time that the language Russians speak today is the "Cawk-nee" of the mother tongue, whose origins actually lie in Ukraine.

After this awakening, it was like I had just swallowed the little red pill in the film *The Matrix*. So many details that looked insignificant at school started to reemerge in my consciousness. I once again concluded that the Russian identity differs from many nations by being completely synthetic, political, and not ethnic. Russia in terms of identity is very much like America, it is produced in a melting pot of many cultures and peoples. To say you are an American is to say you could be from literally anywhere—unless you are an American Indian.

It is obvious to me:

There are no Russians.
Russians are Ukrainians from Kievan Rus
blended with Tatars and Northern Scandinavian
and Ugric nations.

In other words, what is here, in Kyiv, is the original Russian. Some may even joke—Ukrainians are to Russia as the American Indians are to America.

What is in Moscow is just one branch of Kievans, heavily diluted by outside invaders. These modern-day Russians are an alloy of many peoples, whereas original Russians are only one of our components. By the way, you should know that genetic tests also indicate that it is impossible to separate the Ukrainian and Russian genes, at least not with the current level of scientific development. I checked.

Who is the heir of Kievan Rus? Moscow believes that it is.

But wait a minute, who founded Moscow? Prince of Kyiv Yuri Dolgoruky, who is buried in Kyiv, not in Moscow.

Who created the ancient Russian legal system? It was Prince Yaroslav the Wise, from Kyiv. And he is buried in St. Sophia Cathedral—in Kyiv, of course.

Who baptized Russia? Kyiv's Prince Vladimir.

Here is the Kyiv grave of Pyotr Stolypin, former prime minister of the Russian Empire. Here are the remains of the key Russian folk hero Ilya Muromets in Kyiv.

In other words, everything that, for many Russians, is the foundation of their country is, in fact, the foundation of Ukraine. So when Ukraine makes the unfortunate choice of defining itself as "not Russia," it voluntarily chooses to leave its primordial heritage up to Moscow to define incorrectly.

This is why I disagree with former Ukrainian President Leonid Kuchma, who wrote a book in 2003 with the title, *Ukraine Is Not Russia.* Nor do I agree with many Russian and Ukrainian nationalists.

Instead, I believe:

Russia is Ukraine.

Not the other way around.

Six

I again want to call attention to language because it is a particular problem in Ukraine.

There is a predominant ethnic group in the country—Ukrainians—but for a significant part, the native tongue (the language spoken in the family) is not Ukrainian but Russian. Therefore, the mentality of this ethnic group could be divided into three groups, and each has its attitude toward the language.

For the first one, it is important to speak Ukrainian only, but they are a minority.

The second one is most comfortable with Surzhik, which is a blended spoken language that includes elements of Ukrainian and Russian. It is common in several regions of Ukraine and neighboring areas in Russia and Moldova. It differs from the proper Ukrainian and Russian languages, although it is difficult to draw a clear line between Ukrainian, Russian, and Surzhik.

The third group does not accept restrictions on its free choice of which languages to speak.

In addition, besides Ukrainians, there are Russians, Hungarians, Poles, Bulgarians, Jews, and, of course, Crimean Tatars who also live in Ukraine—and each has their view of the "correct" language to speak.

There are countries in the world which are built on a multilingual and multinational basis. This does not prevent them from being united and strong. On the contrary, it helps them to compete with other nations. For example, four different ethnic groups and languages have coexisted in Switzerland for centuries without strife. Its people cultivate diversity. The Swiss are a political nation.

In my opinion, the path of Ukraine is the path of Switzerland.

Ukrainian-Russian bilingualism is a historical and cultural fact. For the majority of the country's population, it is important to recognize that the first language is modern Russian. However, almost everyone speaks Ukrainian, and its role is gradually increasing. This is very important for nation building.

It's only bad when coercion begins.

For instance, speculations on the language issue were common in Ukraine since the country gained its independence. Those of Western Ukraine were manipulated by corrupt, but "very patriotic" politicians; those of Eastern Ukraine were always promised to elevate the status of Russian to being the second official language. And in times of war, the more Russian propaganda justified the aggression in Donbas by protecting the rights of Russian speakers, the more often the patriotic Ukrainian public called Russian "the language of the occupiers." Giving a new pretext for attacks by Moscow propagandists—and forcing Ukrainian politicians, including the president, to take sides—further divided the nation. By losing the possibility to speak to diverse language and cultural groups and focusing on just one, Ukrainian politicians always lost their popular support in favor of the consolidated and disciplined Kremlin's agents of influence. Divide and then conquer—nothing new in this world.

Seven

Against the backdrop of hostilities in the Donbas and Russian intervention, the "pendulum" of public sentiment swung sharply toward Western Ukraine. At the same time, Eastern voters still hoped to avoid war, and in 2014, Petro Poroshenko became the president of the country, for they saw in him the most moderate among Maidan leaders. A pro-Western Ukrainian politician but not a radical, such a public consensus allowed Poroshenko to win in the first round—no easy task, given the number of candidates.

Tellingly, Poroshenko won everywhere except for one constituency. In the East, his result was lower than in the West—an average of about 40%, but it was still several times higher than the result of Yulia Tymoshenko, who came in second.

Poroshenko was elected president of Galicia in Western Ukraine, Malorossia in the North, the lands of Cossack freemen in the Center, and the industrial East.

Then, from the first days of his presidency, the cannonade of Russian artillery and shots from the East quickly shifted his centrist views toward reliance on voters in the West. I do not think that the Russian-speaking Poroshenko—for whom Ukrainian became his fourth or fifth language—could ever imagine such an evolution of his politics. A classic moderately neoliberal entrepreneur, he began to look like a radical national conservative by the end of his term, putting forward the slogan "Army, language, faith!"

This evolution showed many of the Ukrainian elite's superficial and situational approaches to fundamental issues such as national identity, who perceived them as mere opportunities for additional buzz on TV screens. Unfortunately, playing games with such profound questions eventually makes a politician put on a mask (and I don't mean a Covid mask) that can be difficult to remove later. This is especially true in a country at war, where combat veterans are by no means inclined to joke about these issues.

As a result, Poroshenko's rule turned into a series of attempts to introduce a Galician take on Ukrainian identity, which is close to the hearts of just about 20% of the country's inhabitants. In fact, that's exactly how many percentage points of the vote he got in the next presidential election.

This is indeed the key problem of Ukrainian society. Galicia in Western Ukraine considers itself, and only itself, the real Ukraine.

However, Ukraine can only survive as a balanced combination of three significant parts: West, South-East, and Center-North.

Eight

This brings us to the elections of Volodymyr Zelensky in 2019.

He was a man without experience, a team, or knowledge of international relations. Yet, unlike Poroshenko in 2014, he relied on all three pillars—the West, South-East, and Center-North—of the diverse Ukrainian nation.

This man is a special phenomenon.

It was precisely the extreme "pendulum" swing toward the West under Poroshenko that helped Zelensky to become president. Disappointment in the post-Maidan government firmly steered society in the other direction.

Zelensky set a record—73.22% of the vote in the second round, against 24.45% for his opponent, Poroshenko.

Many Western-oriented Ukrainian voters cast their ballots for Zelensky instead of Poroshenko.

Why?

The main reason, I think, is that the Ukrainian people are still looking for their identity. Unfortunately, I think the position of some Western Ukrainians could be counterproductive for their own goals and beliefs. They tend to look for an identity based exclusively on ethnicity and language—and to build that identity as if in opposition to Russia.

Instead of saying who Ukrainians are and what they want to achieve, people tend to be satisfied with saying, "We are not Russian. We are different from them, period." And each additional difference is cultivated. It is difficult to call such an approach positive. Identity cannot be built on the principle of, "We are different."

I believe that as the result of the war and the Kremlin's inevitable failure to sustain its take on the imperialistic "Russian world":

Ukraine will acquire a true separate identity
and become a great country
when it claims its rights also to
the Russian heritage and Russian language.

I realized all this when I began living in Ukraine, and it was an important and dramatic discovery for me. However, I think it's also an important and dramatic discovery that the Ukrainians will have to make for
themselves.

Nine

Such an approach to the history and ideological foundations of a recently-
established statehood would lead to problems in any country. The search
for national identity is vital for any young state. Given the deeper national
roots in Ukraine, in any discussion on the issue of collecting Slavic lands,
there is a sufficient argument to assert that the center of such a gathering
lies with us in Kyiv.

Russia cannot be the point of such an assembly. Moreover, due to its
complexity and size, any claim to its pan-Slavic leadership will look like
a threat to its neighbors—including the threat to Russia's own numerous
non-Slavic ethnic groups, who would be alienated by such an approach.

But Ukraine can.

Operating from the center in Kyiv, it is easy to speak with all of
Eastern Europe—Poles, Czechs, Slovaks, Bulgarians, and Slavs of the
Balkans, across the borders of the European Union. With Russia—across
the Eastern border. Likewise, the Hungarians, Romanians, and Greeks
who, although not Slavs, live in the same Baltic–Black Sea–Balkan
macroregion.

I believe this is fair because:

**In Kyiv, and not in Moscow,
lies the true center of Russian/Slavic statehood.**

Such an idea may seem too paradoxical to some. It will confuse others.
Perhaps it will break someone's picture of the world. In the stereotypical
vision of some, the center of the universe is Moscow. According to the
cliché of others, Kyiv is the eternal enemy of this center.

The reason for their prejudice lies in the narrowness of the political,
economic, and cultural horizons available to them.

Meanwhile, placing the assemblage point in Kyiv—external to
Moscow, Saint Petersburg, Voronezh, Yekaterinburg, Novosibirsk,
Khabarovsk (and other competing centers of power)—equalizes them,
leaving much less room for conflict. It removes the reason to confront

Moscow, as Ukraine has been doing since 1991. There is no need now to go looking for a new identity. It is already here—in the thousand-year history of the Ukrainian, Russian, and other Slavic peoples.

Russia, no matter what cataclysms it experiences, can be an endless source of resources for Ukraine. And Ukraine would stabilize Russia and keep it from falling apart—which is anticipated with the almost inevitable squabbling of interest groups that will follow Putin's departure.

At the same time, strictly according to Lenin, "it would be a stupid policy to refuse the union" of the new advanced class of Ukraine and Russia, whose fatherland (like that of the proletariat) is all of humanity.

So I'll say it again, but with just a little different twist:

> **Just imagine the political center being in Kyiv.**
> **And you will see how the whole picture**
> **of this part of the world**
> **where we live will change before your eyes.**

I am convinced that this idea will act as a stimulus for reflection and strategic planning for those who seriously think about the future of Europe, Ukraine, and Russia and their relations.

Ten

I am going to wrap up this discussion about Ukraine for now with this radical thought:

When you think about Russia and Ukraine—excuse me, I mean when you think about Ukraine and Russia—also try to think about this famous phrase from U.S. history:

> *Actions speak louder than words.*
> —Abraham Lincoln

Lincoln engraved these words into American history when he spoke them during his famous Cooper Union speech while running for president.

The national debate at the time was about the Founding Fathers' views regarding slavery. Lincoln's most crucial point in this speech was that while some of the Founding Fathers never expressly voiced their opinions about slavery, their actions spoke "louder than words."

I propose that we apply the same logic to the actions of Ukraine and Russia.

- Since 1996, Ukraine has fought proudly and valiantly, even in the midst of internal struggles, to stand as a democracy.
- Following the 2014 annexation of Crimea and beginning an unthinkable confrontation with Russia, Ukraine had to reinvent itself as a state, rebuild its military, and restart an economy cut off from the Kremlin's natural gas hook.
- Ukraine's response to Russia's invasion in 2022 has been to fight back fiercely, to aggressively court allies worldwide, to use the invasion as a way to strengthen their standing as a global political and economic force, and to adapt their economy during the war in a way that will bring long-standing benefits and prosperity to Ukraine's citizens far into the future.
- Russia, on the other hand, has only become more and more antidemocratic since 1993. The invasion of Ukraine has driven Putin to do precisely the opposite of Ukraine; destroy the country's standing and reputation in the world, isolate it from other world powers, and allow the war to diminish the economic well-being of its citizens.

With all that in mind, here are two questions for Russians to ask themselves:

1. Under which of these two systems would you rather live?
2. If as a Russian, you would rather live like Ukrainians, what can you do to make that happen?

Of course, my goal with this book is to lay out the Big Project for my fellow Russians and you in the West, enabling and empowering Russians to make the best choice for their future.

CHAPTER FIVE

Debunking Fukuyama's "End of History"

One

So far, we've talked a lot about the past.

However, that's not why I am writing this, and I hope it's not why you are reading it, either.

I am not the person I was in the past: my views, methods, and life changed significantly, especially after the war started in 2014. I am sure you are not the person you were in the past either. Russia as a whole does not have to be the country it has been in the past.

You and I can each be something different. First, I was an entrepreneur. Then I was a politician. Now I am both. Combining the two can produce a revolution that changes the world.

And yes, Russia can certainly change and become a healthy, functional democracy.

Two

Once I settled in the United States after the Crimean events and my related problems with the Russian authorities, I became interested in sharing my views and experiences about Russia with others. I felt there was a very limited understanding of what's going on, and that people are listening either to pro-Putin or anti-Putin stereotypes. And both leave no room for rational thinking and in-depth analysis.

As you know, in the West, giving lectures at universities is a common thing for any prominent public figure—a figure in science, culture, entrepreneurs, and politicians. I was already prosecuted in Russia for speaking as such—so why not resume my career, without prosecution, here?

Elon Musk lectures at Stanford. Steve Jobs lectured at Harvard. Bill Gates lectures at Cambridge.

In the West, this is a long-standing tradition.

Before becoming president, Woodrow Wilson was a Princeton professor, writing *A History of the American People* in five volumes, teaching political science, and later serving as chancellor. "Every university graduate," he wrote, "should be a man of his nation, as well as a man of his time."

Many years later, this phrase from President Wilson was repeated many times in university lectures by John F. Kennedy. In one such speech, at the ninetieth-anniversary convocation of Vanderbilt University, Kennedy said:

> *But this Nation was not founded solely on the principle of citizens' rights. Equally important, though too often not discussed, is the citizen's responsibility. . . . For we can have only one form of aristocracy in this country, as Jefferson wrote long ago in rejecting John Adams' suggestion of an artificial aristocracy of wealth and birth. It is, he wrote, the natural aristocracy of character and talent, and the best form of government, he added, was that which selected these men for positions of responsibility.*

"We are choosing to land on the Moon this decade, like other projects, not because it is easy to do, but because it is difficult," Kennedy said at Rice University in 1962, kicking off the space race—and with it, an opportunity for thousands of new and world-critical scientific discoveries and technological innovations.

It is this progress, as well as free-market competition, that Kennedy considered the main engine of development, leading the people of the United States and the world to prosperity and peace.

But what world was he talking about?

In a lecture at the American University, Kennedy also answers this question: "What kind of world do we aspire to? This is not *pax Americana*, imposed by American arms. Not the peace of the grave, and not the safety of the slave. I'm talking about genuine peace, a world that makes life worth living on Earth, a world that allows people and nations to develop, hope, and build a better life for their children—a world not only for Americans but for all men and women, not just the world in our time, but the world for all time."

He thought a lot about the future and knew history well. To me, it's a great example that each politician needs to follow.

Three

I don't want to compare myself to Woodrow Wilson or JFK other than to say that I also think a lot about the future and know history pretty well—especially Russian history. I probably know Russian history better (at least from a Russian point of view!) than Wilson or Kennedy did. So I suggested to friends in the United States who teach at universities, "Let's talk about Russia and its future place in the world with your students."

We will discuss relations between Russia and America. Their cyclicality. The causes of conflicts and conditions of cooperation. True and false ideas about each other, of the peoples and elites of our countries. They are the ones that cause me the most anxiety and grief. They are dangerous not just by themselves, but because it is difficult to imagine a situation worse than when vital political decisions are made by people who do not know anything about each other, do not understand the opponent's logic, and are driven by stereotypes.

One friend in particular, Secretary Condoleezza Rice, invites me to give a lecture for her students at Stanford.

Condoleezza also knows Russia well and even speaks Russian. And also, like me, she's a former oil and gas professional.

She is a very strong teacher, and she has great students. They are powerful, sharp, flexible, free-thinking, energetic, erudite, and capable polemicists. So at some point, Condoleezza and I decided that instead of just a lecture, we should create a kind of geopolitical strategy game for her students. We divided them into several teams that take the positions of different countries and collectively think and discuss how they could act in various critical situations that are developing in the world.

The game was a huge success with her students.

In fact, after several hours of engagement, her students found themselves in an intense and complicated discussion. At one moment, to give them a chance to work on the issue together without looking to me for guidance, I walked out of the room to take a breather.

I found myself in a darkish stone corridor, a bit reminiscent of the *couloir* of a medieval castle with a Romanesque accent. I slowly began walking around, thinking about Condoleezza's students and the game's progress, when I saw a familiar person walking toward me. He was short in stature, in a dark suit, with an Asian appearance.

Four

Francis Fukuyama was the author of many books, including *The End of History and the Last Man.*

There was no reason for me to be surprised by seeing him there; like Secretary Rice, he was also a professor at Stanford.

But frankly, his concept of the "end of history" always surprised me with its deeply ingrained snobbery, a kind of united, extremely condensed attitude of the Western elite about everything happening in the world, which has become widespread after the collapse of the Soviet Union. This collapse is a significant geopolitical catastrophe for some, but for Fukuyama and others, it is a victory—as if their cause has always been right, and now they've won.

However, two years—even two months—before the disappearance of the USSR, they did not even suggest such a development of events might happen, even as an opportunity. And, of course, they have nothing to do with this unexpected geopolitical victory. Everything was done by us, the Soviets ourselves.

In the 1980s, with our "new thinking," we believed we'd scored a major victory for the whole of humanity by stopping the Cold War. Then, in the 1990s, we felt betrayed and taken advantage of by the reformers associated with (and supported by) the West. The more Westerners talked about their ultimate historic victory, the more Russians started to strive for a revanche for their defeat—one they'd initially perceived as the joint achievement in the struggle for peace and security.

I decided I would tell Fukuyama what I thought about his theory of the end of history. I didn't attack. I just politely asked something like this:

"Francis, how did you get the idea that history could have an end?"

And then I continued:

"This is an absolutely anti-scientific approach. After all, history is continuous and lasts as long as the human race exists. And after that, it will continue, just without us. Although then, it will become another story—the history of the universe.

"And it is all the more strange to say that its end has come right now, based on the results of your analysis of the historically short period that humanity is currently going through. It is strange to talk about the complete triumph of some doctrine, in this case, liberal democracy, even if it is in one separate region of the planet. Even in the world of concepts."

And then I shut up.

He didn't argue. Instead, he said:

"You know, I think I was misunderstood by many. History will never end. And the forces of the past will give us a lot of fights in the future. However, I do think that the evolution of the ideas slows down: liberal democracy proved to be the best alternative to every other concept humanity developed. So I simply offered fellow scientists and publishers a bright image and a biting headline. But it looks like everyone read the title, and didn't read the book!"

For the record, I did read the book. So I knew he was referring to his 1989 article, "The End of History?" published in the foreign policy journal *The National Interest*. His widely acclaimed best-selling book, *The End of History and the Last Man*, was published later, in 1992.

Both compositions made him a world celebrity and a highly sought-after author and lecturer.

When he wrote the original "The End of History?" essay in 1989, the world felt like it was on the verge of huge changes—turbulent and obscure processes were going on, threatening unpredictable consequences.

For instance, for the first time in history in the USSR, (albeit partially) free elections of delegates to the Congress of People's Deputies were held on an alternative basis. As a result, Boris Yeltsin, Andrei Sakharov, Yuri Afanasyev, and other supporters of radical democratic reforms were elected deputies. In the Baltic countries, about two million people built a human chain almost 600 kilometers long, demanding independence. And first Azerbaijan, and then Georgia, declared state sovereignty.

Mikhail Gorbachev and German Chancellor Helmut Kohl signed a document giving the countries of Eastern Europe the right to choose their political system. Soviet troops withdrew from Hungary and the GDR (Communist East Germany). The Polish government finally permitted the peoples' Solidarność movement to grow. Nicolae Ceausescu was overthrown in Romania. The process of reunification between East and West Germany began. The Velvet Revolution ended in Czechoslovakia. It seemed the USSR and the Eastern bloc were bursting at the seams before the world's eyes.

Was it the end of history? For some, it was. For others, the overwhelming majority, it was a new beginning. The conflict between these two positions defines the current events, at least in our part of the world. The war in Ukraine is a futile attempt by Putin to reverse the flow of history, as futile as an attempt to stop it altogether. History goes on, no matter what we think about it. The future is always larger than the past and can never be stopped. In particular, no one can stop the search for new ideas and the passionate pursuit of a better society.

Five

I am glad to be able to tell Francis my deepest-held belief:

"There is no end to history."

In this conversation, I found Fukuyama to be a real deep, searching, creative scientist. It is just curious that his most devoted disciple is the person he criticizes the most: Vladimir Putin. The Russian president wants to retaliate against Westerners who believe in their final victory over the Soviets, but he also wants to be the one to stop history himself.

Putin does not accept, as Fukuyama does, the victory of liberalism over communism. He does not believe in any ideas. Even Putinism was invented by his minions, not by himself. His take is: Americans defeated Soviets, thus—Russians. Perhaps he feels it happened because capitalism was stronger than socialism, and that's why he is the evangelist of his own form of corrupted capitalism—because he seeks revenge and needs to be strong this time.

Marx and Engels also predicted the end of history. They saw history ending with a system (communism) in which there is no money, no exploitation, and no class or ethnic conflicts—which means there is no history of wars or clashes of social or geographic communities.

Six

Let's move from Francis Fukuyama to Marx and Engels, who were right in describing the essence of history as the evolution of humanity's way of living, which follows the development of labor and production. They saw how socioeconomic formations succeeded each other, along with ideas and even ethics, following changes in industrial relations.

In a tribal community, the primary value is in the tribe itself. When there are no machines or tools, the tribe is the means of production on its own: the larger the tribe, the more mammoths it kills, or useful plants it finds—vegetables, fruits, grains. The more abundant food is, the higher the birth rate. Each human is a tool. That makes each person truly valuable, and the tribe lives as one family with communist relations between its members. Everybody contributes as much as possible, and receives as much as they need to survive.

With the development of various tools and tillage, people are increasingly moving toward an independent and sedentary lifestyle. A person's primary value is not as a human being anymore, but as a landowner with control over the land that gives bread and other food. A person with more land also has added value and more control over more human beings.

Those who control land become the ruling class. Feudalism emerges, but time goes by, and it remains in the past. People now create enterprises and process what they have produced on earth. They create new material goods and systems for their distribution. Production forces, markets, and ownership structures are becoming more complex. Capitalism develops and gives rise to the bourgeoisie—the new ruling class.

The Industrial Age begins, develops, and goes to the moment of transformation. Now, we see how the primary added value is no longer created at a metallurgical plant or a weaving factory, but in a laboratory, an office, and through high-tech production.

The primary added value is created, in many ways, by those who constantly come up with innovation, with something new. Thus, a new advanced and—in the future—ruling class, a global hegemon, gradually arises.

Time will pass, and the increased complexity of production as new technologies are developed will cause new transformations. Marx assumed that at some point production would be universal, fully automated and self-sustainable, and eventually the market would be fully saturated—nothing would be in deficit, and everything would be free for consumers. So perhaps I am wrong after all, and that is when the end of history will really happen: not with capitalism, but with communism.

Nope, I still don't buy it.

Actually, I believe humanity will improve gradually. Progress cannot be stopped, although Russia's example after the collapse of the Soviet Union shows it can be temporarily reversed for a short time. We Russians, together with other nations, will fly to the stars, find new worlds, and make new discoveries—as happened with us in the past. We will create new technologies, find new sources and types of energy, and get new opportunities that we never had before—after we are liberated.

Humans are likely to change not only ethically but physically. I doubt we will resist for a long time the temptation to play with the genetic codes of animals and plants—and our own, no matter how much religious and other conservative groups hinder this. And then, obviously, a new society will arise; built, most likely, with the heavy influence of the biotech and IT entrepreneurs.

There will be no end to history as long as the desire to compete and to develop is left in humans.

Seven

When I was a kid, I liked to watch war movies. As I watched those usually black-and-white films, I asked myself and the characters on the screen:

"Hey, fascists, why are you killing our people?"

"Hey, fascists, why are you burning our houses?"

Born thirty years after the victory of World War II (fifty years later than those men and women who lived and fought in those distant years), I somehow felt with my child's instinct that those houses were our houses and that those people were our relatives, our family.

Recently, before another Victory Day, I was browsing the Internet and encountered colorized German chronicles of World War II. I saw captured Soviet soldiers wandering under armed escort along broken roads. I saw native Slavic faces, blackened with dust and sun. I saw the faces of other nations of the Soviet Union. I asked myself, "They are being driven to an execution or a concentration camp. What are they thinking about?"

For some reason, I was convinced that, at that very moment, they all were thinking about their mothers, their families, and their loved ones. This common memory united them into one person. It also connected them in their fight against evil. All our movies, literature, and survivors' evidence screams out loud—our people felt as one family in the face of a mortal enemy.

They were as one until the perestroika of the Eighties woke up bloody interethnic conflicts and sowed the seeds of enmity between different people. Then, the elites of former republics used these conflicts to privatize power and national wealth for their selfish benefit.

Putin understands the power of separation better than anyone else. Having attacked Ukraine, he again set people against each other. Russians against Ukrainians. Ukrainians against Russians. Russians against Russians. Ukrainians against Ukrainians. He is also trying to set Europeans against Europeans, and Americans against Americans.

During the Great Patriotic War, those who wore uniforms, regardless of their nationality, political views or religion, were assigned to defend the Motherland. Stalin, who was not particularly tolerant of dissidents, found the most potent words in his famous speech at the beginning of the war were to address everyone as family members: "Brothers and sisters!" The country has allocated its vanguard, sacrificed its best people to repel evil. Former workers and peasants, officials and intelligentsia, people of different views and education— were an army of good. They stopped the enemy for the sake of their family and mine, for the sake of their country and mine.

When I was a kid, I could not imagine in my worst nightmare that I would be standing here in Ukraine, asking my own people:

"Hey, Putinists, why are you killing our people?"

"Hey, Putinists, why are you burning our houses?"

Eight

The modern enemy is much more insidious than the fascists of the twentieth century. He took over the Russian state, absorbed Belarus, and now strives to conquer others—and not only immediate neighbors. He invents false enemies for us, protecting himself. He turns warriors of good into bearers of evil. Our real allies and friends become the "most dangerous." The enemy judges us under the guise of judges. The enemy arrests the best and most active of us under the guise of policemen. The enemy is destroying our enterprises under the guise of officials.

We, the descendants of those who built the country and fought for it, will make a new caste of defenders—defenders of justice and legality. We will stop the enemy. We are creating the Order of Right to fight it. It is happening right now, believe it or not, in the fields of war in Ukraine.

Only by winning will we realize ourselves as a force. We will recognize ourselves as one family. A family that believes in itself and is not afraid of change. The Russian opposition of the past was fearful of becoming such. The Russian opposition of tomorrow, the revolutionary opposition, will not.

I am calling for such a revolution: the revolution in our consciousness. When this revolution happens, a fresh wave of positive change will come, borne by ordinary people—those who are still silent and do not want to associate themselves with the peaceful protests of the past. Those who are capable of action.

It will come from the very foundation of our country. I would like to say "from the very heart," but instead, I will say, "from the very bones, from the very roots." We have long endured the evil that has penetrated everywhere. However, the cleansing wave is gaining strength. With violent attacks on the officials of Putin's regime and his warmongers all across Russia, it is gaining momentum. Now everything depends on those who are rightly called to fight: the people.

What choice do they make? What choice do we make? And how many of us are we—those who are ready to make the choice? This book is about our choice.

CHAPTER SIX

For Me, a "Beginning of History"

One

As I have already told you, I am a politician. I'm not so tall. I have a beard. I smile a lot, but a lot of people don't like it. "Why is he smiling? He must not be one of us—we have nothing to smile about!" Some people don't like my way of dressing, either.

I, too, don't like many things happening around me. I hate the hypocrisy that is everywhere these days, with everybody who refuses to fight at a time of war. My parents told me that if my Motherland and my beliefs are under attack, I should fight back.

I have been to many places in my life. I have mastered many professions. But I haven't done much yet, and I don't know much. It's impossible to know everything. But I have a position, and there are those who are afraid of it. They call me an oppositionist. They know I want to change the world. That's scary enough for many.

People are right. I am a person who wants to change the world for the better; this is an important clarification. I want to return those who have been rejected and made superfluous by modern Russia to the category of necessary ones—a category I want to return to myself. Some will say this desire is utopian. But what else, if not a utopia, can one offer people living in an illusionary world?

As a child, I was fond of airplanes. At the age of six, I studied them day and night and assembled a lot of models. I was living in Poland with my grandparents, the diplomats. One of my grandfather's duties as the ambassador was the oversight of Soviet military bases located in the country.

Once, when I was a boy, he took me to the airfield next to the German-Polish border. The wing commander, Colonel Kopanev, who was a great friend of my grandfather and a regular guest in our house, said to me, "Do you want me to take you up in a jet fighter?"

"No, you don't have to," replied my grandfather.

Oh! But I really wanted to!

"Then why not?" Kopanev said. "Let's ride!"

I was put in a two-seat training version of a real fighter, the MIG-23. We climbed up to the clouds. I pressed on the handles and buttons. He showed some aerobatic tricks, driving me into true ecstasy.

My goal here is not to boast that I grew up as a golden boy. Instead, I am talking about certain feelings of freedom, might, and unlimited horizons implanted in my childhood and stayed with me forever.

What I experienced that day as a six-year-old can only be described as happiness, clean and uncluttered. The plane shook slightly as it took off. My chest tightened, and I let go. As a student, the day would come when I would again experience a similar feeling, but it was no longer associated with airplanes.

I was eighteen then. My comrades, students of the physics department of Moscow State University, were walking on the Lenin Hills overlooking the picturesque bend of the Moscow River. It was a beautiful spring day, and there was not a single cloud in the sky.

A bum approached us with a swollen face and rotten teeth, smelling awful. But, in his eyes, there was . . . I don't know, *something* about him. Something special. Something you rarely see. Bums and cops (yes, in Russia, they are usually despised more or less to the same degree) usually like me. They probably feel I would not turn them down and will always see a human being in them.

The bum asked for a smoke. One of us spared him a cigarette, trying to keep as much distance from him as possible because of the smell.

He puffed, and then asked, "Guys, where do you study?"

"At Moscow State," we answered. "Physics."

"But you guys, you physicists, do you know how to feel?" he asked.

And I answered, "I think we do."

"Here, you, come here," he said to me, walking me about two meters away from my puzzled and disgusted friends.

"Come up here. Do you see the sun? You have to turn around like this, squint your eyes, and you will feel how the spring sun fills you from the inside, pours into your pores, and warms your insides. And as soon as you feel it, you will understand that you do not need anything else in life. Because your soul can now merge with the sun!"

I turned to the sun. I don't know if I managed to become a part of it, but I definitely felt it fill my soul. Part of that tender spring sun, and part of that bum's mind, is now always with me. It's a pity that my friends just laughed and did not want to open themselves up. They have no idea what they missed.

Two

I am a rational person, so I use metaphors only when I know they are needed.

That feeling of the sun shining on me—not burning but born *inside*, warming and raising something higher and higher—awakened freedom in me, and for the second time in my life, I felt its alluring breath.

Just like the day I was taken to the skies on the MIG-23.

On that day, thanks to the homeless person, I felt boundless energy, healing this pain, unleashing freedom out of slavery through me. And I realized that this feeling of complete inner freedom arises in special people under special circumstances.

**You are free when you give up everything, or
everyone abandons you, and you are no
longer attached to anything in this world
of real and imaginary freedoms.**

You have nothing, and the only thing you can do against your will is die.

Of course, I considered myself special. I did not refuse visible benefits then. However, my fundamental difference from most politicians is that I was always ready to give them up, and eventually, I did.

I clearly realized this readiness of mine at the beginning of the winter of 2011, looking at thousands of people in the center of the largest city in the country protesting against unfair elections. That day was not sunny, but the almost erotic energy of the protest made it wonderful.

There I was, looking at those who rose up to declare that their votes had been stolen, and I realized that freedom grows inside each of us. A person must wake up to it during his life, as early as possible and before it's too late.

I'm talking about December 6, 2011, when I came to Triumfalnaya Square in Moscow and suddenly saw that we were no longer a handful of protesters who, for years, had gathered on the streets of Russia's capital on the 31st of every month. Suddenly, there were thousands of us, thousands of people with stolen voices no longer willing to be silent.

For those who don't know, Triumfalnaya Square before 2011 was the site of a protest demanding authorities honor the people's right to assemble peacefully. The demonstrations were held on the 31st day of every second month because freedom of assembly is enshrined in Article 31 of the Russian Constitution, and on that day Moscow would be shaken with mass arrests. Law enforcement in Russia, unlike protesters, never paid any attention to the Constitution. "Respect your own Constitution" was written by Soviet dissidents in 1965. They were not heard then, and nothing has changed ever since. But it will soon.

Three

On December 6, 2011, the protest started just as it began to get dark. Wet snow mixed with rain was falling from the skies, getting underneath people's coats. A porridge of snow and mud gathered under our feet. We stood ankle-deep in it, shoulder to shoulder. The oppressed Moscow sun had just set, but there was a feeling of such energy as if it was about to rise again.

The drums of Putinists brought in on the Kremlin's orders (and paychecks) from nearby regions rattled, creating a feeling of an impending storm that needed to be overcome in order to sweep all crooks and thieves out of Moscow.

Our protesting comrades were mercilessly screwed by the riot police, who shoved them into paddy wagons and took them away. Yet all of us—scattered, cold, like drops of rain interspersed with snow, knocked down into a single ocean on Triumfalnaya, standing shoulder to shoulder—clearly felt that we were comrades. We were all united not only by the theft of our votes but by something more.

Perhaps it was the very feeling that now, violating all conceivable laws of nature, the sun will again rise above us. It will rise above those who will live after us—in a world better than this. And as we chant the words that have already overthrown tyrants many times—"Russia will be free!"—let's turn the world over and find ourselves on the side where it shines not only for all the bums but also for all others who need its light.

Four

I started my career as an entrepreneur in 1989, at fourteen years old. A year before, a gift was brought to my school—a personal computer, a true miracle! It was a genuine IBM PC/XT. It's IBM! With three striped letters on a gray body with black drive holes. This overseas machine took pride of place on the podium on the teacher's desk in the recently opened computer class. There were also three rows of children's computers BK-00-10-01, the newest products of our domestic Soviet electronics industry, or as we then joked, "personal computers for collective use." That IBM was probably the first and last time a full-blooded American from Silicon Valley took over the Russian presidium.

I must say, I have been interested in computers, as I have been in all technology, since childhood. However, that IBM computer sealed my fate: I immediately bought a semi-homemade type of textbook (there were no others) on the latest BASIC programming language, and I was lost to the world. I sat in the computer class from dawn to dusk, using every opportunity to get to the coveted teacher's desk. I installed, then deleted (because of lack of hard drive space), and once again installed the just-released MS-DOS 4.01 and Windows 2.03f—ultramodern programmer's toys of that time.

A year later, I could already do the work of a system administrator. In fact, my career began with exactly such a job—it started at the Nuclear Safety Institute (IBRAE) of the USSR Academy of Sciences, which my father helped to establish shortly after the Chernobyl disaster. It became one of the centers for the dissemination of new computer technologies in Moscow. Through it, the most advanced personal computers were imported into the turbulent era of emerging Soviet capitalism. It also had one of the first connections to global networks (first FIDO, and eventually the Internet). There was just one minor problem: No one knew how to work on personal computers, because everyone in Soviet science was trained to use mainframes. I took advantage of this by creating a special PC training group for scientists with my senior school friend Dmitry

Bereza. In return, IBRAE gave us several permanent job positions and a large hall to use with eight PCs—so, at age fourteen, I had earned my first office and the possibility to start my first company.

Five

We soon earned the required start-up capital—a thousand dollars, a gigantic amount for me at that time. We were paid for creating an animated (or what I would now call multimedia—if we'd known this word then, we would have asked for twice as much!) presentation for my father's business partners from Italy. Dmitry and I invested this money into creating our company, which was supposed to deal with programming and computers. We called it, modestly, "RussProfi." In the very last days of the Soviet Union, in December 1991, we received a registration certificate and became—think of it!—shareholders. We seemed to be standing on the threshold of a genuinely new world of unlimited alluring possibilities.

My business career has been great. In 1995, when Dimitry left for the States to study computer science, I sold the business and became the executive director of the Russian-American joint venture International Network Connections. In 1996, fearing the return of the Communists during the upcoming elections, our American partners preferred to run away from the country, wiping the corporate accounts. (They could have indeed returned, but "democrats" led by Yeltsin and assisted by the States falsified the election results, so nothing had changed at the end of the day.)

As far as the business goes, we made a deal with the world's leading technology supplier for the oil and gas industry, Schlumberger, and I moved there myself as the Director of Marketing and Business Development.

In a Schlumberger jacket, I traveled all over Russia in search of new technologies in oil and gas upstream. We packaged what we found with cutting-edge Western business practices, then distributed these products and services worldwide. Nobody did this at that time—everyone believed that there were no interesting technologies outside the military industry in Russia, especially no technologies to aid in business practices and management. Furthermore, they assumed there never would be. We proved they were wrong; they existed, although a dramatic brain drain in the 1990s quickly destroyed Russia's R&D potential.

By the time I turned twenty-four, we already made a strategic alliance between Schlumberger and Yukos, the leader of the Russian oil industry. I became Vice President for Upstream Technologies there and was running several IT businesses where Yukos was the investor. However, at twenty-six, I felt I was at a dead end, and I needed to change my life.

Six

I was brought to this understanding by a conversation with the owner of Yukos, Mikhail Khodorkovsky.

This happened on Tuesday, August 10, 1999. I led a working group of programmers and designers that restarted the first Russian online media site Gazeta.ru, created by Yukos and the Gleb Pavlovsky Foundation of Effective Policies (FEP). But the first version of this website, made by the famous Internet journalist Anton Nosik, did not please Khodorkovsky. In July, he took the site away from FEP, invited one of the most reputable media managers, Vlad Borodulin from the *Kommersant* newspaper, as the new editor-in-chief, and told us to redo everything.

Then the day came when I reported to Khodorkovsky with the new design.

It was the third hour of that memorable meeting . . .

"So, what do we have here?" Khodorkovsky asked as he pressed the "Business" button on his screen. The Business News tab opened.

"No, Ilya, how can you not understand? You have a section on deals here, and the font color is light blue when dark is needed! Dark is more heavyweight, inspires greater confidence!"

I made a note in my notepad.

"And why is this font so round?"

I wrote it down as well.

"Yes, yes, write this all down; it is all very important. But what I really want to know is, how would I make this site load on every computer in Russia by default?"

"Hmmm," I said, thinking aloud—and also thinking that this idea was kind of crazy. "Well, for example, we could buy Rambler," I said. Rambler was the most popular website in Russia at that time. "And then we will be able to do it. Throw out the search bar, and put in Gazeta.ru!" I suggested with great irony.

Khodorkovsky did not understand the irony. He was ready to change the face of the Russian Internet in the most decisive way. "Great idea! Go talk to them."

"Mikhail Borisovich, are you kidding me? An hour of your time is worth more than all this Rambler!"

I was not exaggerating about the value of an hour of his time.

While he may not be as well known in the West, Mikhail Khodorkovsky is famous in Russia for having been, at one time, the wealthiest man in the country, with an oil and gas fortune, via his company Yukos, estimated to be worth about fifteen billion dollars. At one time, he was ranked #16 on the *Forbes* list of the richest people in the world.

However, he is now also famous for having spent ten years in a Russian prison for what many consider trumped-up fraud charges and a trial that was seen worldwide as lacking appropriate due process.

Today, he is in exile, like me, and lives in London.

Back in 1999, I took his orders and negotiated the acquisition of Rambler with the founder, Dmitry Kryukov. We persuaded him to sell the project for a mere ninety thousand dollars.

Today, its valuation is at least several billion.

Yet Khodorkovsky decided that even ninety thousand was too expensive. So in my eyes, much of my time was wasted in vain. And, by turning down Rambler (and, by the way, the current leader of the online market, Yandex, which is like Russia's Google, was also for sale then, with a whopping $230,000 price tag), the boss clearly showed he was not serious about this business.

I told him as much:

"You are now wasting your time on nonsense. Gazeta.ru is just a website! We should just launch it now and revise it at any time if needed."

I didn't understand why Michael was so picky about the design.

"Ilya, you don't understand," Khodorkovsky began to explain patiently and even a little condescendingly. "Did you not hear about yesterday's appointment?"

It was about someone with the last name Putin, whom only that Monday Yeltsin had sent to parliament as his proposed candidate for prime minister. The previous one—Stepashin—lasted just three months.

"Okay. So?" I asked. "What difference does it make for our small project who the outgoing grandfather appoints?"

By my naive calculation, there was less than a year left before the presidential election, and someone else would win: either former Prime Minister Primakov, or Mayor of Moscow Luzhkov. There was no third way.

"So," Khodorkovsky continued, "the Duma will approve this Putin in the coming days, and later he will become president. And then Gazeta.ru will remain the only free media site in the country."

To be honest, Michael's theory sounded absurd. But what the hell, he was the boss. Over time, I learned to trust his instincts because his predictions often came true, like this one.

On the other hand, I was right about the enormous business opportunities with Rambler and Yandex, but wrong about the political impact of what we were doing at that moment. Indeed, Gazeta.ru became the brightest star on Russia's media horizon, and was later crashed by the Kremlin.

Ironically, when Gazeta.ru was taken away from Khodorkovsky, its ownership was transferred by the Kremlin to Rambler Media Group.

Both Rambler and Yandex owners are now under international sanctions for being part of Putin's propaganda machine. *Sic transit gloria mundi.*

Seven

In 1999, Putin became president.

In 2001, he seized control over the then best Russian TV channel, called NTV.

So it seemed as if Mikhail Khodorkovsky had been right all along.

It's a shame I hadn't listened more carefully. Unfortunately, as you know, Putin's move indirectly killed my then-favorite project to create a next-generation interactive television system, called Arrava, in Russia.

This was not the first time politics interfered in my professional activities, forcing me to change my life plans drastically. Finally, with the words of Khodorkovsky echoing in my ears, I decided that I should influence politics myself so that I would never again have to submit to someone else's evil will. It was equally important to me that I might be able to save others from the same painful and unjust plight.

I left Yukos, and as it turned out later, because I left, I remained free. At the same time, dozens of my Yukos colleagues who stayed with Khodorkovsky were falsely imprisoned by Putin or forced to leave the country, while hundreds of others in the business world with connections to Yukos were also forced to flee.

If you want to know more about the Yukos Affair, I recommend the book *Putin's Prisoner* by Mikhail Khodorkovsky and Natalia Gevorkyan for follow-up reading.

Eight

Becoming a politician in 2002, I decided to join the Communist Party.

This choice was quite obvious: firstly, it was the leading and most influential opposition party at that time. Secondly, I recognized and could solve its main problems: the lack of professional campaign management and funding. And thirdly, wild oligarchic capitalism was clearly ruining Russia, and the country simply craved a reasonable turn to the left away from the neoliberal policies of the Nineties.

In 2003, I took part in the writing of the historic landmark report, "The State and the Oligarchy." Ironically, the Kremlin used it as a public justification for starting the "Yukos affair," which allowed Putin to put Khodorkovsky and other company members in prison. (Including me, probably, had I not left the company when I did.) The report was also used to justify the act of nationalizing Yukos' assets to show all the other Russian oligarchs that if they didn't play by Putin's corrupt rules and let him grow more powerful and prosperous, they would end up in the same place as Khodorkovsky. Or worse.

Nine

There I was, going from Yukos to the Communist Party. So, naturally, it has caused many people to ask: "How does it make sense for you to combine your business experience, your work for Yukos, and your leftist views all into one?"

And then they conclude: "I'll bet being a leftist for you is just a pose, but in reality, you don't care, and you make a career wherever it turns out."

But no, let me assure you, it all makes perfect sense.

I really am left wing, and here's why:

To be left in my understanding means to put the well-being of ordinary people above everything, to be free myself and to respect other people's will, to enforce social justice and not to exploit

**others, to decentralize power, to break monopolies of any kind and
respect minorities' rights, to fight for equal opportunities and be
internationalist and progressive.**

To my mind, all entrepreneurs should be leftist.

CHAPTER SEVEN

"Why Do We Need Democracy?"

One

Just to challenge (and even piss off) my colleagues, this is a question I like to ask them sometimes.

"What? Why do we need democracy?" they typically sputter in response, full of confusion or moral outrage.

Then they talk about economic growth, development, "living like in the West," and all that.

They get offended when I cite other, very different examples of countries that developed as very limited democracies or without democracy, such as Singapore, Taiwan, South Korea, and Japan, that also offer economic growth, development, "and living like in the West."

For economic development, autocracy is usually a plus. All thriving innovation ecosystems in the world were created under strong state control.

Democracy provides not breakthroughs but sustainability. However, it happens only when people are allowed not just to make decisions but also to make mistakes. You probably would not experiment with democracy during periods of transition or war. As soon as turbulence ends, and the country is on a stable track of consistent development with whatever good and well-intended managers it has, they need to step down and allow people to make their own choices. One should never forget that the word democracy means "the power of the people."

Two

Let me say a few words about Russian politics. Its political system, and the Constitution itself, is a copycat of the modern-day French Constitution. The political parties of the Nineties were numerous, fluid, and always built around personalities rather than ideas (with the one exception of the Communist party), and thus pissed off ordinary people royally. They understood very well that their existence was motivated just by the desire to get to power, not to implement some vision. Again, this is with the exception of Communists—but they had two fundamental problems that limited their political influence. Firstly, when its leader Gennady Zyuganov lost the elections to Boris Yeltsin in 1996, even pro-government media repeatedly said he should have fought against rigging the results, which he was scared to do. Secondly, even among left-leaning people, not everybody wanted to return to the Soviet era, which was one of Zyuganov's main propositions.

The beginning of Putin's era was earmarked with an attempt to reformat Russian parties to make them look like those in Germany. Two large centrist parties would rotate as the ruling forces: the center-right or conservatives (United Russia, Putin himself), and the center-left or social-democrats (A Just Russia, Sergei Mironov).

There would also be three to four smaller players: neoliberals (Union of the Right Forces, Boris Nemtsov, and Anatoly Chubays, who usually call themselves just "liberals" or "democrats," although it is incorrect in terms of pure political theory. During the 2021 elections, the Kremlin's technologists constructed a "New People" party to get rid of opposition-minded liberals); national-populists (with a very strange name for a nationalist force—Liberal-Democrats, Vladimir Zhirinovsky); greens or left-liberals (Yabloko, Gregory Yavlinsky); and the Soviet Communists (Gennady Zyuganov). To be fair, Putin initially even offered Zyuganov to rename his party to "Workers' Social Democrats," which would be precisely what Lenin's party was originally called. Still, Stalin and Leonid Brezhnev appeared closer to Zyuganov's heart, and the leader of the Communists turned the idea down.

Obviously, all these parties are controlled by one office in the president's staff, currently occupied by Sergei Kirienko. They are designed to cover 90% of political demand from the constituents, and officially they do. But because they are all artificial, and being cowards like old turtles that go nowhere and are ready to stop and hide at every given moment, they are hardly seen by the ordinary people as their true representatives. They often vote for these parties and their candidates out of protest. During the 2011–2012 events, one of the most popular slogans was, "We did not vote for you bastards, we voted for the other bastards!"

Any activist not ready to choose one of these parties is doomed to be marginalized. Moreover, creating other political parties without the Kremlin's nod is not allowed, and those who try (like Alexei Navalny or Dmitry Gudkov) are suppressed.

Those who do not fit into the political system tend to flock to three political groups, which identify themselves as liberals, nationalists, and leftists. Each group in Russian realities is subdivided into two: liberals into neoliberal "republican" reformers and left-liberal "democrat" intellectuals; nationalists into conservative, nostalgic admirers of the Empire and those anti-immigrant isolationists who want "Russia for Russians"; and leftists into (also pretty much nationalistic) Stalinists, descendants of the Communist Party of the Soviet Union, and modernized internationalist progressives (some Trotskyists, and some anarchists). I belong to the latter.

When the Ukrainian war started in 2014, every group aligned itself on this issue. However, while most liberal groups criticized the invasion, they did so rather passively. They told each other that the best strategy was to leave Russia and wait until the situation changed.

Other opposition groups got split.

Nationalists were the most actively involved—many representatives of their ethnic wing moved to Ukraine and joined the Ukrainian military. In addition, many of them joined the iconic right-wing volunteer regiment Azov. Imperial nationalists, in turn, played a key role in starting the war in Donbas. Their brightest star, Igor Girkin-Strelkov, is believed to be the one who made the first move by occupying the city of Slavyansk.

Leftists did not abstain from the conflict, either. Stalinists saw in the annexation of Crimea and intervention into Donbas the dawn of restoration of the Soviet Union and supported it wholeheartedly. Progressives did not buy it and called to fight against Putin's imperialism.

It is interesting how twisted Russian politics became after the beginning of the war. All ideological alliances were ruined. So the new issue—once again, as in 1917, the issue of war and peace—became of paramount importance. It changed everything, dividing the activists more on means than on objectives.

Democracy assumes free competition and mutual influence, and even pressure from the main antagonist forces. Take out the left or right flank, and the system will become unbalanced and, eventually, undemocratic. When I was working in Schlumberger, and we were steadily capturing the market, my bosses eventually asked me to stop the expansion, saying, "Our monopoly will hurt us, as well as our clients! Let the competitors have their modest market share, so that we will never get too relaxed in our own development and progress." It turned out that Schlumberger was satisfied with a 90% market share in Russia, but I do believe that, in politics, even 50% is often too much.

Three

Ukraine is the opposite case to monopolized Russia. Its competing oligarchs are not shy to involve politicians and journalists in their fights, making the landscape extremely fragmented. As a result, the country is always on the verge of being anarchic.

I feel very comfortable in Ukraine despite the chaos. It is messy, but very open and quite positive. So these years in exile for me . . . they are not lost. I am learning a lot from this experience.

Sometimes my friends and colleagues here try to involve me in Ukrainian politics. But I'm already in it, but in a different way than they suggest.

I believe that for me to try to represent the opinions of Ukrainians would be both rationally incorrect (even after all these years, I am still an outsider) and ethically wrong since the war started in 2014. So instead, I would rather be on Ukrainian TV and radio every day discussing with Ukrainians (and Russians via social media) how they can live better, how Ukraine can defeat Putinism, and, very importantly—how to avoid the numerous mistakes in building the economy we made in Russia. After all, I have almost ten years of experience in policy-making in business development and the economy in Russia, which are also highly relevant for Ukraine.

I am proud that I have managed to convince the Ukrainian

government to avoid some mistakes that the Russian government had made in the past, and that could have turned out to be very painful.

I often think in Ukraine that if in 2002, when I first became politically involved, I knew what the following years would be like for Russia, I would have stayed out of politics and remained in business instead.

Had I done that, in a few years I would have created a truly significant amount of capital. And by now, when the time came, I could implement way more ambitious political projects without any fundraising concerns—entirely independently.

It's too bad I wasted years trying to improve a political system that needs to be dismantled and its leaders and creators trashed.

On the other hand, it is not fair to say that these years were lost. After all, I have gained unique practical experience in communicating with ordinary people and authorities at all levels: a farmer in a field, a worker in a plant, an executive who owns a business, and the president and prime minister of a nation.

This is a different kind of very valuable capital. And capital, Marx teaches, is a self-increasing value, even if it is intangible.

However, the main task always is to transform everything you get and to multiply it into a result that exceeds the investments made.

Four

Speaking of capital:

At the beginning of Putin's rule, private capital controlled two-thirds of the economy.

By 2020, the state formally regained half of this (while in return, it privatized about a third of agricultural land)—although in reality, of course, this was not nationalization but the distribution of "management rights" to the president's closest friends.

They now manage some officially "state" property, but they do it in their own interests, so the behavior of such companies is even worse than that of privatized ones. So, for instance, there is no interest in investing money in things like technical modernization.

On the contrary, they need investment projects that would last as long as possible and require the maximum amount of capital expenditures (ideally some large construction site), on which they can steal more money.

Very often, such an approach means the creation of monster

monopolies, like the Russian oil and gas company Rosneft. Their creation is justified by "national interests," but in reality they are just feeding grounds for the president's associates.

Was there an alternative to creating such a system?

Of course there was.

The most extensive privatization in Russia was not of industries but residential property.

Starting in the summer of 1991, it bloodlessly and practically without conflict transferred 80% of the country's housing assets to the tenants, making them the owners of their own homes. The scale of what happened has no analogues in world history—and everything happened by purely civilized methods, and not in a narrow circle of people specially selected by "privatizers," but with the participation of the overwhelming majority of the country's population.

This proves that the demodernization of our country is not something inherent in our people, which must be pushed into technological or social progress with Stalin's or Peter's methods. Also, this is not the result of sabotage by our global competitors who secretly steal or seal our brains using George Soros's and Bill Gates's sponsored chips and vaccines. Alas, this is a totally predictable result of our own misdeeds.

And conscious efforts can produce very different outcomes.

However, to make modernization happen, we need to reconsider the foundations of the post-Soviet socioeconomic system that took shape in the 1990s.

There is a reason for this.

During the last thirty years, it was way more profitable for people in business to redistribute (privatize, split, merge and resell, and often just raid) the national wealth, especially in the industrial sector, rather than to create new enterprises—or at least modernize the existing assets.

Even in the energy space, which generates the most national exports—and for technological reasons had to use modern approaches and production methods—the country slept through the introduction of alternative energy, such as shale production. The invasion of Ukraine in 2022 has sped up Europe's transition away from Russian hydrocarbons and more widely from traditional energy sources. After the temporary surge in prices that compensated for dropped physical volumes of the top products of Russian raw materials exports in 2022, we will see a long-term loss of most cash-producing markets and a dramatic reduction in financial resources entering the country. This significantly limits the possibility of continuing the endless redistribution of financial flows and the possibility of solving so many political problems by throwing cash at those who need to be shut up.

Another important constraint is the policy of Russian leadership during the Putin regime, which led to international sanctions and a sharp reduction in Russia's participation in international cooperation. No more new technologies for the industries, which means long-term decay. The inability to import critical parts of different machinery and technology-intensive production—means a sharp drop in competitiveness for Russian enterprises.

This also means there's been a constant risk of an irreparable lag in such areas of research and technological development, as a new generation of energy, genomic medicine, and food technology has been introduced and integrated in other countries worldwide.

This low efficiency of the innovation system in Russia has led to an accelerated loss from the country of the primary resources of its development: capital, educated and trained personnel, advanced technologies, and market ideas. During the years of Putin's rule, this has been the main impediment on the country's economic and social growth.

Five

Going back in time, the worst thing that Gorbachev came up with in 1985 was to simultaneously start "acceleration" (economic reforms) and *"glasnost"* (political transformations).

Weak power in a period of stability is a growth factor. Weak power during a time of reform is a disaster. In the case of a large country like Russia, there is also a high risk of bloodshed and destruction.

China implemented Deng Xiaoping's reforms because it tightly controlled the political sphere. I believe they saw the suppression of the uprising in Tiananmen Square as a necessary prerequisite for success.

The success of the Asian economies has been based on a strategy of authoritarian modernization followed by gradual democratization after the economy picked up.

The source of the Soviet crisis that blew up the country was not just in the economy, as neoliberals suggest. It instead was democratization before the start of economic modernization, which led to the collapse of the state administration system, pillage of the national wealth by greedy elites, and subsequent deindustrialization.

Putin, preserving the democratic entourage set up by Gorbachev and Yeltsin, faced the need to slow down the disintegration set by his predecessors, and turned to authoritarian methods. In the beginning, he was praised by neoliberals like Boris Nemtsov, who realized that their desired reforms were impossible if the people of Russia still had their say. Winding down democracy in the country was the collective project of "democrats" and *siloviki*, or "the ministries of force." These democrats thought they were using the latter, but it turned out to be the former. When the autocracy was sealed in place, the new elites started to use it to their full personal benefit, stuffing their bottomless pockets. But there were no checks and balances, and no institutions to stop them.

Six

Another essential issue is Russia's emergence of pseudo (or what they call "managed") democracy.

Few doubt that Putin has continuously been in the driver's seat since August 1999, including 2008–2012, when the president's name was Medvedev. Most of the decisions were made by the actual boss named Putin. However, the need to formally comply with the letter of the law led to:

a. a severe intra-elite conflict in 2007–2011, which contributed a lot to the emergence of the Bolotnaya movement in 2011–2012

b. additional growth of alienation and a widening gap between the elites and the ordinary people, who witnessed the hypocrisy and deception in their leaders

c. significant diversion of resources, and the public management disarray to support "tandemocracy" (which was what this weird coexistence of Putin and Medvedev in power was delicately called)

It is not surprising that in the end, we saw government paralysis in 2012–2013 and stagnation of economic growth during a time when other nations were enjoying a favorable global environment.

Even an open declaration of a dictatorship, or restoration of the monarchy, could have been not just more honest but also more efficient in terms of the system Putin has created in Russia. He realized the need to give up on the Constitution himself, but as usual he limited himself with half measures, passing the infamous amendments in the summer of 2020, which, among other things, granted Putin the right to run for two more six-year terms.

If you want a little help with the math on this, it means Putin could effectively be president from 1999 to 2036, for a total of thirty-seven years.

These amendments pissed off many people in Russia, both in higher circles and among ordinary people. So, the Kremlin had to spend significant resources to ensure the opposition would not campaign against the amendments but call for a boycott instead. As a result, they have managed to push the amendments through. (Some 58 million voters have spoken in favor, out of 109 million with the right to vote. So, if oppositionists had campaigned against it and turned themselves to vote, it would have been quite possible to win that one. We needed just 3% of the voters to flip, and the referendum would have failed.)

Seven

The main task for Russia after the revolutionary changes and getting rid of Putinism should be a new start of a large-scale process—the growth of technology-intensive industries, which will become the source of development of the nation as a whole.

To ensure success, we need to create a set of economic incentives that focus on new technologies, industrial production, and the development of physical products and intangible services, which should be achieved in a harmonious combination.

In Soviet times, modernization and development were in the hands of the state. The most active and competent part of society was to a certain degree able to ensure such harmony. In many positions, especially with consumer goods, the USSR lagged behind the capitalist and agile West, but gradually the changes were slipping in. The prosperity generated by oil and gas abundance in the 1970s played a bad joke on the bureaucracy. It did not consider the need for innovation except for the military, where R&D expenditures grew enormously (widening the gap between science and consumers' demand even further). This contributed a lot to the collapse of the Soviet Union. Moreover, it programmed the intentions of the elites who privatized the power.

The form in which privatization was carried out in the 1990s made any modernization redundant. As a result, spending money on new products and technologies has become less profitable than cutting in pieces of old technology and propping up fixed assets and equipment leftovers.

The production of anything technologically intensive in Russia dropped catastrophically and was replaced by imports. Under Yeltsin and even more under Putin, the raw material sector thrived and became dominant in the economy, primarily the oil and gas sector. The policy of the ruling circles in Russia consistently strengthened this trend. After Putin's return in 2012, it only accelerated, despite the "import substitution" policy (otherwise known as creating copycat products) announced in 2014, which more or less worked only in agriculture—and even that was "thanks" to Western sanctions that led to evaporation of imports, not to the actions of the Russian government.

It is a myth that Putin differed from the Nineties neoliberals. If he was different, it was only in being more radical in destroying Russian industry because he had fewer constraints from the public. From 2010 to 2018, the share of all secondary and tertiary production sectors of the economy in Russia was dropping. Manufacturing went from 53.2% to 50.7% of the national economy in 2018; heating and power plants (important industry indicators) from 10.2% to 8.7%; utilities from 2.5% to 1.7%. These sectors have the closest, direct relation to the daily lives of citizens.

At the same time, the share of raw materials production increased from 34.1% in 2010 to 38.9% in 2018. And the percentage of oil and gas revenues in total budget revenues in 2019 grew from 40.8 to 46%. In 2022, after the invasion, the general economic decline increased this figure to 48%, and in certain months it even surpassed the psychologically important benchmark of 50%.

These and other similar figures are alarming for many, and these concerns are well justified. However, one should not forget about the international division of labor. Let's face it, except for weapons (and maybe vodka), Russian-made consumer goods have never been seriously competitive on global markets. One can make different conclusions from this fact: Do we want to develop some new things at the end of the day, or do we want to stick with vodka and natural gas? My answer here differs dramatically from what you would hear from the Russian reformers of the Nineties and Vladimir Putin.

Eight

Many liberal economists talk about Russia's ominous "oil curse." The "curse" is that when natural resources are easily obtained and sold to the West and China, it may seem pointless to develop other industries like technology or invest in additional resources or assets for the future.

They are right—when there are people in power who are only prepared to just go with the flow, and nothing can force them to leave their inner comfort zone. Money flows like water, and they can use it both for military adventures and things like a pompous Olympics. And yes, this is not just Russia being so shortsighted—in many countries, innovations start only when an external challenge arises.

For instance, the United States began to focus on education when it was necessary to absorb a flow of immigrants, develop new territories, and advance agriculture during the Civil War. Silicon Valley was the answer to the military threat. Israel also created its innovation system due to military threats from the Arab world. Finland switched to high gear on new technologies after the collapse of the USSR. Taiwan built its model under the threat of invasion from China. South Korea needed to defend itself against a likely takeover by the once more advanced and industrialized North Korea.

However, does this mean we should give up on our oil industry and give up what nature has given us in the name of development so that we can invest time and money into other things like technology? Some oppositionists suggest doing just that. I strongly disagree with them. Is Norway, which has an even higher dependency on oil and gas, also stuck with the "oil curse," and should they abandon it as its primary source of revenue? Reality shows that Norway is more democratic and transparent than even the United States, which proves that an abundance of oil does not necessarily mean corruption and autocracy.

I truly believe that Russia's natural resources potential is not a curse but a unique opportunity.

I have already said in this book that I know the oil and gas industry well. First, I worked at Schlumberger, the world's leading company providing high-tech solutions for it, and then I was vice president of Yukos, Russia's leader in oil and gas. While at these two companies, I did not spend time in offices, but spent a lot of time working in the field. And not just anywhere, but precisely where the needs of extraction of raw materials meet innovations and sophisticated science.

In my opinion, we need to shift Russia's finances from the scary and unfashionable hydrocarbons, into the sphere of sexy, nice, and appealing high technologies—combining them in one package for the good of the country.

Here's how we can do that in a new Russia:

1. **Make innovation for the oil and gas industry a top priority for the national economy.**

The oil, gas, and other natural resources industries—which include exploration, production, transportation, and processing of raw materials—are themselves capacious consumers of advanced solutions. These industries need new technologies all the time, both in equipment and services. Meanwhile, as hydrocarbons are gradually being phased out, we need to procure eco-friendly technologies for Russia and stimulate growth of such twenty-first-century minerals as lithium, graphite, titanium and others.

2. **Tell the truth: Today, Russia is dependent on other nations for innovation.**

Russia, with its more than 150-year history of oil production, is unfortunately in a weak position of technological dependence on other countries. That's why things like sanctions in connection with the annexation of Crimea and the war in Ukraine, for instance, doom us to stagnation.

Meanwhile, Russia's own internal propaganda tries to prove that sanctions actually help Russian companies to overcome this dependence by launching innovations locally. Under the current system, however, there are no incentives for Russian companies to innovate, and there is no reward for modernization. So, innovation and modernization are not happening. Opening up the nation and supporting international cooperation will help develop the internal innovations ecosystem.

3. **Tell the truth: About how the current system in Russia rewards a few and steals from the rest.**

As a reader in the West, you know that in countries like the United States, a lot of innovation is driven by the constant search to reduce costs, which means spending more on innovations and new technologies. In Russia, we are trapped in a vicious cycle where industry is constantly bargaining for various preferences and compensations from the authorities—all at the taxpayers' expense. It is a more accessible and cheaper way to reduce costs than implementing innovations.

Also innovation is crucial to preserve both nature and the urban environment. For Russia, it should be imperative to safeguard the very vulnerable environment of the North. Instead, the elites systematically choose the way with the highest toll, while the government leaders just split (steal) the profits and neglect their duties.

4. **Make innovation and diversification outside of oil and gas a national economic priority.**

Part of the profits received from the sale of hydrocarbons can and should be invested in local companies that develop technologies that are not directly related to the oil and gas industry.

5. **Oil and gas money should be invested in securities on world markets.**

For example, it should be invested in shares in foreign high-tech and other highly profitable enterprises, not excluding oil and gas, which can be sources of new technologies to be brought back home.

6. **Play nice with the rest of the world so they will invest in us and sell us their top-notch technology.**

Russian funds should be spent in a commercially reasonable way on the direct purchase of proven technologies or to finance promising R&D and its application to the various sectors of our country's economy.

7. **Learn from our friends' successes and failures.**

Follow and re-create the experiences of other countries that have found (often by trial and error) successful uses of their proceeds from selling oil, gas, and other minerals on the world markets.

Of course, to do this, Russia must first do a better job of learning how to make friends with other nations.

8. **Be honest with ourselves about why Russia hasn't already adopted a common-sense plan like this.**

What prevents Russia from adopting a plan like this? Is it the complacency of the elite? Swagger? Greed? Probably all three, but the main reasons are the lack of desire and economic incentives, thanks to the elitist mindset that our country is their personal cash cow, and the disbelief of the country's leaders in the future of a plan like this for themselves and their children.

Or, as I said earlier in the book:

The main thing that Putin has stolen from us is the future.

Nine

The money stolen by Putin's accomplices, which people like Alexei Navalny are after, is essential, but it is secondary.

No Crimea, and no stability, can replace this burning feeling that we have no future.

That's why Russian oppositionists have so much anger and passion—because we see that there is no future for the whole nation and for ourselves, unless we leave Russia.

And that's why I felt so liberated on that street corner in California, when I found out that Putin banned me from going home.

For Russians in the West, they know they have a future. They know they own and control their future. This is one of their most important values.

But it must be returned home and invested in the creation of Russia without Putin.

To be more precise, in the creation of Russia *after* Putin.

Part Two: Where Are We Now?

CHAPTER EIGHT

About Responsibility

One

Since 2014, I have not been able to return to Russia.

Many countries have offered me the opportunity to become their citizen and stay with them forever—Poland, Lithuania, the United States—but I have sincerely thanked them all and refused.

On my passport is written, "Place of birth: USSR."

My relatives live in almost all countries of the former Soviet Union. I have decided that the Soviet Union, not Russia or Ukraine, is my Motherland. One should not change one's Motherland, as one should not change parents. Even if your parents separate, they are always your mother and father. To me, Russia, Ukraine, Belarus, and other Soviet republics are like my parents. I can live anywhere in the world, but I can't pledge my loyalty to anyone but them.

My new home and my love is Kyiv.

This city has always fascinated me with its spirit of freedom. It is not the illusion of freedom we in Russia were given a taste of in 1991. Still, we also clearly saw what it was worth in 1993, when Yeltsin in the center of Moscow shelled the parliament with tanks, to the applause of the West and local "democrats."

It's such a strange feeling in Russia when you discover that theoretically you are free to go in any direction—can go right, can go left, can go straight, you can even run as fast as you can, but you will stay in place. Just like Alice in Wonderland, if you wish to go anywhere you must run twice as fast. Yet, that's what you should do in Russia if you want to get somewhere, vote, speak up, and do business. Run harder and harder and harder, without ever getting anywhere—and you'd better find yourself a track to follow and don't go into uncharted territory.

You may think you can move, live, and work alone, but in reality, you need a team, a pack, a horde. You need people who are on your side, no matter what. You may not call them a family, but they will give you the feeling of a close group where you are valued by the fact of your birth.

Such feelings at work sometimes can even compensate for your low salary, but they could never supplant the deceit of imaginary freedom in Russia. No matter how much you repeat to yourself that you are free, in Russia, you remain a prisoner of circumstances and a subordinate of those above you. You will never have the freedom to play by your own rules, but will always be forced to play by the rules of the corrupt government and elites.

It is not enough just to set a person free, you need to give them the tools that will allow them to use this freedom.
This is what the state is for.

The state is a system that should enable everyone, using one's own knowledge and talent, to unlock one's own potential in full and teach one's children to do the same.

However, as we saw with the Yeltsin reforms, the state must also protect the people from a "predator class" that also takes advantage of this freedom to prey on the innocent and unsuspecting.

They might be oligarchs, swindlers, and thieves. Suddenly liberated and left without any state control, they grabbed the power and the national wealth after the collapse of the Soviet Union, while others were just waking up.

The unarmed (both legally and literally) weak are not able to resist such a threat—they have never encountered predators and do not know how to defend themselves.

Putin is also a predator.

He limited the emergence of new oligarchs because he could, and because he wanted to become a more powerful predator himself. He has his minions, who spread in Russia like wasps in a hollow and are feeding their creator, not forgetting themselves.

Now he depends on his cronies, and his authority to provide them with feeding grounds has turned into his main weakness—instead of being a master, he becomes a slave to the interests of his ranks.

Into Putin's ear, they whisper the words of Spain's General Franco, "Give law to our enemies, and the rest to us." And the Russian president publicly complains, "I became a slave at the galleys of the state."

Putin has basically distributed feeding ranges among his people in exchange for some rent and for giving him the right to make political decisions. He assigned tasks to supervise the businesspeople of the 1990s, including Yeltsin-era oligarchs, collecting the toll and passing it up to the very top. A true oligarchy, and just one refused to understand and submit to the new order—my former boss, Michael Khodorkovsky. For that, he was immediately jailed for ten years.

Khodorkovsky, of course, had to be imprisoned to send a message to other elites that what happened to him could also happen to them, but only if they stepped out of line. Of course, the non-elites also saw what happened, and they toe the line as well.

Since the imprisonment of Khodorkovsky, Putin's faithful followers have ruled the country without any obstacles. It was treason by both former and new elites, an act of treason against Russian society, both dishonest and unfair.

Every citizen of the country should be able to find their place in society and realize their greatest potential. This will prevent people from becoming "downsized" and feeling left out. In such a system, if someone wants to be a peasant and work on the land, they should be free to do so. If you want to be a factory worker? Go do it. However, we should also encourage—and enable—people to grow beyond themselves. Everyone should be able to be the owner and entrepreneur of his or her own life.

We want the system of social selection and social lifts to work.

Each may fit into the chain, but not into the one that Putin offers: "You must go where we direct you, even if there is nothing for you there."

After all, Putin and his team do not provide a track into the future for Russians. They do not even promise it. Instead, they only shamelessly exploit those who cannot find it themselves and condemn them for not being patriotic enough.

We want people who make decisions on behalf of the state to be in their positions solely because of their personal talent and merit.

Two

I do not blame anyone for the fact that we are at an impasse.

Having received freedom—and at some point, everyone in Russia had it—we did not know where to go.

We have destroyed our country. Or let it fall apart.

Nobody forced us to vote for Yeltsin or Putin. We did it ourselves—no need to justify ourselves. We came to the polling stations, put a tick with our own hands, and put the ballot in the ballot box. So you can object, "Well, neither Yeltsin nor Putin told us they were going to ruin the country, and at that time, we treated the statements of politicians in a completely different way."

Yes, but there were people, like Yeltsin's opponents, who warned us that this would be the case if we chose him, but we did not believe them; we believed Yeltsin. Many who did not believe Yeltsin later decided to support Putin because they believed he was different, but he was not. It was a false choice offered by treacherous elites who wanted to make money and keep their power, no matter what.

Well, we were deceived, but the fact remains—with our votes, we elected the leaders of post-Soviet Russia who acted against our interests. We acted with our hearts when:

Political decisions must always be made with the brain.

And we, in Russia, repeat the same thing over and over again. We go for the bright, not for the smart; for the talkers, not for the doers; for the entertainers, not for the insightful. Then we are disappointed, and remain forever proudly and resentfully sitting on our couch—not trusting anyone, but still not ready to commit to understanding politics and politicians for ourselves.

That's why I do not blame anyone for the fact that in Russia, we are where we are today.

Instead, my goal here is to pull back the curtain on current Russian politics so everyone can see what goes on behind the scenes, so that all have the knowledge and insight they need to make smart political decisions for themselves in the future, always using their head and never their heart again.

Three

I know it's hard to admit mistakes.

Self-judgment takes a lot of energy. In general, it is human nature to look for easy ways. But, at the same time, people forget that there is no such thing as a free lunch.

Yes, the reformers have promised milk, honey and sausages for everyone.

When we reached the end point of the path begun by Yeltsin, we discovered . . . oh no, we did not find anything except an abyss, and in it, Putin, who promised to "save the country."

Maybe he did save us from the abyss, but he took all the sausage and honey for himself and his friends. And then he "asks" to stay with us a little longer so that he can drink all the milk too before it turns sour.

Therefore, I propose now, at this point, that my fellow Russians each quietly, calmly, and without sprinkling ashes on our heads, admit our mistakes and go in the direction that will pave highways to success and prosperity in the future for us as Russians, and also enable us to be part of the success and prosperity that all our friends in the West enjoy.

> **Everyone in Russia should be aware
> of their personal responsibility.
> Putin is not the only one responsible for Russia.**

As Russians, we can't be afraid of the consequences of our fight. We can't be afraid of the system. We have to leverage its weaknesses to the best of our abilities to stand up for what we believe in.

Four

As a child, I learned an important lesson.

As you already know, my grandfather—my father's father—was a diplomat. His approach to life and work was formed in 1956 in Hungary. My grandfather, an intern in the Soviet embassy, was originally a railway engineer, and he followed Stalin's call after World War II, ending up in the Higher Diplomatic School. He then found himself at the epicenter of the nascent uprising.

It was the result of the tossing of the Soviet Union when after Stalin's death, the new leadership in Moscow decided to remove the dogmatist Mátyás Rákosi from power and replace him with "New Course Socialist" Imre Nagy. His approach quickly became popular and spun out of control. Then the Politburo decided to revert things, provoking major unrest.

In general, the Kremlin behaved awkwardly in Eastern Europe, considering it almost a part of the USSR, and relying on brute force where it was necessary to show flexibility. This led to problems in Yugoslavia, Czechoslovakia, Poland, and East Germany, and ultimately to the collapse of the Warsaw Pact, a treaty for mutual defense established in 1955 by the Soviet Union and seven other Socialist states in Central and Eastern Europe. For many in Russia, the union of brotherly nations that was paid for by the blood of Soviet soldiers during World War II was wasted by either fools or traitors at the helm.

In 1956, the future almighty chairman of KGB (and later Secretary General) Yury Andropov was the ambassador to Hungary. It was the suppression of that uprising in Hungary to which he owes his meteoric career. My grandfather's immediate boss was someone named Vladimir Kryuchkov, who worked as the embassy's third secretary. He drew his own conclusions from what had happened. Kryuchkov succeeded Andropov, became the last chairman of the KGB of the USSR, and organized his own—unsuccessful—uprising in 1991, known now in history as the August Coup. The result was the ultimate collapse of the USSR.

Hungary's uprising in 1956 was brutally suppressed: 2,652 civilians died, 19,226 were injured, and 200,000 (2% of the population!) left the country. In addition, 669 Soviet soldiers were killed.

Few people remember this, but it was the events in Budapest that led to the first case of a boycott of the Olympic Games.

Soon after these events in Hungary, my grandfather was transferred to Poland, where another anti-Soviet uprising had just been suppressed—in Poznan. However, no matter how highly moral this position would have been, he never became a dissident. Instead, Nickolai Ponomarev continued to serve his Homeland but decided not to allow anything like this to ever happen again, wherever he worked. Following his oath, he later played a crucial role in saving Poland from the Soviet invasion in the 1980s. As you are about to see, he also conveyed this conviction to me.

The shadow of Soviet policy in Eastern Europe hovers over Russia today. Putin learned his ways in another Eastern European country—the GDR, or East Germany. The country was different, but the approaches were the same—the same riots and results: natural collapse and impoverishment of people. Putin, on the other hand, drew different conclusions than my grandfather did.

Andropov is known to be Putin's hero. So, initially, at home, the Russian president tries to apply some of his former boss' brutal approaches. Later, he expanded them to other countries, Ukraine being just one of them. Poland, Hungary, the Baltic States, and many others are on the potential hit list.

Five

I already wrote that I went to Poland for the summer when I was four years old. It was 1979. My grandfather and grandmother lived in Szczecin, in the country's northwest, almost on the border with Germany. Grandfather worked as a Consul General, being, in fact, the representative of the USSR for unofficial contacts with the opposition in the rank of an ambassador. He witnessed the creation of Solidarność, a trade union that united wharf workers. Their dissatisfaction with their poor life turned into dissatisfaction with the USSR and the Polish communists.

We lived in the consulate—an old dark brick building, the former summer residence of Admiral Canaris, the famous chief of Hitler's military intelligence. The gloomy German architecture, with the entrance to the consulate through a narrow passage between two tall ivy-covered walls, created the atmosphere of a small besieged Teutonic castle.

Even the lines of *harcerzy* dressed in light-green uniform shirts— Polish scouts that in those days were the communist youth organization, like Young Pioneers in the Soviet Union—marching on the square in front of our house resembled preparations for the assault. Dead cats were regularly thrown over the fence of our house at night, and threats were also written on the walls.

Arriving for two months of summer vacation, I was stuck in Szczecin for a long time. Being the only child among Russians felt like being adopted by the Soviet military command and diplomats stationed in the vicinity. My extended stay in Poland was my grandfather's decision. Given the worsening relations between the USSR and Poland, he understood that sending me home after two months, which had always been the plan, could be perceived as sending me away to safety in preparation for an invasion.

My grandfather took me everywhere with him, to all the negotiations, in violation of traffic rules sitting on his car's front seat for all to see. So, for two years, I performed as a walking illustration for Poles that the Soviet tanks remained at the bases.

In the evening, when it was time for me to go to bed after dinner, I would often fall asleep on his shoulder while listening to his stories about the world around us.

As I learned much later, at that time he took a step that eventually buried his career; it led to quarreling with many colleagues, and even some of our relatives who were afraid for their social status.

This happened after Grandfather's meeting with a person whose worldview was strongly influenced by another popular uprising. It was with General Wojciech Jaruzelski, who became the Minister of Defense of Poland after the suppression of the Prague Spring of 1968, during which he commanded the troops of the Warsaw Pact. Like my granddad, he swore not to allow such a thing to be repeated in his native Poland.

These two gentlemen, whose world attitude was formed during two invasions in the nearby countries, conspired to prevent a third one. And my grandfather engaged in shuttle diplomacy between the Polish officials and Solidarność leaders, negotiating a road map to remove the pretext for the potential attack.

Six

"Never be afraid of anyone, don't go with the flow, serve the country, believe in your cause and act according to your conscience, no matter what people say," grandfather once said, ruffling my hair as I was falling asleep.

On that day, he sent a letter to Brezhnev—directly, over the head of Foreign Minister Gromyko. In it, he wrote that a brute solution in Poland was not an option, that the invasion of Soviet troops would harm, first and foremost, the USSR, and that the war with the people could be won, but this victory would be Pyrrhic.

There was no answer.

Instead, my grandfather, as a significant violator of subordination, was recalled to Moscow. Nevertheless, Brezhnev decided to keep the troops in the barracks. Instead of Soviet intervention, Jaruzelski introduced martial law in Poland for several years, as he had discussed with my grandfather. Solidarność leader Lech Valesa was moved to a small then-undisclosed town in Eastern Poland, where he was kept in custody for eleven months until the situation calmed down. Later the country experienced a peaceful transition to a democratic state with free elections, in which Jaruzelski himself did not participate.

Years have passed. The efforts of my grandfather—who fell out of Gromyko's favor and was forced to retire—are now appreciated by all sides of that conflict, both the leaders of Solidarność and members of the Politburo.

Power in Poland passed peacefully, first to Lech Walesa, and then, through free elections, into the hands of the former minister of the communist government of the PPR, Alexander Kwasniewski. And then to the next president, already a conservative—and all through fair elections, without violence and upheavals.

True, there was an attempt to bring Wojciech Jaruzelski to court, but they did not find any evidence of the crimes he was accused of committing. What a contrast with Russia.

I am proud that Poland was able to change, partly because then, in 1980, my grandfather showed responsibility, and at the cost of his career helped to stop the invasion or the unwinding spiral of civil war, which seemed then quite possible to many.

I am always trying to do the same in Russia, Ukraine, and elsewhere. Alas, Putin does not have even these few checks and balances that Brezhnev had. Out of Eastern Bloc countries, he follows the tragic paths of either Romania's Nicolae Ceauşescu or Yugoslavia's Slobodan Milošević. Of course, humanity learned how to deal with those bastards as well. Unfortunately, the toll is always the loss of many lives, which was avoided in Poland. It could be minimized only with our resolve and prompt actions now.

CHAPTER NINE

About Methods and Goals

One

Does the end justify the means?

Once, this question was put to me by my father. So now I'm repeating it.

This is one of the most important things in my life.

What is acceptable in the name of a great idea? What is the extent of this tolerance? To what extent can you ignore the opinion of the majority when you are sure that you are right? Do you have the right to impose your view on others? How far should you go to conform and adapt to a mainstream opinion when you are sure it is wrong?

As you can see, one short question includes several rather capacious ones.

Let me put it straight:

Over many years, the Russian liberal opposition has diligently collected in its ranks most of the controversial people and dubious topics that are rejected by the Big Project majority.

This includes admirers of what Putin calls the "dashing Nineties," "revolutionaries in fur coats," militant atheists, LGBT activists, pro-Western "fifth column" and "national traitors" seeking to disband Russia and calling for its foreign occupation, Islamic separatists, ultraright and ultraleft fighters, you name it. Naturally, state TV during protests enjoys interviewing them. They don't even need to edit much; just pick up the right person and let him speak more on behalf of us all.

We cannot deny that these people usually act according to their sincere beliefs and do not bend to pressure. However, they also tend to lack any chance for political success because they cannot connect with the ordinary person. Putin always plays on contrast. Using his control over the media, he appears a better liberal and a better conservative, a better socialist and a better nationalist, just more reasonable and sane than those who oppose him.

The Russian opposition needs what you have already heard me call a Big Project. Bright Future. Great Vision. Perfect Dream. One that nobody will ever be able to hijack, as well as a strong team capable of bringing it all to life—but whose members would not pretend to be more meaningful than the Dream itself.

Two

It is very important to understand and accept the motivation of those who go into opposition in Russia.

The protest usually begins for one of two reasons: when you are gravely insulted or endangered so that you can't stand it, or when you believe that something can be changed, and you see how your contribution will help bring that positive change. Of course, the best scenario is when both motivations are combined.

For instance, I am thinking now of the frosty morning of January 22, 2005, in Krasnoyarsk.

It was two years before I was elected to the State Duma. At that time I was the founder of the quickly growing, unregistered Left Front movement.

It was the third week of pensioners' protests against the monetization of privileges, which I will explain in a moment. This reform that most people in the West are unaware of almost ended Putin's days in power: a dozen regional administrations were seized by the people, and the government spent a tremendous amount of money to calm everybody down at the end.

The neoliberals suggested the reform in the government and were very much praised by the neoliberals in the opposition and even the International Monetary Fund. It was very simple: traditionally, in the Soviet Union, many categories of the population—like pensioners, veterans, people with disabilities, or single mothers, you name it—received certain privileges, such as free rides on public transport, or discounted drugs, or sponsored tickets to the theaters and cinemas. Based on past logic, this made perfect sense; those buses, trains, and drugstores belonged to the state, so it all worked fine. Who cares how many passengers will pay for a ride on the bus if the cost is determined only by the route and schedule, and is not affected by the occupancy? However, the situation changes if you plan to privatize the transportation company, especially if it is intended to go into the hands of your greedy friends who want guarantees of their future revenues.

So the government decided to evaluate the financial value of these privileges and replace them with financial subsidies, which would be given to people in cash. They thought people would actually like it—they could spend the money the way they wanted, with no strings attached. In reality, people were outraged, and not just because it turned out the government cheated during the evaluation.

I will say the following is a typical mistake of liberals in power in Russia: Older people were simply offended when money was offered to them instead of honor. Granted, this was not a rational consideration—while in many cases the decision was stupid from a fiscal point of view, it did not matter much to the elders. But, even when the money they received was significant, the whole notion was perceived as an insult. So, the pensioners took to the streets.

**In Russia, depriving people of respect is
sometimes worse than depriving them of money.**

Some five thousand people gathered in front of the Krasnoyarsk regional administration; given the size of the city, it was more than during the Bolotnaya protests. The protesters were mainly elders, with the apparent dominance of some very angry old ladies. If Putin had appeared there, no police would have been able to save him.

Despite the –20° Fahrenheit frost, the heat on the usually boring rally of the Communist Party was rising every minute.

These people wanted some real action. They'd heard stories from other regions about how pensioners rebelled and stormed the local government offices. The regional communists, on the other hand, just wanted to say all their usual curses against the government in Moscow and retreat to the safety of their warm homes.

The first secretary of the party's regional committee, Vladislav Yurchik, finally declared the rally closed, but the grandmothers were going nowhere. "We are not leaving!"

Someone starts singing the "Internationale":

> *No savior from on high delivers*
> *No faith have we in prince or peer*
> *Our own right hand the chains must shiver*
> *Chains of hatred, greed and fear!*

Experienced party bosses were clearly not eager to do something, especially with their own hands, and scuttled sideways like some old crabs in fear, retreating "to an extraordinary plenum."

My comrades and I from the Left Front—Roman Burlak, Maxim Firsov, and Andrey Seleznev— unexpectedly found ourselves at the helm of the protest.

The eyes of the old ladies, who clearly felt like young Komsomol members of the 1920s, were on us and burning with rage and fire.

So we led the protesting crowd to the steps of the Krasnoyarsk Regional Administration, and we broke inside without much difficulty.

Before us was an empty lobby, finished with marble in the classical Stalinist style, aptly called by one writer, "Empire during the plague."

Several frightened guards had abandoned their weapons and were hiding in the supply closet.

This was nothing like the January 6th, 2021, insurrection in the States—it was more like the American film *Cocoon*. It was a pack of passionate pensioners led by a handful of unarmed young oppositionists. And there's not a soul there—right there in the corridors of power!

There was silence for a while. In it, you could hear your breath, flowing clouds of hope.

"We need to draw up our demands," I finally said, deciding at that moment to look like a knowledgeable commander. "Roman," I ordered, "you write: 'We, the people of Krasnoyarsk, demand . . .'"

Someone gives Burlak a scrap of paper of dubious purity. Firsov drags a pencil stub somewhere right out of his hair styled after Angela Davis.

What could we demand that the governor could fulfill?

The issue of political demands is not as straightforward as it seems. When I worked in the oil industry, an experienced colleague taught me how to deal with impossible tasks that were put on us regularly:

"So, let's say they tell you to jump over the moon," he would say. "You sit down, you try to rationalize, and you split the task into stages. You then write to guys in the procurement department, 'I request you provide a spring of such and such stiffness, of such and such size, within a week.' And if the suppliers do not find the spring you need, then this is not a matter for you to handle. You have done your job."

This simple technique often reflects the opposition's approach to its demands.

It is easiest to boldly and uncompromisingly demand what would never be delivered.

And you are clean, and the people say, "Wow, how brave!"

However, you have displayed zero responsibility and created zero results besides the hype around yourself. It may be good enough for many, but never for me.

This mistake was made in May 2012 during the "March of the Millions" on Bolotnaya Square in Moscow, when nothing was achieved. People stop taking you seriously when you demand something regularly, and nothing happens. My approach is to always ask for something feasible and probable, and then fight tooth and nail to make it happen.

In Krasnoyarsk in 2005, we demanded a reduction in electricity tariffs, which had risen sharply since the New Year—a genuine topic of concern.

We then handed the letter full of our elders' demands over to the trembling guards, after chasing them out from under the tables, under the lenses of television cameras, while also telling them nicely that the grandmothers may, at least temporarily, leave them alone—if they promise to cooperate. So, of course, they did.

Three

Thanks to our experience with the protest in Krasnoyarsk, and many other lessons learned after that, we were ready in 2011 when we had a chance to create an opposition in Russia as a broad and robust coalition.

When it comes to protests, sometimes you are working with those babushkas, and sometimes it's young women and men who are stepping forward.

Take the first rally in Bolotnaya on December 10, 2011, which I led together with Vladimir Ryzhkov.

People were constantly pulling me by the sleeve from below the stage we were standing on, asking me if they could come on stage, too—some to speak, and some just to marvel at the huge crowd never seen before at an opposition rally. Then, at one moment, someone pulled at me with such force that he almost tore off my sleeve. He pointed to a pretty woman with sensual lips but stubborn eyes who sharply contrasted with everyone around her.

"I brought you a speaker!"

"Who is it?"

"You don't recognize her? It's Tolokno, well, Nadya Tolokonnikova. From Voina!"

Well, of course! Voina ("War" in English) was a famous leftist Russian performance art group. They were not just familiar to me. They were right at the height of their fame.

A number of their activist events have caused great resonance both in the artistic and political environment. For example, a year before Bolotnaya, I helped to extract "on parole" from the St. Petersburg police detention four activists of the group: David Soldaev, Natalia Sokol, The Thief, and Lenya the Fucked. At their recent activist event, they over-turned and set several police cars on fire and afterward were facing pretty serious prison terms.

I think what actually saved them that time was not my pledge. It was a funny and very sharp performance they made shortly before. St. Petersburg is full of drawbridges. So, they painted a huge, stiff dick on Liteiny bridge, one of the largest bridges in the city, which was right in front of the local FSB (and former KGB) office. After that, they just had to wait a bit: the bridge was lifted, and the members of the Russian secret police saw what others thought about them. It was not so easy to close the bridge quickly because of the marine traffic. We all enjoyed the view for quite a while, and it appears that the police, who genuinely hated the FSB, were enjoying it too, so cops had to close their eyes a bit when Voina members were captured and arrested.

Speaking of Tolokno, the first time I saw her was in a photo of another sensational Voina performance when Putin designated Medvedev as his replacement. The performance was called "Fuck for the Heir Puppy Bear!" and being pornographic, it created a lot of buzz in the media and inside Moscow and St. Petersburg cultural and political circles.

By the time of our rally, I had heard that Tolokno and her husband Peter Verzilov had split with the rest of the Voina group and were starting a new project in Moscow called Pussy Riot. I did not know the details then, but I had long respected their radical views, and I was glad to introduce Nadya to the large crowd at Bolotnaya Square.

I dragged her by the hand onto the stage, up the slippery, steep stairs. Turning away from me, she was unwrapping something.

"What have you got there?"

"Well, Ilya, don't worry, it's just a flag," Nadya said evasively.

"We decided that we were rallying with no partisan or political symbols—you know that, right?" I said, wanting to make sure we stayed on message during the whole event.

"No big deal, no politics. Don't worry!" she reassured me.

Not suspecting a trick, I announced Nadya's speech. She immediately jumped to the mike, shouting passionately like a true revolutionary Valkyria leading us to an Anarchist Valhalla. And what's a march without a flag to follow? She finally managed to open her bundle. It was a rainbow flag of the LGBT movement.

For many years I was the leading ambassador of all minorities in the Russian parliament. Before voting against the annexation of Crimea, I was also the only person not to support the so-called "gay propaganda law," Russia's most discriminatory anti-LGBTQ piece of legislation.

Personally, my approach was always to work to make sure society would gradually learn to accept all genders and preferences as one's private affair. And in general, it was working: a decade before Bolotnaya, 23% of Russians viewed gay people negatively, and 45% were neutral, and these numbers were slowly improving. Moreover, the number of opponents decreased steadily, especially in the younger population. I believed that the critical thing was to communicate this as something normal. Additional attention would have hurt the cause, as it would force people to take sides, and many of those on their way to accepting the gay community would inevitably take a step back.

It appears it was not only me who was thinking that way. Political technologists in the Kremlin were also watching the rally very closely. They also heard the overwhelming whistling and hooting of people standing in front of the stage where Nadya was speaking. And they recognized the opportunity to discredit us in the eyes of the conservative majority even before we realized the danger.

I did not think that Putin would agree to use widespread prejudice against gay people for his benefit. Many of his trusted allies are gay, and he, to my knowledge, is at least bisexual. But, as Russian national wisdom says, the thief is always the loudest to shout, "Stop the thief!"

Chilled by the wind, Ryzhkov perked up and looked at me with growing interest—how many more such popular speakers did the leftists have in stock?

Three

A few months after the protest at Bolotnaya, Nadya's actions as part of the Russian all-women protest band Pussy Riot made her even more famous, not just in Russia but around the world.

Around this time, one gloomy February morning in 2012, my then press secretary Maria Baronova rushed into my Duma office on Okhotny Ryad. As often happened, Maria was in a state of heightened exaltation, rolling her eyes and wringing her hands as she asked me, "How can I bring some electric guitars into the Duma?"

"Sorry?"

I didn't understand her request. Maria had only worked for me for two weeks and had not yet learned how my team worked. (Or maybe, in fact, everyone has already passed her off to someone else with this question that seemed absurd.)

"Ponomarev, you entrusted me with your PR—and we now need some electric guitars!" she explained somewhat vaguely, now with her hands on her hips, and her eyes especially fiery.

I like rock, and I love guitar music. At that moment, however, the connection between the State Duma, electric guitars, and my PR person was unclear to me.

I also didn't appreciate that plans to develop my public relations were being decided without my first at least hearing the essence of the idea.

But I also really believed in Maria.

"Maybe you should tell me what you have in mind first. Who in the Duma needs electric guitars?"

"Ponomarev, you will sing to Naryshkin! Objections are not accepted!"

Sergey Naryshkin, who shortly before became the speaker of the State Duma, had already managed to become famous among the deputies for his "conciliatory" initiatives. The first of them was the idea to get all the deputies of the Duma together for the holidays and sing something in unison. In my humble opinion, this was politically a terrible idea because it clearly demonstrated to the whole country that all deputies were one gang, and party differences were pure fiction. Maria knew my position on this quite well.

This is why I raised my eyebrows and made a defiant yet surprised face, waiting for the true reason.

"Relax, I'm kidding!" she reassured me. "Actually, we have come up with an idea for a performance here with the girls!"

"The 'girls'?"

"Yes! Performance! Modern art! Pussy Riot!"

"Pussy Riot? Do you know who they are?" I asked.

"Ponomarev, don't be stupid! Of course, I do! I'm ordering passes for them, don't you understand?"

"Passes to the Duma?"

"You think the Duma is no better than Red Square? If you can, let's immediately order them passes to the Kremlin!"

I could not order a pass to the Kremlin. However, Maria's logic here could not be beaten.

Four

Eventually, Maria's plan became clear to me. It appeared that Pussy Riot wanted to perform a song in the State Duma's plenary session with our help, and it was my responsibility to ensure that this happened.

To be honest, the thought of this happening both horrified and excited me at the same time.

The following scandal would be humongous, and that was good. What the consequences would be—well, it was hard to calculate and predict. Nevertheless, it would be something to remember and grin about in my old age: an anti-Putin punk rock concert at the plenary session, with the security detail unable to do anything because of the limited access to the main hall of the Duma—it was a cool alternative to Naryshkin's vicious musical circles.

The guitars were provided, the action plan was thought out and prepared. But it didn't work out with the girls themselves. It turned out that, for their previous achievements, they were already put on the security service's "extremist list" and would not be allowed into the parliament. So the deputies of the Duma didn't get to see them perform. And I didn't get to know them; at least, not then.

Meanwhile, this played out in a very negative way just a few days later. Not allowed to come to the Duma, Pussy Riot decided to attack the Church, which many saw as an attack on society and its traditions. They went to the Yelokhov Cathedral to sing their new hit, "Mother of God, Drive Putin Away!" Their attempt was unsuccessful, of course—security interfered. Then, a day later, they actually performed the song in the Cathedral of Christ the Savior, a symbol of modern-day hypocrisy and the main cathedral of the Russian Orthodox Church. It was built by Turks in the 1990s at a location in Moscow rumored to be cursed. It was occupied once by the mansion of Malyuta Skuratov, the most hated cruel top executioner of Ivan the Terrible. After his death, the property was burned to ashes by Muscovites.

This time, Pussy Riot's performance blew up public opinion. The angered hierarchs of the Orthodox Church demanded that authorities imprison the girls. A noisy and vile process began over three of them: Nadya Tolokonnikova, Maria Alyokhina, and Yekaterina Samutsevich.

The trial sharply polarized society, and the Kremlin used it masterfully against the opposition. We did everything we could to express moral support for Nadya, Maria, and Yekaterina, and there was a significant international campaign to help them. Celebrities from Madonna to Paul McCartney spoke publicly, calling for their release. Nothing helped. All three were found guilty of "hooliganism motivated by religious hatred" and were sent to camps.

Putin needed not only priests on his side but also to use our own solidarity campaign against us to paint the opposition black (actually, not black, but the colors of the LGBTQ rainbow flag). His media used the case to draw the line—we were against Russian core values and traditions, did not trust in God, were against the family values, and were all gay and perverts.

Sadly, these three bright and courageous women totally diluted our message. In the eyes of ordinary Russians, we no longer stood for their political rights and social well-being but the rights of sexual minorities and against the Church. To date, we have not managed to communicate our goals to our potential supporters, aside from getting rid of Putin.

Now we have to restate our Vision and Dream and stay on this message no matter what.

Five

Two years later, as a deputy, I visited Nadya in her camp.

She was dying. Literally.

For many days, she had been on a hunger strike against the conditions of prisoners and stood on the edge of the grave.

As the doctors later told me, she had a day, maybe two left to live.

In exchange for her stopping her hunger strike, besides other things, I promised her I would talk with other women in the camp and help them in any way I could.

I will not describe all the emotions that I experienced over the course of those days I spent at the womens' camp. It's enough for at least one more book. I am still in touch with some of the women I met there.

As promised, I communicated with all the prisoners in Nadya's barrack and with many women from other units. By threatening the camp's leadership with negative global public opinion and their inevitable future inclusion on the Magnitsky list for their handling of the prisoners, I got the opportunity to communicate with the women without witnesses. I believe that the stories I heard from them were the honest-to-God truth.

"She is good, Nadya," the other prisoners would say, "but strange. Why did she go to that cathedral? Why is she stirring the pot and rocking the boat with the administration? Living here, of course, is harsh but manageable. She is only making it worse for everyone."

This reminds me of the arguments with other countless "ordinary Russians" that I hear day after day, year after year. "Why fight? Don't fight! Just go along! If you don't go along, you will only make your bad life even worse!"

It's as if the whole country is sitting in a camp!

Six

Ironically, in the same colony from my leftist friend Nadya Tolokonnikova sits the ultraright Yevgenia Khasis—the wife of Nikita Tikhonov, a neofascist and the murderer of one of the founders of the Left Front, my lawyer friend Stas Markelov. An intelligent and strong-willed woman who received eighteen years as an accomplice of her husband and did not renounce him, Yevgenia is my and Nadya's ideological enemy.

I met with her. She talked a lot about life in the camp. And again she showed me the gap between the opinion of the majority and the protesters at Bolotnaya.

"Ilya, imagine it—*eighteen* years," she says. "All my youth will be spent here. Will I have children? I don't know. . . . I read a lot and correspond with my comrades, but here my task is simple: to survive. Think long. Why do we need conflicts and hype? Can we change the system here? A strong person must adapt and survive. The only thing I can do here is to pray once in a while and bring others to do the same. For our own sake, for the sake of those we love—to survive!"

Listening to her words, I thought that, for some, Putin's rule is almost like a life sentence. Is his rule, in fact, some sort of capital punishment for the entire country?

**Over these years of self-imprisonment in Putinism,
the whole country has lost the values it once had,
replacing them with the idea of
survival and stability at any cost.**

Reality under Putinism is often pointless, so even meaningful values become meaningless. Even the most justified protest gets sliced and diced through the state-controlled word processor of social media into inflammatory slogans and sound bites with no real substance.

Russian media—both pro-Kremlin and those who identify themselves as "opposition"—tend to promote those who are either the most radical (and thus unpopular) or those who have the hidden support of elite (business and media) groups, to the detriment of those who have a legitimate and justified cause for their protest.

At some point, as legitimate protestors watch the shrill, substance-free social media posers grab all the attention with their ridiculous ploys, they realize it may be better to have a fragile peace with jailers than to try to stand for values that are worthy and right, if nobody speaks about them.

**What are people willing to fight for?
And even when they think they are willing to fight,
what determines whether they really do fight or not?**

It all starts with an idea that, after having heard it several times, people accept as their own.

An idea for which people can and should and will stand for without retreating.

An idea that will give people more purpose in life than they can get from any leader or boss.

Who will generate and deliver this idea?

And how do you make sure that this idea or message does not turn into a cult, and its supporters into fanatics, sweeping away everything in its path?

Seven

Throughout my political career, I have persistently and consistently worked to solve one task—the task of coming to power, so that I could stop talking and start doing, as I am used to doing while doing business.

At various levels, on a national and a local scale, even while in exile, I have continued to stay focused on this one primary task—getting our hands on the levers of power, so we can put our plans and goals to work to change Russia and the world.

Having this long and only sometimes successful experience, I affirm two things:

1.
To change society, the opposition must become power.
2.
**It is impossible to change society
within the framework of the existing political system in Russia.**

Therefore, any significant changes can only be made by dismantling the current system, either partially or completely.

Demolition, like construction, is an engineering operation. Those who produce it get to decide what means to use.

The management system created by Putin and his entourage in Russia can theoretically be dismantled with the help of legal tools: that is, through elections.

But, judging by what has been happening in the country for twenty years, this is less and less likely.

Other measures can also be taken: for instance, taking a revolutionary path and forcibly demolishing everything that refuses concessions and compromises.

When I say "revolutionary," I don't just mean a soldier with a gun or a guerrilla fighter. My revolutionary is everybody willing to go beyond the impotent mechanisms the current Constitution provides.

Eight

Putin. Stalin. Peter the Great. Ivan the Terrible. Many characters in our history caused constant disputes among contemporaries and their descendants.

Does the end justify the means? Here it is again, this question that started this chapter and was first put to me by my father. Every new Russian ruler seems to ask this, too.

As a rule, those who unequivocally answer "yes" to this question end up in a bad place and shed a lot of blood, but we remember them and their deeds for a long time. Sometimes we even praise them, and our respect is proportional to the blood spilled.

In contrast, we often underestimate and even despise humanists who live according to the commandments.

"Soft-bodied," we say about them. "You can't steer Russia in white gloves," we preach to them.

Who should ultimately be held responsible for the bloodshed in 1917—the soft and indecisive Nicholas II, or his irreconcilable antagonists from the Bolshevik Party?

I am convinced that the ruler, unable to cope with power, is fully responsible for everything that his overthrowers will later do.

Here is a fresh example—Mikhail Gorbachev, who had enough heart to start perestroika, but not enough brains to keep the country from disintegration and plunder.

However, few historical figures are more controversial than Vladimir Lenin. Even with Stalin, everything is much more unambiguous than with the leader of the Revolution and the most famous Russian on the planet. (By the way, the most famous Ukrainian is Trotsky, which gives an extra color to the Russia-Ukraine war.)

Once, on Facebook, I remembered Lenin's jubilee with a piece from this still unfinished book. I wrote that he was a great dreamer, and we have much to learn from such passionate people.

You would not believe what followed on Facebook in the comments!

"Cannibal," "inventor of concentration camps," "executioner of the Russian, Ukrainian and other peoples." One friend even called him an anti-Semite. Finally, I realized that this person, his means, and his goals must be discussed in more detail.

Everyone knows the purposefulness and ruthlessness of the leader of the Bolsheviks and his unwillingness to see obstacles on the way to his dream—a just society without the exploitation of human beings by other human beings. Everyone knows about the rivers of blood spilled during the attempt to build such a society in the USSR. It is also known that—so far—the attempt has been unsuccessful. After the successful overthrow of the monarchy that hindered the development of Russia, an even less democratic and rigid system was soon created in the country. Still, a great modernization breakthrough happened, replaced by a long stagnant extinction and decay. Each historical twist was paid for with blood.

The problem is evident, but I have always believed that in order to treat something, one must know the nature of the disease. To oppose the fanaticism of Lenin's supporters with the fanaticism of his enemies, the deafness of those who believe in Leninism with the deafness of those who believe in liberalism, is senseless and leads to one thing: some Bolsheviks will be replaced by others who are even more indiscriminate in terms of methods of action. And we saw this in the 1990s, when the most vocal anti-communists were the most like Bolsheviks.

Therefore, I consider this a useful and necessary challenge: At which point did Lenin's mistakes lead to the defeat of his ideals?

Nine

The most objective take on Lenin's heritage is (unsurprisingly) by people who profess leftist views. They can separate ends from means and don't stick to stereotypes. One such individual was the famous British thinker Bertrand Russell. He personally knew the leader of the Russian revolution, and, being a convinced leftist, Russell visited Lenin in 1920.

During his visit, he recognized the Soviet development model as not corresponding to true communist ideas and was very disappointed in the Bolsheviks. Recalling this trip in *The Practice and Theory of Bolshevism*, Russell wrote, "If Bolshevism remains the only vigorous and effective competitor of capitalism, I believe that no form of Socialism will be realized, but only chaos and destruction. . . . One who believes, as I do, that the free intellect is the chief engine of human progress, cannot but be fundamentally opposed to Bolshevism, as much as to the Church of Rome."

Russell points to one of the main reasons, saying, "Bolshevism is not merely a political doctrine; it is also a religion, with elaborate dogmas and inspired scriptures. When Lenin wishes to prove some proposition, he does so, if possible, by quoting texts from Marx and Engels."

I think this is one of the main reasons for what happened in the Soviet Union.

Lenin was not an imperialist and did not try to keep the Russian Empire within its borders. On the contrary, he considered, for example, Western Ukrainian nationalists as his important allies in the fight against autocracy and Russian chauvinism, and called on self-determination of the nations of the country, not ruling out their secession (for example, Finland and Poland).

When Ukrainian national patriots call him the executioner of the Ukrainian people, they forget that it was Lenin who supported the Ukrainization policy and, on his initiative, the Ukrainian language became the primary language in the territory of this country. After all that, overturning the position of the majority of his own party, it was he who insisted on the recognition of the independence of the Ukrainian Republic.

His closest associates in this were Ukrainian-born Leon Trotsky and Volodymyr Antonov-Ovseenko (who, like many of Ukraine's political figures, was originally not a Bolshevik, but a Menshevik).

The same Lenin did not allow the Donetsk-Kryvyi Rih Republic, which had rebelled against Kyiv, to secede from Ukraine. (How relevant after 2014!)

Nor was Lenin the inventor of concentration camps. (They were invented by the British during the Anglo-Boer War; some debate it was done by Unionists during the Civil War in the United States.)

He did not start the civil war in Russia. (The White Terror began before the Red one.)

At the same time, his means of class struggle were brutal and typical of his time, and he gave orders for ruthless reprisals against the enemies of the revolution (Here, however, people did not need to be incited—reprisals and lynching were arranged everywhere without additional prompting.)

In this sense, he was not much different from his opponents—the White Army did precisely the same thing. All Russians know how a peasant complained in the famous movie *Chapaev*:

**"The whites came and robbed,
the reds came and robbed,
where could the poor peasant go?"**

I have not heard of commanders of that war who would have professed the Christian approach of "turn the other cheek." Therefore, the Bolsheviks' cruelty did not alienate most of their countrymen from them. This allowed them to win the fight.

And of course, Lenin himself, partly Jewish and a convinced internationalist, for whom the Jewish movement (primarily the Bund) was the most important ally in the revolutionary struggle, was never an anti-Semite.

Lenin's main crime lies elsewhere.

He was a bad Marxist. As a lawyer, he had an excellent understanding of politics, but little understanding of economics. Zombified by his dream and great goal, he convinced himself that Marx could not foresee a world war, and therefore did not know about the possibility of a forced giant leap from feudal Russia, which had just begun industrialization, immediately into the "beautiful Russia of the future."

It was possible to push off and jump over the abyss of economic backwardness but not to land on the other side of the gap properly. And so, this is the main lesson:

**We should never replace a scientific approach
and rational reason with blind faith in our dreams,
no matter how beautiful they may seem to us.**

Returning to Russell, despite what he saw in Russia and his criticism of Bolshevism, he remained a communist. He wrote, "I believe that Communism is necessary to the world, and I believe that the heroism of Russia has fired men's hopes in a way which was essential to the realization of Communism in the future. . . . I went to Russia a Communist; but contact with those who have no doubts has intensified a thousandfold my own doubts, not as to Communism in itself, but as to the wisdom of holding a creed so firmly that for its sake men are willing to inflict widespread misery… Russian Communism may fail and go under, but Communism itself will not die. . . . The existing capitalist system is doomed. Its injustice is so glaring that only ignorance and tradition could lead wage earners to tolerate it. As ignorance diminishes, tradition becomes weakened."

I must say that, for Lenin, communication with Russell did not pass without a trace. I think the great philosopher influenced the fact that "war communism" was soon curtailed, and the country moved to the "new economic policy," which gave a tremendous impetus to free enterprise within the welfare state. But, alas, Lenin suffered a stroke and later died, while Stalin had a different plan in mind for the country.

The idea and science behind it was eventually replaced by faith, leadership by a cult, and creativity by dictate. But this was no longer linked to Lenin nor to Trotsky and not to the revolution they inspired.

Ten

For those in Russia who call or consider themselves "non-systemic opposition," it is essential that you be aware of the following: This state will never let you in, even if you are willing to compromise.

Instead, the Kremlin gladly uses everyone, from moderates like Sobchak to radicals like Navalny, for its own purposes.

Meanwhile, here's the one thing that is important for the state: that no one is allowed to show up with a *systemic* alternative. No one can pretend to take over the system. And it starts low: you cannot have a comprehensive vision of something different. You can just suggest some changes and submit your proposals for *them* to decide.

Everybody likes a well-known myth so loved by neoliberals: that real reforms are always unpopular.

I think this ludicrous idea is imposed on us by those who are unable to successfully put forward a program in the interests of the majority and unable to unite society around it.

Was Roosevelt's New Deal unpopular in the United States? Or reforms in Singapore and South Korea? Did Finnish society protest against the successful transformation of its economy after the collapse of the USSR? Or the Brazilians against its leap forward in the 2000s, when the country overtook Russia?

Of course, among the unpopular reforms there are also successful examples. But, firstly, there are fewer of them, and, secondly, it is undoubtedly impossible to establish an unambiguous relationship between the success of the transformations and their pain.

However, this is extremely important: the success of reforms is impossible without society's trust in the prospects for reforms. It can be built on both high and low popular support of the leader: support for the left-wing democrat Roosevelt, respect for the iron will of the conservative Thatcher, and fear of the bloody dictatorship of the reactionary Pinochet have one thing in common—people believed that Roosevelt, Thatcher, and Pinochet meant precisely that which they said in public. They didn't lie. In the end, they achieved their declared goals.

One should not confuse the popularity of the reforms with their being painless. We go to see the doctor understanding that he may inflict pain on us. But we consciously agree to this, and he is responsible for the result and is not playing tricks on us.

So there is no need to flaunt readiness for "unpopular" measures. You have to decide on the popular (or at least achievable) ones. Trust in the feasibility of goals and the impeccability of means is the key to mass support, without which our actions will never be successful.

CHAPTER TEN

On the Successful Transfer of Power

One

Not a single president of Ukraine, except Kuchma, has been in office for two terms. In Russia, only one president did not serve two terms. (Although we still argue about the one-termer, Medvedev. Did he even exist?)

Many are confused by this. After all, the political system in Russia is called "democracy." To me, democracy means changing power according to people's will. But in Russia's domestic "democracy," "politicians" and "analysts" look exclusively at Vladimir Putin and his presidential terms and don't even want to think about an alternative. They know precisely how many years he has been in office and do not want to think how much longer he will stay.

Everyone knows they need to do something, and they need to find something to do, to transfer the power from Putin . . .

. . . to Putin.

At the same time, elections as a means of transition are rarely discussed. After all, "politicians" and "analysts" in Russia are serious adults and do not waste time on empty talk.

"Free and fair elections"—when applied to Russia, these words sound like an absurd joke, a figurative and witty combination of contradictory concepts.

Everyone is used to the fact:
Under the current regime,
there can be no free elections in Russia.

Some say that a post-Soviet nation is not capable of a free and fair election. They point fingers at Turkmenistan and Belarus.

Yet there are also the examples of Georgia and Ukraine, where genuine competitive elections occur regularly.

In Russia, elections today are needed, as you know, not to ensure the change of power but to establish its inviolability.

In my memory, there were only once somewhat free elections—in the summer of 1991, and ironically that was under Soviet rule.

However, if we look to history, we can see that sometimes unfree and unfair elections are the catalysts that cause a powerful reaction in society, which entails a change in the dictator, his entourage, elites, and the entire regime.

Such was the case in Mexico, when the deep-rooted dictatorship of General Porfirio Diaz, who ruled the country for a total of forty years (more than Putin!), fell as his rival Francisco Madero, the leader of the liberal democratic opposition, refused to recognize the results of another rigged election.

Madero appealed to the people with a call to arms to overthrow the ruling corrupt clique.

This was the beginning of the Mexican Revolution, which led to the resignation of General Díaz. In May 1911, General Díaz emigrated to France, where he lived for the rest of his life.

Thanks to the successful combination of several essential factors, Madero's call was heard, and a revolutionary movement began in the country, ultimately completely changing Mexico.

No, this movement was not peaceful. It included conflicts between various leaders and interest groups. Oligarchic and military clans fought for "their" states, cities, territories and industries. There were coups and counter-coups.

Yet the result was the removal of Díaz from power—and with him, a layer of the old elites that seemed impenetrable and stable just a month earlier. They included those who distributed resources, appointments, and financial and commodity flows among themselves; bureaucrats who steered budgets into their pockets and sat on unofficial royalties coming from the regions; and the military and police officials, who constituted a merciless machine of graft and violence. Everything was just like modern-day Russia.

Meanwhile, the evolution of the movement against the dictatorship into a series of conflicts was not a foregone conclusion.

The change of power, regime, and the entire organization of life in Russia could be peaceful, including through elections. However, the longer the power structure did not change, the greater the likelihood of its catastrophic change. I think with the invasion of Ukraine in February 2022, Putin has crossed the final red line. Now, only revolution seems feasible.

Two

"Analysts" and "politicians" also understand this fact. Therefore, from time to time, they still consider taking a chance to run for office, only to realize again and again that there are no elections anymore.

Yet, in Moscow, St. Petersburg, and every other Russian city, town, and village, the future transition is being discussed more and more. It is difficult to name an analyst, whether pro-government or opposition-minded, who would not, at least from time to time, speak out about the transfer of power. It's just that nobody believes it will happen due to the electoral process.

The reason is that politics still exist in an authoritarian system and a totalitarian or neo-totalitarian society. It is simply undemocratic, connected not with elections but with other forms of struggle for power. And therefore, it has a different nature. Still, there is a political class. Its members strive to get their share of power within the existing system, to create their own "centers of power."

Russian bulldogs are fighting under the carpet, but they do fight and are not sitting still.

Yes, from time to time, the Kremlin throws some "bone" to the political class to occupy its teeth and paws; remember the reason for my appearance at the Valdai Forum and my meeting with Putin? It was all built on the back of the Kremlin, feeding us in local politics a bone.

If this is not done, then some of its representatives may begin to fantasize and plot, and this is dangerous.

The packs of the political class and their leaders begin to joyfully tug at this bone "under the carpet" since its removal to open air is strictly prohibited. Yet, sometimes something (or someone) flies out "from under the carpet" to the surface. It gets into the media, social media, and foreign Russian-language publications. Meanwhile, the fuss continues. It may go on for a long time, but illusions aside:

**The removal of Putin by some other person,
and the replacement of the current power clan
by another group is inevitable.**

It will happen, and most likely by force, because no other options are visible. Indeed, some people within the Kremlin are preparing "a plan B" for a peaceful (or maybe not) transfer of power from Putin to some successor of his, whether it is Sergei Kirienko or Dmitry Medvedev, or somebody else. However, for this to happen, Putin needs to agree to this. I can hardly see how he can resign before scoring the victory over Ukraine, and that's just not gonna happen.

Are we then perhaps talking about an internal Kremlin intrigue, a "palace coup"?

Maybe.

I am a physicist by training, and looking at Putin's Russia, I see a system with a minimum or maximum of potential energy. In order to move from one stable state of matter to another, both should look stable enough.

In political terms, we need an alternative—that is, the possibility of moving from current point "A" to some other point "B," in which the political class feels better and more comfortable than in the present situation.

At this moment, no such prospect is visible. Therefore, a comfortable change is impossible. No matter how much discontent accumulates, even in the political class, nothing will happen if there is no visible—and feasible—alternative.

**A change occurs when there is an alternative
recognized either by the majority or by the ruling class.**

A change will also occur when there is a significant sense of insecurity and outright danger in the current state of things. Not just some (even severe) pressure from sanctions, but an immediate threat to one's property and life—larger than the threat coming from Putin himself.

Therefore, Putin is mainly busy constantly reproducing and ensuring a situation where there is no alternative to him or his group, scaring ordinary Russians and disseminating depression in the most intellectually active circles so that they will not call for the uprising that will force the elites to have to protect themselves from the rebellious people.

A ghost of 1917 should reemerge in Russia to enable the change, and that's precisely the demon that Putin summoned in February 2022.

Three

Putin is not trying to present himself as the best ruler of Russia of all time. Instead, he just makes it his goal to show the Russian people that all the other rulers in the rest of the world are worse.

He throws shit on Navalny. Maybe Khodorkovsky. At me. Or Ukraine and, of course, on the United States to show (and even convince people for a while) that perhaps everything is quite bad here, but over there, everywhere else, it is even worse.

Part of the secret here is that he must not only throw shit on everyone else everywhere else, but he must also deprive people of any positive information or examples that contradict his narrative.

He does this successfully, and it's not difficult to do because this is facilitated by his complete and undivided control over the media, ready to easily throw shit at any Russian you might think of as an alternative. Of course, he also throws shit at any other leaders and countries you might use as a comparison.

For instance, take the most promoted figure of the Russian opposition, Alexei Navalny. Even at the peak of his popularity in Russia, every second Russian citizen had never heard of him. That is why the authorities have made it a rule never to mention his name on TV—so that no one would even recognize it.

A simple non-politicized person sees a politician only if shown on TV or in the news—and thus could be considered as an alternative. But if this surname is immediately pronounced as "a swindler and foreign agent Ivanov," then it will never enter the category of acceptable options.

Until someone is allowed to say: "But this guy, Ivanov, or this gal, Anastasia, is a serious person!" then he or she is put on par with the current leaders. Then the ordinary citizen and our potential supporters will be ready to recognize Ivanov or Anastasia's existence, listen to their ideas, and even vote for them.

That's why the authorities are always working to put blinders on people: hushing up, not allowing them to participate in elections, derogatorily and contemptuously ridiculing potential opponents on TV. Why would you listen to someone about whom you heard was a bungler and a fool, or dirty, a crook, or a potential spy?

Alas, this strategy of the Kremlin is very successful so far.

Moreover, the Kremlin skillfully also uses factors such as the scary memories of the 1990s, which became an alternative to the Soviet era, and with which so many fears are associated.

So even though the new generation does not remember that time well, too many people still have the horror of the collapse of their usual life—and people know for sure that things can be much, much worse than under the current government, and they hold on to a titmouse in their hand.

Four

However, this does not mean that it is impossible to present people with an alternative to Putin and his system even during the current circumstances. This can happen in different ways. For example, someone might be introduced as an alternative as an act of subversion. Let's introduce this person as an alternative, and then we can knock him down. But wait! This agent of subversion can also go rogue with power amassed for themselves.

Or it can happen spontaneously. For example, in 1989, the image of Yeltsin on the public stage was created out of stupidity and as a result of a personal insult.

As an alternative to Gorbachev, Yeltsin emerged when he spoke at the Plenum of the Central Committee of the CPSU on October 21, 1987. There, the future Russian president ran into the wife of the General Secretary, who was pretty much hated by the ordinary people. There was a leaked speech by Yeltsin where he demanded that Gorbachev rescue him from Raisa Gorbacheva's "petty tutelage, from her almost daily calls and scoldings."

If he had done or said anything other than a complaint about the behavior of Gorbachev's wife, who was genuinely loved by the Soviet leader but hated by everyone else, he would not have been removed immediately—and everyone knew about it. There were enough informal channels for disseminating information and rumors in the Union, and the message quickly spread. And now, for criticizing one of the most despised people in the country, Yeltsin very quickly gained tremendous popularity.

Why did he rise so quickly? Other viable and active supporters of reforms—the Interregional Deputy Group and Andrei Sakharov—were not visible and understandable alternatives. The people could not imagine them as rulers of the country. They lay on a different shelf of public consciousness. But Yeltsin was something else. He was already in charge. Therefore, he became an alternative. Everyone who wanted changes, albeit very different ones, was forced to unite around this one disgraced apparatchik. Who else was there?

Despite the variety of choices, there appeared to be no alternative.

Perhaps, the people thought, Yeltsin could lead the country as a result of simple apparatus evolution.

As the head of the Moscow City Committee of the CPSU, he was definitely in the top ten in the queue for the Soviet party throne. And so, entering the race, he opposed the big boss with a speech attractive to the people, and automatically became a desired alternative to Gorbachev in their eyes. Everything then depended on his determination, firmness, flexibility, ability to build alliances, and other qualities of a politician and statesman, and he did not miss the chance.

Five

If someone now from Putin's entourage—the prime minister or, say, the deputy prime minister—plays a risky game and states at a meeting in the Kremlin or the White House, "Mr. President, your pension reform is robbery and a crime against the interests of the people," he also has a chance to become the "new Yeltsin."

Putin, however, does not keep anyone around who might do that. He is farsighted and skillfully kills all potential movers. If one of the deputies says "reform is robbery" (as Sergei Zheleznyak and Natalya Poklonskaya did), it doesn't matter. Well, who are they to become an alternative? We need a man of power! In the eyes of the people, the Duma members have no power.

The same can be said about conspiracies and palace coups.

As we think strategically about what would provoke a revolt from within, we must guess about the participants who would need to see that their chances to win are real, and the prize is greater than what they have now. They must also see the possible outcome—money, the growth of personal influence, and the development of careers, all adjusted by the risk—as significantly better for them than doing nothing and waiting for some other opportunity to arise.

But who might be ready for such a move?

Putin feeds his entourage very generously. Therefore, any rebellion is too dangerous. It is much easier to wait for the system itself to crawl into a different state.

Suppose the United States were really aiming for a change of power in Russia (which they are not). Then, if they are afraid of the revolution, they should bet not on one of the pro-Western oppositionists but someone close to Putin with significant assets in the West.

They could say to this person, "Comrade, we will dispossess you here. You are to lose everything. But you may choose another way. Switch sides, give up on evil, get off the sanctions lists, and join the others to change your country."

However, the West is afraid to act this way, fearing confusion and destabilization when dozens of new potentially aggressive and unpredictable countries with nuclear missiles may appear instead of Russia. Moreover, besides the nukes, nobody wants to provide China with free access to the vast natural resources of Siberia and the Far East. For many in the West, Putin (if he stops swinging the nuclear baton) could seem to be the lesser evil—and so they stand still.

Six

Given this logic, Putin was always better for the West. It knew that he could rattle his saber as much as he wanted, but he was unlikely to do anything. Some even supported him in his bullying—it was good for profits, as you are about to see. Yet everything changed on February 24, 2022.

Before the full-scale invasion that day, we witnessed a Cold War 2.0 (or some suggest we should call it a Hybrid War).

The period of 2014–2022 was a flashback to a threatening and scary time, but a profitable world order for those making money on confrontation.

The more Putin shakes his fist at the Americans and Europeans, they thought, the larger the U.S. military budget will be, the more abundant the NATO funding, the more jobs for the military-industrial complex, and the easier it would be for conservative Western politicians to get reelected. At the end of the day, he is no fool, they thought; he would not dare to fight NATO. Would he?

Also, many perceive the war with Ukraine as an inter-Slavic cabal. Before the invasion, Ukraine never really mattered. After the initial honeymoon in 2014, when millions of Ukrainians during the Euromaidan demonstrated their readiness to fight the police and literally die for European values, the West comfortably justified keeping its distance from the war, citing corruption and chaos in this country—as if corruption in Ukraine is so much worse than in Romania, Bulgaria, or even Italy sometimes. I don't think so. It is definitely better than in Putin's Russia; I can confidently attest to that.

Such an attitude was driven by the obvious and quite natural fact that, in making its strategy in the post-Soviet space, the West first thought about its own shortsighted interests. Putin recognized this and was not afraid—he knew the ties with Russia were way more valuable, especially for Europeans. Therefore, he believed the EU would have a minimal choice when the time came.

He was wrong. The West was ready to close its eyes on many things, but not on full-scale invasion, acts of genocide, and the terrorizing of civilians.

To a large degree, the February invasion was a wake-up call for Putin. In one popular Russian movie, the main character kidnapped a lady to marry him. She turned him down, and he said to his people, "It is either me taking her to the priest so she will be my wife, or she would take me to the judge as a criminal." That's precisely Putin's situation at the moment.

Putin understands this, and his bet is, once again, to bully other global leaders—to bluff and to scare them. To make Ukrainians suffer so much that they would prefer to agree to his claims and rebel against their government for being stubborn in refusing Putin's demands.

The thing is—it is not going to happen. And Russian elites have already recognized it. I think even Putin, deep inside himself, recognizes it—but the judges in the Hague are already preparing for the trial. So, he has to continue and pray for a miracle to happen. History shows, after all, that he is one lucky bastard at the end of the day.

But nobody believes luck is with him this time. Everybody is looking for a personal escape, not to become Putin's replacement. So the chatter about a possible transfer of power remains chatter.

The most likely trigger for any change in Russia is collapse: a deep, violent systemic internal crisis, possibly provoked by the military defeat (or inability to achieve a military victory, which is the same) and amplified by Western economic sanctions.

While this is the most likely option, it is not the only one. And I sincerely hope there will be another, more peaceful way.

Personally, I think this will not be a crisis of the economy but of the government itself—the illness of the leader, conflict (or even a coup) in Putin's inner circle, or something else which would be the result of a grave mistake the Russian president made on February 24, 2022.

But thinking about the scenario of change
excites me less than envisioning the future results.
Who will come next?
With what agenda?

There is every reason to believe that, with a large-scale systemic crisis in Russia and the collapse of power, it will not be Khodorkovsky, Gudkov, or Navalny who will be well positioned to pick it up, but someone cut from the same cloth as Putin.

It is obvious we desperately need to create an alternative ourselves, that our promise to ordinary Russians is someone who is finally on their side.

It is not so difficult to do. We just need to recognize the despair of those hurt so badly during the reforms of the 1990s and convince them that their well-being—not some chimera of modern imperialism or modern capitalism—will be the priority of the new leaders.

Some people suggest that I am the right person for that job. We'll see, since it's really for the people of Russia to ultimately decide. However, it would be my honor to serve and lead them, and promote my Big Project outlined on these pages, until a permanent new government is formed.

Seven

Despite being really rusty, Russia's Rust Belt is located along very picturesque slopes of the Urals mountains that separate Europe from Asia, slicing the country into two, from the Arctic Ocean in the North to the borders of Kazakhstan in the South. Abundant with natural resources, especially different metals, it was a central industrial area from long ago.

It was also considered the safest place in the country—too far away from the Western borders and protected by the mountains from the East. Moreover, a lot of military factories were conveniently located here.

The crown jewel of the Soviet tank building industry—"Uralvagonzavod"—is also here, in the grim and tough town of Nizhny Tagil. Even its name in Russian sounds like "don't mess with us." And when the Bolotnaya protests started, Putin decided to look there for support.

It was a curious and intelligent decision. In the post-Soviet era, no one was hurt as much as Uralvagonzavod. The country just momentarily and unexpectedly stopped ordering more tanks, which were produced in ridiculous quantities until the very death of the USSR. Paradoxically, the workers initially supported Yeltsin wholeheartedly, as he was from the same region. Then they became distraught and angry when reforms in the Nineties backfired on them with all their might, like all the tanks they had managed to create. Uralvagonzavod folks were on the verge of revolt all the time, and only alcohol and heavy drugs (which conveniently flooded the town after the Soviet police vanished) helped the government keep the situation under control.

Reformers paid it all back with a symmetrical hatred. "Rednecks," "old-timers," "renegades," and "scum" were the usual labels from the people who called themselves "democrats" and "liberals." Naturally, this made the workers a straightforward target for Putin's manipulation: He just needed to show the Uralvagonzavod workers that those assembled in Bolotnaya identified themselves as those same democrats and liberals that were demonizing them.

To give the Uralvagonzavod folks a bit of extra incentive, he shut down its main competitor—a tank producer in Omsk, called Omsktransmash (more precisely, he transferred its ownership to the rival Uralvagonzavod). Of course, he could have chosen otherwise and shut down Uralvagonzavod and kept Omsk, but probably the conservative Urals was closer to Putin's heart than leftist Siberia.

Then just a couple of days after the December 2011 protests erupted,

Putin was talking with Uralvagonzavod's labor union leader, Igor Kholmanskikh, on TV, and the latter swore loyalty to the Russian president on behalf of all industrial workers of the country. "We are ready to come to Moscow with our guys! We will not let anyone destroy our hard-earned stability!"

Moscow liberal leaders reconfirmed that all industrial proletariat was their enemy and cut off the social agenda, isolating the movement from the ordinary people and dooming its outcome. All the country faced the difficult choice between the two flanks and preferred to step back. As a result, the protest movement started to fade. Putin soon appointed Kholmanskikh as his plenipotentiary representative in the Urals Federal District and later as Chairman of Uralvagonzavod. In 2020, the well-used and unnecessary Uralvagonzavod returned to the edge of bankruptcy, and its workload (along with wages) was slashed almost by half.

This all reminds me so much of my childhood. A picture of endless frozen Polish factories in the summer of 1980 under the red banners of "Strike!" is forever engraved in my memory.

Several years of consistent work led to the very first strikes at factories, mines, and shipyards in 1980 being genuinely massive. They soon managed to inspire the creation of an organized and effective labor movement— Solidarność (Solidarity), led by Lech Walesa.

By its official registration in November 1980, Solidarity consisted of more than 7 million people (its numbers snowballed to 9–10 million). From September 1980 to December 1981, its branches organized about 150 significant strikes on a national and regional scale. In addition, the agricultural workers had established their union—Rural Solidarity—and in 1981, it included up to half of all agro-industrial producers.

This experience cannot be called new—in Poland, they repeated what the Bolsheviks did in Russia, the founders of the Congress of Industrial Trade Unions in the United States, and many other people and organizations in different countries of the world.

However, even though it cannot be called unique, it was creatively rethought in accordance with the conditions, and can be applied in a variety of countries.

But two things should be noted: firstly, they now like to talk about Solidarity as an anti-communist trade union, but this is inaccurate. It indeed opposed the Polish authorities, who hid behind communist ideas and relied on Soviet bayonets. But the union's original demands were purely left: "socialism with a human face"; first of all, lower prices and a guaranteed food supply. The primary political demand was the legalization of independent trade unions. Moreover, out of 7 million members of the trade union, more than a million were members of the ruling PZPR (Polish United Workers' Party).

Secondly, (and this is probably the main thing) the lesson of Solidarity is precisely in the *solidarity* of working people. People got involved in a serious collective cause in which they saw strength, and did not support small political groups with unclear prospects.

It is also worth learning from the protests in Belarus in 2020. There, the union between the industrial workers and the urban crowds started to happen, which did not work out in Russia in 2011. In fact, President Lukashenko has tried hard to keep the Soviet industrial potential of the republic intact. But he also created a new high-tech industry, which was already generating about 10% of the country's GDP by the time the protests began.

By doing so, he gave birth to a serious *new class*. The same *new class* took to the streets of Belarusian cities and was subjected to severe police repression. However, after the industrial workers joined them, the authorities immediately removed the security forces from the streets and backed off. The implications of this *new class* are significant for Russia's future, and we will discuss it more in chapters thirteen through sixteen.

I believe this book will reach the collective "Uralvagonzavod"—the broad masses of Russian workers and ordinary citizens, and they will understand who their ally is. They will see our ideas and goals coincide, and we will respect each other and form a true force together.

Eight

Real change can only come from below. The "transfer of power" from above only prolongs the agony, after which the collapse will be even more painful and profound.

This change will not appear by itself. It has been developed over the years, as we did in the Left Front, with the Union of Coordination Councils (that we established as nonpartisan grassroots solidarity groups after the protests against the monetization of privileges), independent trade unions, and other public organizations throughout the country.

In the end, I know that there are people that work in factories and industry as well as in offices and live in cities and towns, who wait for their time to come. They regularly come with hopes of new high-profile political projects in which they talk about justice and honesty, but then periodically move away from them, having seen it's yet another deception.

Our situation resembles that of the Bolsheviks in 1917. They were absolutely unprepared for the February Revolution. They didn't have an organization. There were leaders—but some were in prison, some in exile. And some professional activists passed through the party school in Longjumeau, but there were just a few behind them. Emptiness.

Nevertheless, there was a clear ideological base, a straightforward program, the courage of leaders, and a willingness to fight to the very end.

Suddenly, for everyone, there was a popular uprising, and the Tsar was overthrown. However, modern historians suggest that it was more of a coup, an act of treason organized by a large bourgeoisie, unsatisfied with how Nickolas II was handling the First World War. They were behind a mysterious lack of bread in the capital and unexpected clashes of soldiers with their officers, and it was them, not leftists, who financed an organized labor union movement.

But Bolsheviks demonstrated a rapid, almost instantaneous mobilization. The unambiguity and radicalism of slogans attracted millions. So very quickly, in fact, in one or two months, a dual power was formed—the official Provisional Government at the top, and the People's Soviets everywhere else.

We must achieve the same. In war, an alternative center of power will emerge sooner or later. And the world will recognize it because it will be the only possibility to delegitimize Putin. Then the system will collapse, as Bolivar cannot carry double, as O. Henry once suggested.

As soon as there is a significant change in the country's leadership, exiled Russians must immediately return home from emigration. We must build a combat-effective infrastructure. We'll have to do it in two or three months.

But we cannot say who will take the political helm. The new leadership could bring the country back on track—or to a dead end.

Therefore, we need a clear picture of future development—an action plan. We must clearly understand where we and all of Russia are going. So that the unprincipled and loose mass of managers, who will inevitably try to jump the wagon as soon as it appears, must also receive a clear understanding of our goals and the benefits for themselves. There will always be a place for competent people in New Russia. But the swindlers and thieves, slick in their rotten machinations, will be mercilessly thrown out.

The outline of this plan, our strategy, is right here in this book. And the plan will be continuously amended as the situation and our capabilities evolve.

How will it happen? We don't have a crystal ball. A responsible and experienced politician knows that everything is determined by the current situation, our fundamental principles, and our commitment to follow them. And the willingness to deliver them not only to those who already follow you but also to those who still do not trust you or disagree with you.

CHAPTER ELEVEN

About Foreign Policy, War, and Nukes

One

In the early 2000s, Putin wanted to join NATO, and there were negotiations about it. The leadership of the alliance was amazed that the Kremlin wanted to participate as an equal partner with the United States while maintaining its own standards of military organization.

But NATO was created as an elite club led by the United States. Part of the deal with the Europeans was that they may not spend enough money on defense, but they must obey the guys from across the ocean who will protect them.

The Americans invested in the North Atlantic security system, and now they are not ready to share these investments with anyone. Quite logically, they instead want the retainers to be paid—even 2% of the national budgets that are supposed to be allocated for defense purposes are usually paid by the newest members, the Eastern Europeans, who see the value in NATO but are pretty much ignored by the traditional member states. So now, when Ukraine asks for defense assistance, countries like Germany or France cannot really deliver anything serious—they've neglected to buy weapons for a long time.

It would have been funny if it weren't so sad. After the invasion began,

Western Europeans started looking for producers to provide them with all different types of military equipment, only to realize those weapon manufacturers were long gone in "peaceful" Europe. As a result, not only tanks or cannons could not be produced, but also armored vests or rifles—they lost all of that manufacturing capability. Frankly speaking, in Russia, the situation is not significantly better. Still, at least the Soviet Union left Putin a considerable legacy of hardware, which can be used in the fields of war for quite some time.

Western Europeans wanted a free ride. If Americans were so concerned about geopolitics, let them pay for it and provide the EU with military cover—but without a second thought of who was in charge. Clearly, the worst-case scenario would have been the United States losing interest in protecting Europe, which almost happened under the Trump administration. However, nobody wanted to deal with problems before they emerged.

At the beginning of the 2000s, Russia was not ready for a significant financial commitment either. Yet since it was not really considered a threat anymore, even the temptation to put the Russian military and nuclear arsenal under joint command control did not produce enough appeal to NATO leadership.

Additionally, there was an issue with military standards, which were different. It was painful but feasible to enforce them on Poles or Czechs, but how to conform the entire Russian army, the second largest in the world? Obviously, if there were a political will, it would not become a deal breaker, but it was also an essential element in the decision process. Moreover, alliance members should not be competitors in the arms market. Russia is one of the largest arms producers in the world, and that's not going to change.

Taking all these factors in consideration, the West decided for the second time in its history that there was no place for Russia in NATO. I wonder, when the question arises for the third time, will the lesson finally be learned?

Ironically, Russia is now more important for NATO than ever. Without the annexation of Crimea, hostilities in the Donbas, and then the all-out invasion of Ukraine, the alliance in its current form would lose its meaning. However, with aggression against Ukraine—which means a confrontation with the entire belt of Eastern European states from the Baltic to the Black Sea—Putin has actually resurrected this organization.

Now the generals are on horseback, and with money. Politicians who indeed for some time believed in the "end of history" were harshly brought back to reality.

Confrontation or aggressive competition between the two poles (or even between the three poles, if China is considered) is just the usual model of the world. In this rut, all people in uniform in all countries know how to exist. They are lost when it is not clear who the enemy is, as it was twenty years after the collapse of the Soviet Union. They strived to invent enemies for themselves, to create a starting point in them.

This is the essence of traditional foreign policy. It always was and remains pragmatic.

Even in America, it does not depend so much on who the president of the country is, and even less so on who the foreign leaders are. It goes on and on, guided chiefly by public prejudice, stereotypes, politics, and the lobbying power of the military-industrial complex. Even George W. Bush, who, under Dick Cheney's dictation, declared a "global war against terrorism" and began the cleansing of Afghanistan in 2001, and the invasion of Iraq in 2003, could not change this tradition.

For those who do not understand how this policy works, Julian Assange publishes, as they say, "top-secret materials on spy scandals, corruption in the highest echelons of power, war crimes and secrets of great power diplomacy," including videos, secret dispatches, and State Department telegrams. This costs the careers of a number of officials but reassures specialists: the principles are for the public, while the "pragmatic" approach to world affairs remains secretly in place. Undercover deals and underhanded intrigues continue, and all is quiet on the Western front.

It is important to understand that a black-and-white view of the world does not reflect reality. It never worked before, and it does not work now. Those in power, however, pretend it is the case to the public. In fact, it turns out that the "irreconcilable conflicts" of systems, countries, and forces we see are often not so irreconcilable after all. They are just comfortable.

The elites are only afraid that something will change and that the source of fear among the people will disappear, as their "secret knowledge" (which they actually do not possess) will no longer be needed. Of course, even the most seemingly antagonistic forces know how to cooperate profoundly and comprehensively when necessary.

Two

At the end of the Russian-Ukrainian war, the question of the demilitarization of Russia will inevitably be on the agenda.

We are too big, and we have defied all the norms of decency to be left alone. Putin could deceive the Russians using his undivided control over television. Still, the whole world was horrified, even the pragmatic Chinese and the people of India, far from Ukraine.

"Why can they, but we can not," Putin constantly asks.

The argument, of course, is at the kindergarten level: "Why, if Vasya pulls the girls' pigtails, can't we do the same?"

If Vasya is ill-mannered, you need to educate him, not become a bully or abuser yourself.

If the Americans are wrong in invading Iraq, this does not mean that we should invade Ukraine!

In addition, in foreign policy—in contrast to life within the country clearly regulated by laws— the principle of expediency, recognized by the majority, is more applicable.

Gather a large support group around you, convince other countries that you are right—and then claim your rights.

In the case of Putin, maybe the Chinese president taps him from time to time on his shoulder. But, in reality, when it comes to voting at the UN, only Belarus and Eritrea are on his side. So why is he so surprised, then, at the sanctions and troubles for—okay, forget ordinary Russians—his closest cronies?

And do not envy America, where there is a constant support group: this is a consequence of the strength of its economy.

We ourselves have a million opportunities to attract international investors and partners to our side, but for some reason we want to act not with affection and persuasion, but with arm-twisting and blackmail.

As we all know, after February 2022, things have become so bad that not only Putin, but all Russians, have become world outcasts.

So the old way of simply returning the soldiers to the barracks will no longer work.

Some hotheads shout that everything is simple: disarm the Russian army, take away nuclear weapons, cancel the right of veto in the UN, and all will be well.

I don't think this is correct.

Three

The global balance of power is a damn delicate thing.

These are such multidimensional scales, on which not two, but two hundred different interests of different countries are weighed simultaneously.

The disappearance of the USSR as a superpower saved the world from the threat of mutual destruction, but destroyed the fragile balance.

The West (and above all the United States), feeling like a winner, lost the need to coordinate its actions with other centers of power.

Like any monopoly, this does not benefit progress.

Ultimately, the irritation and annoyance resulting from this among Russian citizens played an important role in the degeneration of the country. In the late 1980s, Russia voluntarily renounced the status of world hegemony and turned into a resentful, aggressive, but still weak hooligan who could neither defeat Chechnya nor Ukraine.

It is disgusting to watch how we spin in front of the mirror, convincing ourselves how we got up from our knees, and endlessly trying to boast about how strong and mighty we are today while only having the past victories of our ancestors to show as evidence of our strength.

This situation is dire when we cannot implement a single big project or even feed ourselves!

Americans can afford to throw hamburgers all over the Middle East without damage (but rather, with benefit) to their own weight; we in turn can only argue with the Ukrainians for the copyright for borscht, which not all Russian housewives can afford to cook anyway.

One way or another, even in this pitiful state, Russia, from the point of view of the West, is now needed for an immensely important thing: to protect the natural resources of Siberia from Chinese control.

NATO politicians argue that "Putins" come and go, but geography stays, and everything possible should be done so that the world does not return to a state of competition between the two superpowers, which these days refers to China and the United States.

Therefore, the idea of nuclear disarmament of Russia, however tempting for many, will not be supported by many "pragmatists."

UN reform is also a matter of doubt. The veto right is used by no means only by Russia.

Will other countries (U.S., China, UK, and France) abandon it for humanitarian reasons? You can ask, but there are doubts. I think the only realistic reform is to give the UN General Assembly the right to override the veto if a resolution is supported by a supermajority.

Four

When it comes to the future of nuclear weapons, the situation needs to be addressed in greater detail.

The shortsighted steps of a number of countries, Western and Russia, have clearly demonstrated to others that the role of this argument has not decreased but increased after the end of the Cold War.

The examples of North Korea, Iran, the conflicts between India and Pakistan, the Kremlin's nuclear map after the attack on Ukraine—all suggest that the situation requires a new approach.

My view is this:

Nuclear weapons are a means of collective defense of all mankind, not individual countries.

I think there should always be two keys to the launch of nuclear missiles—one in the possession of the country, the other in the control of the UN Security Council. Without their mutual decision, this weapon cannot be used.

This does not exclude the possibility for a particular country on whose territory the nuclear arsenal is located to have exclusive access to it. But it will not be able to do this suddenly and imperceptibly: Such steps will become known to the whole world, and there will be no more opportunities for blackmailing others.

Either the country confirms its intention to use its arsenal, and then the world will have to react and have time for it, or other countries will know that whatever conflicts they have with a nuclear power, it will not use this terrible weapon against them without the consent of the rest of the world.

A decision of this magnitude will not happen quickly either. We will need to organize a new global movement for world peace—not like the great powers once did in their own interests, but for real, from below.

I am sure this initiative will be supported not by millions but by billions, and world leaders will have to join them.

In the meantime, after the change of power in Russia, I would apply to join NATO—together with Ukraine and other post-Soviet countries—and maintain that Russian, American, French, and British nuclear arsenals will become the collective defense of the Northern Alliance.

This would solve so many problems of our common—and global—security!

CHAPTER TWELVE

About the State

One

How does a small person live in the big state of Russia?

Not so comfortably.

In this state, we all feel bad. Our lives will never change. As soon as we raise a timid, trembling voice—if we raise it!—the heavy and dirty boot of power hangs over us. Then the boot presses us into the ground and grinds us into worm puree.

Therefore, the little man is silent. Keeping his fingers covertly crossed, he is silent, and patient.

The Russian people are always patient. They say that someday we will be rewarded for this. They say that those who are patient go to heaven. Unfortunately, they take it literally and continue to suffer like those old Russian women in the Warsaw church at the beginning of this book.

Our lousy life in a specific state, shod in specific boots with blunt toes and heavy horseshoes, is by God's design. This is how the little man thinks.

"So," he says, "I won't utter a word."

"Not even a chirp?" I ask.

"I won't peep!" he confirms, and continues to endure.

No one will know how annoying the little man is in a hospital. Our

Russian hospitals, where they drink from us our once hot, scarlet, and now sluggish black blood.

How the courts frighten the little man—where we, trembling creatures, are ordered to compete with those who have the right. How stupid Lady Justice strains us, drilling into all with her eyes from under the bandage and her sword, turned only to our necks. How our hamstrings tremble when we smell that sword's edge, quick and wrong, imagining only that it can touch . . . me! And you!

No! I'd rather crawl back to the safety of my room and quietly, privately, and pitifully express my indignation. Or I will sell my opinion at a higher price—I will vote "correctly" and go for the "righteous" rally. And I'll get a bonus from the state for being loyal to it.

Although, perhaps, it is there that I will timidly open my mouth and express everything about this boot, which will make me—weak, disillusioned, disenfranchised—tremble with endless fear. I will praise him and the foot inside the boot! So, I lean on the power, vast and unbearable, to feel safe. Maybe one day, I will still say something vindictively—speaking directly to the boot.

That's what my little man tells me. And I'm listening. I understand his point.

Because I remember how I sometimes felt like a disenfranchised person with the parliamentary pin, given the right to vote from time to time in the State Duma. Sometimes even to go against the majority.

There is neither strength nor courage in going against the majority. There is only painful disgust at the sight of 450 intelligent, successful people who have made themselves small, into worms eating the decaying flesh of my country and its citizens.

I can be the same. Being close to the power of the state, feeling its reflection, I raise my displeased voice—I am so close, it may hear me. Maybe it will not crush me. I am able to take a step, even to my own detriment. The little man may not able to do so, but I can.

If I know exactly what idea I'm doing it for, I courageously take a step.

This is my strength. Compared to the boot of power, my strength is small. But listen, those in boots—they are even smaller! Parasites, moths, there are many of them, they are strong with their swarming mass, they are crooks and thieves, bureaucrats and partocrats, but still people vote for them. Because they know what to say and what to do, and this is their strength.

"No!" you say. "They are weak. Because they promise, but they never deliver."

They do almost nothing they say they will. Everyone is used to it. We all know they could do what they say, but they don't have any reason to do it for the people, only for themselves and their friends.

In Russia, we have a common joke:

"What do you call a man who wants to, but he can't? Impotent, right?

"And what do you call a man who can, but won't? We call him a son of a bitch."

Putin is the man who can, but won't.

So, we will continue to endure until we understand:

> **Without our faith in the power of the enemy,
> he has no power and never will.**

Two

Remember—I am a physicist by profession. I was taught:

> **It is impossible to change the way a system works
> from the inside.**

You can swap its elements, but the system as a whole will continue the same uniform and linear motion that it was making before—or stay at rest.

This is Newton's first law, taught in physics classes everywhere. Interestingly, it is also clearly applicable to the work of political systems, but, for some reason, no one thinks about it that way.

Here's another entirely unexpected place in life where you might apply the same law: If you rearrange the beds in a brothel, the quality of its services will not change. And if you keep the same politicians within the same political system, the result will also be the same.

It is only possible to change the system
by influencing it from the outside.

Without external influence from the popular masses (or as a result of a military defeat, which looks like the most probable outcome of the invasion into Ukraine), it will continue to move in the same direction as before. No matter how many changes you make on the inside, you are accomplishing nothing but moving the beds around the Kremlin's brothel.

Is that what you want?

No!

Therefore, we must plan to change the system from the outside.

Yet here's a trap that lies in wait for us: the favorite delusion of the Russian liberal intelligentsia, which listens so attentively to other oppositionists like Navalny:

"Let's replace those bastards with ourselves . . . we will use the same tools, the same media, we will just send a different signal . . . after all, society is not ready for liberalism and does not understand what serves its own good."

Wait! What?

Someone thinks it is worth using the mechanism of evil for good, and everything will be okay?

No. It won't be fine.

As Russian Yevgeny Schwartz said in his play *The Dragon* in 1944, it is not true that the only way to get rid of dragons is to have your own.

The biggest risk is to kill a dragon
and then become a dragon yourself.

Those who watched the *Game of Thrones* series could see how it happens.

You cannot change the system by just pumping people up with different propaganda, disinformation, and belief in false goals and victories. They must be allowed to make their own decisions, and you need to offer them other ideas. Unfortunately, this continuously happened in Russia until 1986 and after 1993.

Instead, people need to absorb information consciously: by reading a book, articles, or posts on the Web; watching TV shows or videos on

YouTube; or listening to a live speech or lecture on the radio. And they say to themselves: "Yes, now we believe in it. And that's what we want."

For me, this is an essential principle. The state cannot do without ideas. Let there be many. Let them compete. Let them be broadcast by those who come to power due to fair and free elections.

But let them do it honestly. Let people say what they really mean as if they are speaking to their family.

Let them do it. Let people be responsible for their words.

Three

Power is the fruit of the free choice of people. Not what is being forced on them.

We need to figure things out together and agree on where we want to go.

I cannot go to the podium as a speaker and then tell the people who came to the rally, having given up their time and overcome the cold or heat and made it past the police metal detectors, that I have nothing to offer them.

This is cowardice.

Instead, our new state must bear the fruit of collective creativity.

The leader of a democratic country is not a despot who dictates his will. He is a moderator who hears the minority and gives everyone the right to self-realization.

I have a clear vision of what country I want to live in. I know how to build it. However, I also know that other people have their own dreams of an ideal state, and I'm not afraid to hear them or consider them. We must allow every dream a chance to come true and ensure that every idea strengthens us as a people.

Only then will our country be able to consider itself free.

In this country, we will have three main components of strength—the multitude, the idea, and the truth. Let each of us be different, and let each of us even be somewhat strange. But we are relatives to each other. Unity is people holding hands, standing ankle-deep in wet snow, driven into a trap, as if into the mouth of a giant riot police officer in a helmet and with a rubber baton, breaking our hands and shoving us into paddy wagons—and yet we are warm from the feeling of not being alone and putting up a fight together.

**The idea is our core.
Truth is what keeps us warm.**

Let's not become fixated on the fact that Putin and his people stole everything from us. Let's not divide the nation into "us" versus "them." Instead, we will allow everyone and anyone who sincerely seeks truth, protection, and ideas to join. Including people from the current top—those who understand the government as we've known it has led us in the wrong direction and that it—damned by all—should be left to perish alone, abandoned, and forgotten as a bad dream.

Then we will take our future into our own hands.

To achieve this, it is necessary to discuss in precise words and with clear examples how to live, what to do, and where to go.

Part Three: The "Unexpected" Generation

CHAPTER THIRTEEN

Let's Meet Russia's *"New Class"*

One

In Kazakhstan, there is a delicacy—turtle liver.

In the spring, when the steppe blooms, turtles wake up from hibernation and suddenly crawl everywhere, rushing (which, for a turtle, is actually waddling) to produce a new life.

Among the people of the East, the turtle is a symbol of sexual energy.

Meanwhile, hunters sharpen axes, prepare galvanized buckets, and race to the steppe.

The turtles can't hear them coming. But if they could hear the hunters, what could they do?

Then the turtles are caught.

It's a simple matter, really.

With a deft trained movement, the hunter uses a very sharp knife to cut the shell, take out the liver, and throw it into a bloody bucket.

Then the hunter lets the turtle go free.

And the turtles?

Believe it or not, they are unaware of what has happened, and they cheerfully waddle away in search of a mate, still alive, but already dead. Still existing, but without a future. Not understanding what has been done to them—not understanding all that has been stolen from them. Their liver. Their lives. Their future.

Everything has been taken from them, in the cruelest possible way.

So it is with the Soviet middle class.

They cut them to pieces, took their most vital parts, and the middle class waddled off thinking they were about to fall in love and live long, healthy, prosperous lives in liberated Russia.

But no.

That middle class, like the turtle, is gone.

Today, instead, we have what I will call the *new class*.

Two

In the early 2000s in Russia, the term "creative class" came into vogue.

To push back against this, Kremlin propaganda tried to make a mockery of "the creative class" by calling them "creakol."

Roughly speaking, "creakol" can be translated from Kremlinise to something like "hipster."

My impression is that in America and Western Europe, many want to live the life of a hipster, but no one wants to be called a hipster. That's what the Kremlin tried to do with creakols: isolate and shame a particular group of people and turn others against them.

The term "creative class" was initially introduced by Richard Florida, a prominent American sociologist and economist who published the book, *The Rise of the Creative Class: How It's Transforming Work, Leisure, Community, and Everyday Life*.

The term denotes people included in the postindustrial sector of the economy. The author believes they are becoming a large group in developed countries. For example, in the United States, their share, according to his estimate, is 30% of all employees. (I consider this figure to be greatly overestimated, but I agree that it is the fastest-growing part of U.S. society.)

Regardless of its percentage of the population of any given country, this group is powerful because its members often serve as role models or influencers for others, and they use their expertise with the latest technology to help create their countries' agendas and shape public opinion.

The Florida hypothesis is exciting and controversial. But I am not here to argue for or against it. Instead, I merely mention the words "creative class" because they are often used to describe a *new class* of demanding and protesting Russians.

However, the artistic bohemia—the designers, artists, writers, and

journalists we generally think of as the hipsters, creative class, or creakol—are only a small part of this mass movement, at least in Russia.

Many others are also involved as well in creating something new,
including engineers and scientists, healthcare workers, teachers, and others.

Perhaps when we say "creative class," we are talking about the eternal
strength and weakness of Russia—the intelligentsia.

Once, in the heat of the moment, arguing with the famous Soviet
writer Maxim Gorky, Lenin declared:

**"Such an intelligentsia is not the brain,
but the shit of the nation."**

Lenin did not mean that the cultural elites of the Russian Empire smelled
bad. His point was that they were not original; they did not produce new
ideas but just nicely processed and packaged what was actually created by
the most advanced class of his day—the industrial workers.

Today we have the new vanguard—the *new class*. It includes so many
others who would never have been considered intelligentsia: small business owners and entrepreneurs, merchants, office workers, programmers,
and media professionals. Individuals who not only move the economy
of the twenty-first century but also join protests against the oppressive
system.

I am fine with letting the authorities mock and discount this group
because I know doing so is actually to the Kremlin's detriment. It's not
a small, voiceless group. On the contrary, it's a powerful, growing, independent, and vocal force to be reckoned with.

The invasion of Ukraine in 2022 triggered a massive exodus of these
people from Russia. In a very short time frame, the country lost approximately 150,000 people, and the total toll since 2014 is at least one million.

I remember how the turnout of so many protestors at Bolotnaya in
2011 shocked the authorities and ourselves. "Look how many of us are
here!" was the amazed yet joyful observation one could hear coming
from every corner.

Many, and still growing!

Three

Here's the thing about some of those hipsters who are right now sitting
near you in front of their expensive new Apple MacBook Pro computers,

talking on their expensive new Apple iPhones, with equally expensive shiny new white Apple earbuds in their ears, at your downtown Starbucks all day:

They are the ones who use TikTok, YouTube, Telegram, Instagram, Snapchat, Twitter, and yes, Facebook (but only when they have to), Twitch, Substack, Medium, and WhatsApp to take control of the conversation and the agenda.

If you want to start a powerful movement, you've got to get people like this on your side.

But be careful because:

> **If you approach them with the wrong message
> or the wrong position or the wrong point of view,
> you are likely to become the one
> who is the turtle without a liver.**

When they organize, they have incredible power. However, they have never really organized—and don't appreciate how much power they really have.

I think that's a shame. They should be encouraged, within a system designed to encourage all, to participate in a social and political system that's designed for participation by everyone.

We must not let the elites of the past separate this new generation—and the *new class* in general—from the other oppressed. Different lifestyles, beards, and coffee brands should not restrict our understanding of the fundamental economic and social interest: to be able to self-govern and unlock one's potential to the fullest.

Four

Introducing these "hipsters" to the Russian economy and society is essential.

But really, what should we call them?

Although I have used the term "hipster" here in jest, that's not correct. They don't all have tattoos and pierced noses and man-buns.

Nor should they be called "creakol," because the Kremlin invented that term to demean them.

"Creative class" is not quite right, either. They're not all artists and designers and members of the vanguard.

The reality is, they come from all walks of life in Russia.

As I've written different versions of this text, I've racked my brain searching for the right name for them.

We need a valid name that reflects who they are, what they are capable of doing, and their mission, which is also wholly nonjudgmental.

Meanwhile, no one else has come up with a good name for them either, so:

**Since no one can come up with a special word
for this special group, let's continue to call them:
*"the new class."***

Five

For a moment, let's compare the Russian *new class* with the Russian "middle class," and by "Russian middle class," I mean the middle class from the Soviet era because:

**One of the leading causes—and one of the primary
tragic consequences—of the end of the Soviet system
was the destruction of the middle class.**

The middle class in Russia is gone, destroyed by the very efforts that were intended to enlarge and benefit it.

Like Churchill once suggested, many see the Soviet system as an equal distribution of poverty.

But it was also a system of more or less equal distribution of opportunities, public goods, and services.

Now, we can debate what was meant by the middle-class during Soviet times.

Yes, those who earned average or "middle-class" wages by Soviet standards were nominally poorer than the owners of average incomes in the West. In the USSR, a $300 monthly salary was good; with $500, you would be considered indecently wealthy. $1000—that's for either seasonal workers in the most challenging conditions in the North or for crooks. Just by having such money, you were inviting very inconvenient attention from law enforcement.

The income of the middle class in the States and Western Europe, expressed in dollars, always greatly exceeded the average income of the people of Russia. But no matter how many rubles were in their pockets, ordinary Russians could enjoy many of the same pleasures of life as the Western middle class, like regular vacations at the seaside, camping and hiking, decent healthcare, and high-quality education.

During the years of neoliberal reforms, the Russian authorities brought the people to actual poverty. And the Russian people never recovered: according to the World Bank, in 2017, more than 50% of Russians lived poorer than they were in the USSR. So it is no surprise they were receptive to Putin's referrals to the good old Soviet times.

Of course, just as in the issue of how to define the middle class, it is also not so easy to define poverty, and in different countries, it begins with varying levels of income. Lucky owners of relatively decent salaries in Russia are few, and they do not always fit nicely into rigid social theories.

There are many reasons why this demise of the Soviet middle class happened. One of those reasons is that Russia was a country where nobody knew the basic principles of a market economy and trade, so there was a colossal advantage for a small group of those who knew how or figured out how to adapt to new circumstances and prosper. At the same time, everyone else was trapped in an endless cycle of fighting for survival as the Yeltsin government destroyed the economy.

Six

The USSR was investing income from the sale of oil and gas into the transition from the industrial to the postindustrial—informational—phase of development. In the Soviet Union, like in the West, investments were not just in the consumer space. Scientific progress and industrial development also gave birth to professions related to the production of nonmaterial products. They included new types of engineers, scientists, teachers, doctors, and other high-tech professionals.

The development of these productive forces and technologies gave rise to the *new class*—included in the postindustrial sector, creating intangible assets and working with them, plus having an income comparable to the income of people in the West involved in similar activities.

For a while, those lucky enough to be part of the *new class* think everything is fine. The steppe is blooming. But soon, they see that it is all an illusion.

Yes, there are blooming oligarchs protected by thieving bureaucrats. But the steppe is trampled down by the selfish, swaggering crowd of people that privatized not just the national wealth, but also the title of national elite. And an authoritarian, greedy, repressive regime created by them hinders the development of the sector in which the *new class* works.

As a result, the Russian *new class* begins to understand quite quickly:

It's time to discard illusions about the future, and to start building this future instead.

Seven

In the modern world, the *new class* has many advantages.

For instance, a Russian with a communications or technology education can go anywhere in the world and get a work visa and a high-paying job.

At the same time, the way of life of the *new class* is very different from the way of life of others.

Their families are organized differently, they spend their leisure time differently, they communicate differently. They view power and leadership differently. They tend to work not in hierarchical environments, but in horizontal networks. All this leads to different political expectations and the demand for evolution of the political system.

As new waves of communications and technology transform the world, their expectations and numbers grow.

This, in turn, encourages even more significant changes in political and administrative structures.

Meanwhile, robotization and production automation means the number of people employed in the production of physical goods will decrease, just as the number of people once employed in agriculture decreased during industrialization.

More and more people will engage in these new forms of employment. There is already less and less need for industrial jobs. Tensions rise. People who were daily and hourly enslaved by the industrial machines are liberated, but they have nowhere to go to make their living. They continue to be the slaves of the elites and heartless State.

A virtuous cycle of change starts as the nature of employment changes. Employment within the corporate sector changes. A new freelance sector is born and quickly grows. This growth of the freelance sector means a surge of people who are accustomed to, and even expect to, control their destiny—and will demand this control in all aspects of their lives, including the politics of the nation where they live. Meanwhile, at the same time, "liberated" freelance workers cannot form unions to defend themselves from the greed of their employers. So freedom becomes slavery, as one of the most famous socialists in history, George Orwell, suggested a long time ago.

This encourages even more changes in political and administrative structures.

Here, I foresee a marriage of the digital skills and experiences of the *new class*—and the demand for "digital" or "direct democracy"—as an extension of their digital-first and digital-always worldview.

However, in order to arrive at a situation where such fundamental changes become possible, the Russian *new class* will have to work hard and go a long way, using all their talents and skills.

Eight

Now that we've come this far together, let's be clear:

I am writing this book for those who are ready for change, who are ready to lead, for those who want to be part of this *"new class."*

I am also writing this book to introduce the Big Project to the world, of course, but specifically to the *new class*.

Because the *new class* is not just made up of white-collar workers and creatives.

The people I think of don't just work in offices. Some produce technology or services, while others produce goods. They cannot live without each other; otherwise, one will have nothing to do, while the other will have nothing to eat and nowhere to live.

It takes all of us to be responsible and take ownership of our country. So I extend my hand to everyone who is ready to build a new Russia—not for the elite, but for the many.

It doesn't matter on which square we gather, on Bolotnaya or Poklonnaya. In Kyiv, Donetsk, or Moscow. Or in an online meeting room hidden from prying eyes on Okhotny Ryad. Everyone is invited, without exception.

We need to become one unified organism—not scattered, not split.

We are sick, seriously sick. But organs alone do not recover. The whole body must be treated. We can only develop and grow together. Therefore, we need a single organism formed of all people with common ethical—historical and civilizational—roots. People who have been ethnically mixed with each other for thousands of years. We need a large single organism, and we, neither in Moscow nor outside it, should build borders between ourselves. We shall not oppose anyone living in our country. We shall build a new commonwealth of equals instead.

Let's remember our history: Which of the previous rulers of Russia was interested in the growth of civic consciousness and people's unity?

None. Instead of multiplying, they were just dividing.

CHAPTER FOURTEEN

"Why the Hell Did I Have to Be Born in Russia?"

One

Let me be the first to point something out:

From the perspective of rigorous theory, one must admit: the term *"the new class"* is unscientific.

The founders of Marxism define the term "class" specifically: "Classes are large groups of people that differ in their place in a historically defined system of production, in their relationship (for the most part fixed and formalized into laws) to the means of production, in their role in the social organization of labor, and consequently, according to the methods of obtaining and the size of the share of social wealth that they have."

This is very important. Education, background, and income may differ—in fact, they divide people. And what unites us? What and how we live and work. Activity determines the way of life, the community of interests, circle of acquaintances, and political views.

And what does *the new class* do?

They primarily create intangible assets: according to one of the definitions, products that have value and can increase in price can be sold on the market. But often, for the *new class,* this means "things" which at the same time are not actually "things"—they do not have a physical form.

An essential feature of such assets is that they bring specific economic benefits to the creator or owner and are used in the production of goods, improving work performance, providing services, and for management needs.

The creation of such an asset requires creativity, a high degree of resourcefulness, ingenuity and, often, business skills from people belonging to this *new class.*

It also makes sense for us to define intangible assets better in our ever-changing "digital world."

Let's start with "the world of word and image"—journalism, writing, television, and art. And "the world of technical and technological invention." And the "world of decisions"—managerial moves and strategies. As well as the "zone of money," which is just a flicker on the scoreboard of financial platforms and supermarket checkouts today.

From the point of view of Marxist theory:

The majority of the representatives of this *new class* are the proletariat.

Historically, we have used this word to mean factory workers, but this understanding is an outdated relic from the past century. Programmers, journalists, and office workers also correspond to this concept. They do not own the means of production and do not make a profit. Instead, they create a surplus product with value that can be very high. However, then they are alienated from what they produce!

This means they are generally deprived of any right to participate in the management of the results of their labor. A specific counterexample that the curious reader can cite is "options" on high-tech stocks, where employees are given a small stake in the companies where they work, thereby becoming personally interested or vested in the growth and future of the company and even receive voting rights. Of course, it is easy to see that in this case, the shares of the enterprise distributed among employees is very small, and the total number of employees who own shares in their companies across all companies is only a small minority of the *new class.* Therefore, the logic and behavior of the *new class,* overall, remains the logical behavior of recruited laborers.

And therefore, the logic of their economic, social, and political behavior is still the logic of the proletariat.

Two

One day, while looking for new technologies to work with within the framework of the Skolkovo project, I ended up in an ultramodern medical clinic that was using the most innovative developments to help families who could not have children.

It's an interesting story, how I got there.

My good friend, B., is the head of a rural branch of the A Just Russia party in Siberia. The district center is just a station on the Trans-Siberian Railway; the nearest large city is a hundred kilometers away.

The place is famous only for the endless swampy steppe, among which the peasants manage to grow enough somehow to survive.

B. has a bunch of businesses, but he does not stick out much. However, he worries about the state of his country, so he joined the party.

By local standards, he is almost an oligarch—in his "empire," there is a driving school, an auto repair shop, and a car wash. According to rumors, ambitious B. was also actively using farmers' markets to sell some groceries, but this is not certain. It would have made him too influential, which was dangerous in the circumstances. He lives in a stone house on the outskirts of the town and drives a five-year-old Japanese four-wheel-drive truck.

He's known to be fair in his personal and business affairs, people respect him, and they often come to him for advice.

And now I'm flying on Duma business to Prague and making my way down the aisle on my way to my seat at the back of the plane when I see my pal B. sitting in first class.

This is Russia, so my first thought is about wealth via corruption. But he's also a good friend. And I knew he was honest. So I am confused.

Frankly, I would be less surprised if I met Putin or Obama sitting there.

"Oh! What are you doing here? Where are you flying to?" I ask.

"Oh!" he says back. "I'm just on a trip. I haven't been to Karlovy Vary (in the Czech Republic) for a long time."

Something was wrong here.

He was painfully embarrassed.

And truthfully, I never thought of him as a person who regularly travels first class to the Czech Republic and back.

B. looks like a teenager caught at the scene of a crime. So I'm intrigued.

Moreover, I know Karlovy Vary quite well. It's a city known for its spas, and I don't see B. as the kind of guy who relishes a visit to a spa.

"Oh!" I say. "I hope you're not headed there because you need some healing waters."

"Not really," he says. "I'm just making a business trip."

I say to myself, "Oh! What kind of business can the owner of a provincial car wash in Siberia have in Karlovy Vary?"

Now I am having fun. "Did you find an investor in the Czech Republic?" I ask, continuing my interrogation.

"Yes. Well. To be honest, rather the opposite. I have a few businesses there," he confesses.

"Businesses?" I ask. I am honestly puzzled.

"Yes. Well, just three hotels."

He waits for me to respond.

"And a clinic for moms," he continues.

I say nothing, to give him a chance to add more.

"Clinic?" I finally ask.

My image of B. begins to acquire new colors.

"Well, yes—a medical clinic, a fertility clinic." he starts to explain. "Friends advised. Business of the future, you know! They come from all over the former Soviet Union. And the locals too."

But I don't understand how a small businessman from Siberia can suddenly have a medical project in Europe. "Why not with us?" I ask. "Why not at home in Russia?"

"Don't you understand?" he says.

No, I don't, and for a good reason. If he has these successful businesses in the Czech Republic, why does he stay in Russia with a bunch of car washes and stalls in a godforsaken swamp?

And then B. utters a phrase that becomes one of my mottos in life, and which contains all our inescapable Russian patriotism:

"I am needed where I was born, in Russia."

He thinks for a moment as he says it, moving his lips.

Yes, I agree with him. But often, I also think to myself:

"But why the hell did I have to be born in Russia?"

This conflict pretty much sums things up for many Russians.

**There's the need to do something else
for either survival or just to pursue a better opportunity,
and there is no way to do it at home.**

Three

So, I went to B.'s ultramodern clinic with him.

It's along an attractive and upscale alley, where cast-iron taps of flowing spring water stand along the entire length. I see young and not very young women drinking the water of the natural spring from expensive-looking porcelain cups. Along with the murmur of water and its splashes, words in different languages reach me. Hearing them, I reflect on the transparency of the borders. I think about how all these women are united not only by the desire to give birth to a child, but also by belonging to the *new class*.

Only the *new class*, not being put on the brink of survival by poverty, is able to transform the reality in its favor in search of a solution to any problem.

Here, I not only see members of the *new class* avail themselves of the latest technologies but also not having to put up with circumstances that are deemed unacceptable. This is an opportunity which, alas, the working class is almost always deprived of.

This is the *new class*, possessing information and knowledge that gives them confidence. The confidence to believe that any problem can be solved. They've learned the habit of not seeing boundaries—and not considering themselves slaves.

I walk down the alley to the reproductive health clinic. This desire of the *new class* to reproduce themselves seems to me both an exciting and unique characteristic of this class and their sense of how they can control so many aspects of the world around them. I also see it as a very good sign.

The clinic is hidden in the shade of tall trees with thick rough trunks. On their branches—unexpectedly large white flowers with soft juicy petals. They look like lilies, but bigger, and it seems incredible that such gnarled giants could birth them.

The walls of the clinic are almost invisible. It seemed that someone was deliberately hiding it at the end of the alley. After walking along, I stop to examine the walls and windows. At the glass partition dividing the concrete wall from the foundation to the roof, an elevator can suddenly be seen.

"Strange," I think, "one had to go all the way along the alley, past the carved taps of springs and trees with fabulous flowers, to bury oneself into an inconspicuous gray wall. Or maybe it is designed so the clinic can only be found by others with the same sense of self and position in the world."

If, in essence, and honestly, a woman can reproduce herself—by helping to artificially conceive children of a *new class*—the clinic guarantees itself a future full of new clients.

As I stand there, my thoughts are simple: this clinic is proof that *the new class* is alive, strong, and growing, and as the *new class* grows, there will be demand for more recent high-tech solutions in medicine and many other fields.

Four

We go into the laboratory. Two drops on a glass. Between them is a water bridge drawn with a pipette.

Through the microscope glass, two dozen spermatozoa are visible in the first drop.

Every one is unique, not recognizing the existence of brothers. Every one is focused on their personal—personal!—success. And success for each of them always depends solely on their own efforts.

But each one is also ready to play by the same rules—making one's success everyone's success.

Moving their tails, they rush to the bridge.

At first they swim in a bunch, poking their foreheads. But where the drop is lengthened by a bridge, three come forward.

Looking at them, it is hard to believe that they are not rational beings endowed with a competitive thirst for victory.

At the entrance to the bridge they jostle, pushing each other. One makes a dash and flies onto the bridge first. The other two are quick to follow—but not fast enough. The rest keep swimming, but they are far behind and only approach the drop. The leader, pushing off with its tail, instantly overcomes a quarter of the bridge. The second shakes its tail, fusses, and catches up with a solid jolt. These are the top three.

For a while, the two in the lead go nose to nose. Then, at the finish line, the one in the second position makes another dash and enters the drop first. And we have a winner!

Behind him, the one previously in third moves into second place. And the one that was the first on the bridge—loser! This one is the last.

This drop of water, of course, contains an egg—a small brown-black dot, similar to a speck of dust that has flown into the water.

"This is a good sperm cell," the embryologist says, catching the leader with a pipette; and he then performs a few more practiced and graceful moves with his specimen and announces:

"The child is made."

In the first drop—two dozen spermatozoa at the starting line. In the second drop is one single spermatozoa in the egg.

To myself, I call the one in the egg—Zuckerberg.

He saw the target and ran toward it with everyone else. He is not a superman's sperm, but he was taken from one man like everyone else.

He had equal opportunities with others.

They all differ little from the abilities of their neighbors.

Maybe he's just a little stronger. Maybe he's just a little smarter. Maybe he just got lucky.

Maybe he just wanted to be in that egg more than all the others.

Or maybe he just rushed forward to get in front of the others, breathing down their necks, the thrill of competition egging (no pun intended) him on.

If it weren't for all the others racing forward, he might not have swam to the egg at all.

But there was a crowd; he participated in the race, and he came in first.

Zuckerberg is not a genius. He was not the only competitor in the race. Just ask the Winklevoss twins. Or Tom from MySpace (if you are of a certain age to get that reference).

However, in order for Facebook to emerge, a thousand start-up spermatozoa, a thousand start-up founders like Zuckerberg, were needed who were trying to penetrate the egg of the Internet to create the first viable social media network for the millions who were ready to use it.

In the end, the one particular Zuckerberg we all know was the winner.

**This is how it works with the *new class*;
they are always ready when opportunity arises.**

Running and becoming a "Zuckerberg" is not everyone's calling. The calling of many may simply be running. Stubborn running, where you line up ear to ear at some segments with those ahead, feeling how they breathe into the back of your head. You breathe into the back of the heads of others yourself, urging those who escaped to keep running by simply running yourself. Coming up with new goals for yourself that you transmit to others through your increased efforts while running alongside them. This run is called life. This is where both luck and natural selection take place.

Looking at the magic drops in the clinic, I think:

If you take out all the spermatozoa from the drop and leave just one—any random one—it, I guess, still hobbles to the egg. However, when a lone spermatozoon approaches the egg without risk, it will not pass to the generation what is most important in life: the relentless drive to succeed. Instead, it is a weaker spermatozoon that lacks any ambition not just to survive but to thrive.

Now, look around at the others at Starbucks with you as you read this. At the risk of being judgmental, you may think you know by watching for a moment which of the others around you would kill you to get to that egg first. And which of the others around you *might* be interested in getting to the egg if it's *convenient*, or if it's *easy*, or *if someone else shows them the way*. And then others who couldn't be bothered with the egg because, well, "*Why should I?*"

Passing by large plastic tanks in the corridor, I ask the doctors what is in them.

"Embryos," they answer. "Eight are prepared for each client, and two are implanted. In the tanks are embryos that were not useful. At first, we store them, and when the biological parents can no longer or do not want to pay for storage, we destroy them."

"How do you destroy them?" I ask.

"We just pour them out."

Looking at these tanks, I think that there are many more of us—*a new class*—more than we ourselves think.

We are no better than workers and no worse than traditional businessmen or state officials.

If we measure our mental abilities, they are more than likely to coincide. Our location—by the machines, in palaces, or offices in front of a computer at a desk—as a rule, is determined not by IQ, but by circumstances and birth, as well as by the random opportunities that life did or did not give us.

I wish for the moment that we would all get what we deserve in life and that where we were born would not influence it. And that nobody will be flushed down the drain by those above us. Alas—the number of those flushed still exceeds those who are *allowed* to thrive, and I am talking about those who walk among us, not the stored embryos at a fertility clinic.

Five

The new class is the most capable part of society.

But it's often also the cruelest when it comes to its treatment of others, and even themselves, because its members are often threatened by the idea that everyone else has the same goals.

This conflict within ourselves as individuals and as a group is because we consider ourselves the one and only, but we overlook that we have a common genetic code.

The new class does not want to be a crowd, but it is a crowd. Members of the *new class* consider themselves free and independent, but they are also always looking for idols.

The new class considers itself self-sufficient and does not recognize the state being above itself, but it seems to always need someone who will raise capital or launch its idea into production or appreciate creativity or buy the goods they create.

The new class is looking for personal success, but instead of achieving it, it often competes with itself.

**Russia, after decades of decline,
is ready and needs to give birth again.
Our bell called in the fields of the lost war.
Time for those who want to feel like humans again.**

We can say that the role of the peasants of a hundred years ago has passed to the workers and pensioners—they are dissatisfied, live in poverty, curse the authorities, but so far do not want to change the system—they do not see a positive alternative.

But the *new class* is different. They know they have the means to create a better life for themselves; here in Russia, or they will go elsewhere to do it. Yet Russia is their home. If only Russia would transform itself into a place with a climate of freedom and opportunity that's like (and please excuse the crude analogy here) millions and millions of eggs waiting to be fertilized by millions and millions of members of the *new class*.

CHAPTER FIFTEEN

The *"New Class"* Is Powerless.
And Powerful.

One

The inclusion *of a new class* in politics seriously scares the old elites.

A vivid example is when members from both parties of the United States Congress's House Judiciary Antitrust Subcommittee attempted to kneecap, mafia-style, the heads of the four most powerful companies in the innovation industry in the United States in July 2020.

Appearing before this powerful committee was Alphabet/Google CEO Sundara Pichai, Apple CEO Tim Cook; Jeff Bezos, founder of Amazon and owner of the *Washington Post*, and Facebook/Meta CEO Mark Zuckerberg.

For this subcommittee, here's the big question:
Are these four companies—
Google, Apple, Amazon, Facebook—
too damn big?

Here's how the chair of the subcommittee, Democrat David Cicilline

from Rhode Island, summarized the meeting after grilling these tech
CEOs for five and a half hours:

"This hearing has made one fact clear to me: these companies as they
exist today have monopoly power. Some need to be broken up, and all
need to be properly regulated and held accountable."

"Simply put: They have too much power," said Sicillini.

I am a tech guy from Siberia, the Silicon Valley of Russia. While
first in exile, I lived in the actual Silicon Valley. I've also spent lots of
time in the tech center of Boston. Now I live in Kyiv, another tech center. In the Russian State Duma, I was the Investments and Venture
Capital Subcommittee Chairman. Before that, I was the Director of
Russia's High-Tech Parks Task Force for the Ministry of Informational
Technology and Telecommunications, where we successfully created a
network of technology parks in Russia. Today I invest in tech companies
all over the world, and I was behind the first Ukraine-originated company to go public in the United States. I will not trouble you with my
personal opinions about these hearings in the U.S. Congress, which continue to this day, because my opinion is not the point of the story here.

But what conclusion should the *new class* draw from this cautionary
tale?

That it needs to quickly and significantly expand and strengthen its
political power, because the power they derive from technology—and its
ability to use that technology to communicate and mobilize—terrifies
those who are currently in power.

Two

A big problem for the *new class* in Russia is that it is not integrated into
the political system at all.

As a class, they are not represented in political parties.

However, even as the *new class* fails to build political clout, it still
remains a problem for the elites.

The problems they cause for the elites are illustrated by a 2009 study
in which sociologists from the Public Opinion Foundation (FOM) discovered that about 15% of the Russian population behave differently from
the rest. They work differently, rest and heal differently. They have different political views, but similar values based on the thesis, "how you
work, so you eat."

**FOM called these people "People-XXI".
But this group, 15% of the population,
is part of the same group I call the *"new class."***

You can see the problem.

While the majority believe that one's trajectory and success in life depend more on circumstances than on one's efforts, 15% of the population thinks the opposite is true. Suppose this group, an advanced, potentially revolutionary force, can use the new tools and platforms of technology to find each other. In that case, they will discover how much power they have when they join together.

Consequently, the vanguard, politically active part of *the new class* faces the same task that Lenin and the Social Democrats once faced: To convince the working class and all those dissatisfied with the regime that they and we, the entirety of the *new class*, are allies. That we are one.

We must show them that they have a place in the future that we are building. We need to show them that they need the alliance with us to demolish those who hold power in Moscow, but also live in Nice and eat in Monte Carlo.

We must show them that we understand and value the work they do, and that:

**The new system will work harmoniously,
because we will bring the existing industries back to life
and create new jobs.**

After all, people wear not virtual but real clothes, pour real gasoline into the tank of a real car, build a road from real asphalt and drive along it for real food, live in a real house and sleep in a real bed. Workers in industry and agriculture create all this.

However, it's also crucial for all to understand and agree that this is not about subsidies to unprofitable industries but about equalizing economic conditions with the help of tax, investment, and other instruments.

Everyone should know that industrial production is key to sustainable development. But it needs a constantly developing and growing high-tech component. Therefore, the preservation of industrial potential and the development of high technologies for its production base should be a priority for every country. This is the basis of future economic policy and growth.

> **This is why we have to start working together
> to kick-start the evolution of our production system.**

Our working class allies must be sure that, after the victory, they too are members of the *new class*, and the *new class* is not just another group that shows up when it needs something, makes promises that will never be fulfilled, and then (again) leaves them to their fate. On the contrary, the *new class* needs them and will help them gain prosperity—a high and stable income and the blessings of life that they deserve.

Three

Paypal. Netflix. iPhone. Airbnb. Uber. Tesla.

What do they all have in common?

Yes, these are all brands that many members of the *new class* love.

And yes, each brand is a reinvention (also by members of *the new class*) of an entire industry; industries most of us would have thought could never be reinvented by anyone.

And each brand has also taken power from the established elite and given it to the people; therefore, each is a platform for personal empowerment.

If members of *the new class* can transform the credit card business, Hollywood, Ma Bell and the cell phone business, the hotel, the auto, and the oil and gas industry?

If members of *the new class* can take power from the established elite of these industries and give that power to the people?

You could say these companies have democratized their industries.

Well, that's a pretty damn big deal.

It gives us clues about what is possible. However, it also raises expectations, especially for members of the *new class*.

If I am a member of the *new class*, I am thinking:

> **"I want my government to be democratized too,
> and I want it to work like an app on my phone."**

If Airbnb and Uber can do it, why can't my government?

But can the Airbnb app on your phone really serve as the model for better government?

Absolutely.

Within the Airbnb app, for instance, there are rules, responsibilities, an accounting system, and a rating system.

Okay, I am oversimplifying to make a point. And the point is this:

**There should be a way for you to use your phone
to interact with your government, to propose a new law,
to edit a new law, to comment on a new law,
to vote on a new law.**

It's called direct democracy. And it's not a dream. It already exists, and we will discuss it more in Cchapter 20.

And let's acknowledge that for the *new class*, in particular, an app like Airbnb for the government on your phone is one of the most important things we can do to empower citizens and promote passionate citizen engagement.

Four

However, in Russia, authorities are moving in the other direction, tightening the social screws.

They are also forcing belt-tightening things like pension reform.

Before the 2022 invasion of Ukraine, the budget was full of money. Putin had a considerable surplus. But the funds were not invested anywhere. As a result, there was no mass construction of roads that could lead to innovations—new concrete, asphalt, and materials. There was no modernization of things like metallurgy that created new nanomaterials. There was no development of new energy.

Unfortunately, the money was sent into the pockets of Putin and his friends.

Consequently, the application of the forces of both classes—the *new class* and the working class—is limited. And with it, there is no possibility of a decent and prosperous life for the majority.

This situation is analogous to where the oppressed classes found themselves in Russia at the beginning of the twentieth century, which Lenin and his associates dealt with.

Five

When I was eight, my parents and I took a trip along the Volga River on the Afanasy Nikitin steamer.

For me, this voyage was a fantasy come true. I saw ancient Russian cities; zigzags of history and politics: Tsarevich Dimitri was killed near this porch; white Czechs revolted here; here Ivan the Terrible conquered once-proud Tataria; and in this Stalingrad mound soaked with blood, the Nazi army broke its head.

As we sailed, my father told me the fascinating story of our family. I found out my great-grandfather and Lenin's father (by the way, by today's standards—representatives of the middle class) were well acquainted. My great-grandfather, Pavel Yakovlevich Ponomarev, even knew Lenin as a child!

Maybe such a discovery for young people today, even in Russia, would be trivial or an eye-roller.

But for me, a young Octobrist and future bright-eyed member of the Vladimir Lenin All-Union Pioneer Organization (aka the Young Pioneers), this news about my great-grandfather Pavel Ponomarev was more shocking to me than if I had found out my great-grandfather had been Paul the Apostle.

Here's why this is relevant:

A hundred years ago, Lenin and his supporters were aware of their lack of rights. Some (Jews, Poles, Balts, Caucasians) were discriminated against based on nationality and religion, some on property grounds, and some simply read about progress in other parts of the world and sympathized with those within their own country who found it hard to live. However, it seemed there was nothing they could do to change life in their country for the better on their own.

Along comes Lenin (whose father was the head of the regional department of education and whose mother was the daughter of a Jewish doctor), who decided to master the most advanced theory and practice of class struggle by Marx—the most innovative humanitarian technology of his era.

He learned that the leading class had to be the proletariat. The goal, and the path to it, will be indicated by a political force armed with the theory of the transformation of the world. An important episode in his biography—the protests at Kazan University—is comparable in significance to the protests in Russia of 2011–2012. If Lenin lived now, he would be with us and the first to come to Bolotnaya.

But let's not over-romanticize the history of Lenin. We know his experience, including the knowledge of the interception of power by the apparatus of the "red bureaucracy." Given it, we will not give power to anyone. The *new class* will certainly manage its power better than workers and peasants did in 1917.

But I repeat: to take power, we need to realize the commonality of our true interests. And gain a common or shared class consciousness.

Today, the *new class* representatives are working for their personal capital and their own personal power, even when employed by others.

It's time for us to work together, for ourselves, as a group.

In this case, I define "group" more broadly than you might think to include the interests of the *new class* and the entire Russian society.

By saving and promoting ourselves, we are saving science, culture, education, production, and democracy. Even now, the *new class* implicitly determines the life of the country—draws plans and develops production, manages production and sells oil, creates the Russian version of Google called Yandex and the Russian version of Facebook called VKontakte, prepares so many solutions in so many areas of social and business life.

But at the top, decisions are still being made by the elites from the past.

At the same time, these elites feel threatened. They know the *new class* can do many things they, as the elites, cannot do and cannot control. They know, for example, that many members of the *new class* have mastered the fine art of communications—including mastery of the tools of media like video and visuals, provocative and compelling messaging, and the use of network channels from TikTok to Facebook to Google to Twitch, as an art of persuasion. Even more frightening to the elites is that many members of the *new class* also know how to negotiate their way through computer networks poorly controlled by authorities.

At the same time, the archaic benefits of the monarchy, its spiritual staples, and pseudo-elitism are all alien to the *new class*, as well as the illusion of enrichment in the service to the Tsar. You can't brainwash its head with TV soap operas (*Game of Thrones* aside). Moreover, the *new class* will not allow itself to be cut off from the world. You can't even put its members on a steamer and send them to distant places, as the Bolsheviks did with Russian philosophers in 1922—there are too many of us. Our main value is the freedom of self-fulfillment. It is a precondition for everything: high social status, financial well-being, and respect for fellow citizens.

Six

The government does not know how to subdue us. That's why we are scary.

This is why it wants to subdue our children, to ensure they don't become like us.

Therefore, their goal of education reform is to minimize the likelihood of the emergence of dissidents. To deprive every child who was not born into one of Russia's select few "chosen" families of the right and opportunity to achieve life fulfillment and professional success.

I have children, who, like me, went to an ordinary Moscow school in preparation to live in Russia and work for the glory of Russia, like myself and my ancestors.

I am a man of the world, however, and I want them to feel free at any point in their lives.

So, they are fluent in several languages and know and respect foreign cultures.

Now, the future is wide open for them.

That's not how it works for most families in Russia, especially families who are members of the *new class.*

An essential task for Putin is to convince the *new class* that they, and most importantly, their children, have no future in Russia. If the future is taken away from you, you give up the struggle for the present and rush to hide in the place where you feel valued and safe.

While each of us is looking for a way out of this stalemate in life, the bureaucrat solves his most important problem—us, who disturb his rest. As long as luck and flexibility allow him, he will stay in his chair and be fed. And what's next? After all, no one elected him. He can be replaced at any time, with others just like him who also can't do anything but want power. Where should the professional government crook go to then? What about his children, who are stuffing themselves on privilege because they were born with a silver spoon in their mouths? The one who comes after him, you bet, has his own children, too.

It's a common misfortune of a cog in the feudal system. Those Putinists like feudalism, where ranks and posts could be passed to their heirs. Such people are turning the life impasse of the *new class* into a civilizational crisis for the entire nation. To the delight of the rest of the competitive world, which receives the best brains drained from our country.

Seven

In a previous chapter, I wrote that the *new class* in Russia is the most disenfranchised today.

There is a reason for this. The best time for developing the *new class* in Russia was from 2006–2014.

It was then that the elites, frightened by the growing shortage of personnel and aware of the uncertainty that arose in business circles after the Khodorkovsky case, decided to tame the new generation (meaning many members of the *new class),* even though they also feared them.

So, they launched a series of initiatives to modernize the economy and support innovation.

This is evidenced by the creation of several significant strategic plans at that time, in which I actively participated. In my opinion, the most important is the "Yaroslavl Plan 10-15-20: Innovation Roadmap in Russia," created under the auspices of the New York Academy of Sciences as a conceptual framework for what became known as the Skolkovo project, created in collaboration with the Massachusetts Institute of Technology (MIT).

You remember the Skolkovo project, right?

It was part of what I discussed in my meeting with Putin. It was also the basis of unproven allegations against me related to Skolkovo, for which I was barred from ever returning to my home.

With all that in mind, let me tell you more about Skolkovo and the Yaroslavl Plan.

The numbers in the name "Yaroslavl Plan 10-15-20" mean "10 Years to Implement; 15 Steps to Take; 20 Pitfalls to Avoid."

This is a very fast and very ambitious plan.

In the United States and Taiwan, it took twenty-five years to get from the start to the path of sustainable development. In Israel—twenty years. In Singapore and Finland—ten years each.

The experience of these countries, including their mistakes and failures, are summed up in the Yaroslavl Plan. Mistakes and failures are crucial. Unfortunately, those who make these mistakes rarely admit and dissect them in public. Yet such an analysis is needed because it prevents you from stepping on the old rake again.

In addition, the plan analyzed the state of affairs in the field of innovation in Russia, offering recommendations that take into account existing experience and development priorities of the country.

Unlike many other countries, Russia began developing an innovation policy with a robust education system. In addition, it developed scientific institutions, initially created in the Soviet era, then partly collapsed, and partially transformed in the twenty years since the end of the USSR.

The presence of Russia as a potentially large domestic market brought it closer to the United States.

In Russia, there were already a number of factors mentioned in the plan that were important for the success of the innovation policy. However, just using the potential of existing domestic scientific and technical thought would not be sufficient to transform the national economy into a knowledge economy.

One of the main findings of this report is that no innovation ecosystem has emerged on its own.

In all the other countries, without exception, the main role in its development was played by the state, which provided a well-planned, flexible, and adequately funded policy.

This plan advised the Russian authorities to create and support aggressive and innovative government programs like Skolkovo.

These recommendations were sent to the new President, Dmitry Medvedev.

Under Medvedev, several government programs that began under Putin were combined with one common strategy and a set of working tools for developing institutionalized innovations.

The new framework looked a lot like how Western start-ups raise early capital in the early stages.

First, innovators were taught to raise money by going to those called FFF—friends, family, and fools. In the West, innovators typically target the first two F's, so the investment round is commonly known as "Friends and Family," but sometimes the fools come along.

Later come the professionals: first venture capitalists and their venture funds, and finally, private equity funds. The latter are giving a lot of money to turn a fully working project into a large-scale production or global service.

In the Yaroslavl Plan, the strategy was developed on top of four pillars—so-called "development institutions."

The first one was called Rusnano, a state institution that invests when there is not just a concept but working prototypes, and it is time to build a big plant.

Another important institution that was part of the Yaroslavl Plan is the Russian Venture Company (RVC). It was created back in 2006. This is a "fund of funds," and its task is to co-finance projects with foreign money coming into Russia.

To understand this, imagine a BOGO or "buy one get one free" deal. So let's say there is a Silicon Valley fund ready to finance start-ups in Russia. The fund management is told, "Okay, begin investing with us and invest 100 million. And we'll add a hundred million. No interest. To increase your capital and rate of return while reducing risk."

For an investment fund, that's a tough offer to walk away from, which was the point.

Another critical element of the Yaroslavl Plan for an innovative economy started under Putin were high-tech parks.

The idea was to create a Russian Bangalore—to finance the infrastructure of towns where innovators could live and work. Even before I was elected to the State Duma, I was asked to take charge of this project and was appointed Director of the High-Tech Parks Task Force.

President Medvedev then added a fourth piece to the plan: Skolkovo, which offered integration of the high-tech parks, funding for Russian projects, and incentives for foreign investment. In other words, Skolkovo was designed to be a Russian blend of the most successful elements of Wall Street, Silicon Valley, and Bangalore.

Skolkovo was founded in 2010, and when asked, I agreed to take on the project as the advisor on business development and commercialization.

Eight

Two interesting stories from this period, to give you yet another taste of how things work in Russia:

First, over the New Year's holiday in January 2010, I decided to mix a little work and pleasure. I had to be at MIT on Skolkovo business around that time, so I went early to visit family and friends in the Boston area. One day, I got at least eight panicked calls from my friend John Preston—a local legend, former head of the MIT Technology Commercialization Center, and then head of a large venture capital fund in Boston.

John, you see, got a call out of the blue from some high-ranking Russian officials who wanted to stop off at MIT on their way to Davos so they could learn more about the MIT-Skolkovo partnership.

John was panicked for several reasons. First, the Russians had invited themselves with very little notice. Second, John is not a diplomat and doesn't have the time or experience to make a plan for such a diplomatic gathering.

As usual, the Russian officials came up with the most plausible explanation for why the trip to MIT made sense: Boston, you see, is located precisely halfway between Moscow and Davos! Meanwhile, to reinforce that it was just a "casual" visit, the head of the Russian delegation, Igor Shuvalov, wears a tracksuit, while everyone from MIT is dressed in jackets and bow ties to meet the visiting Russian dignitaries.

Another funny situation arises at the event: Preston wants me to participate in all the activities. The Americans, of course, consider me to be one of the Russians. However, no one on the Russian side can take responsibility for me being there (I'm a well-known oppositionist, after all!), so, as a result, the Russians pretend that I am there on behalf of the Americans.

It turns out it was fortunate for both sides that I was there. I ended up serving as the most effective translator available, as I could translate the American language of business and innovation for the Russians, and the Russian language of bureaucracy for the Americans.

At one point during the visit, the folks from MIT proudly explained that they were able to generate $400 million a year by commercializing new technologies.

Yes, this was a very proud moment for the Americans!

But it was an even more exciting moment for the Russians, who heard this number and thought, "That sounds like so much money for us to steal!"

So, here's a lesson we should all learn from this Russian visit:

If you don't give money to those who can really do something great with it, because you're afraid someone wants to steal it, then not to give money to those who can really do something, means that only thieves remain around, and normal people scatter.

And one more story that I will tell, for the very first time.

This happened later, during President Medvedev's visit to America. I helped organize this visit and was part of the official delegation as a member of the Duma, so I flew with him on his plane, stayed at the same hotels, and participated in all the events. Medvedev was taken to Silicon Valley, introduced to Steve Jobs and then California Governor Arnold Schwarzenegger, given an iPhone, and started a Twitter account.

From there, we were about to fly to Washington to sign a historic framework agreement with MIT. Everyone was delighted.

When the time comes to leave our excellent five-star Silicon Valley hotel, the hotel presents me with a bill . . . so I can pay for the pleasure of staying there with Medvedev.

You see, the Presidential Administration pays for the members of the delegation. However, I am a deputy of the Duma—so according to the law, my party, United Russia, must pay my bill.

The party is not going to pay for this, of course. But I didn't know all this until I was shocked when presented with a very expensive and unexpected bill.

I am just a deputy! Not the President of Russia, or a wealthy Silicon Valley billionaire! I don't have this kind of money!

So, I did the only thing I could think of: I ran away from the hotel.

Was I ashamed? Of course!

But I also knew I couldn't fix things by saying I was the organizer of Medvedev's trip, and that my own country wouldn't pay my bill.

That's not the end of the story. Two or three weeks later, I received a call from a high-ranking official asking, "Ilya, why is the presidential protocol swearing at you?"

Again, I am embarrassed, but I tell him the whole story, and he laughs for a very long time. Then, we come to an agreement that covers costs for my work in Skolkovo so that this does not happen again.

Except it did happen again. As you know, my work for Skolkovo eventually led to false accusations of embezzlement, and enabled Putin to illegally bar me from entering the country.

Sometime after this trip to the United States with Medvedev, Putin returned to power, and it was clear that the Skolkovo project was at risk: partially because of jealousy of conservatives and scientists who believed the state should fund fundamental research and not fool with innovations. However, it was mainly because Putin (to the contrary opinions of some liberal opposition, criticizing whatever government initiative could happen) clearly understood that Skolkovo was becoming an incubator and financial gym for the *new class*. Therefore, it would be an ever-growing challenge to his power.

Nine

Meanwhile, explosive growth in the high-tech fields in Russia had already begun. As a result, many young people responded positively to the opportunities created by the Yaroslavl Plan, and started offering their ideas and registering new projects.

Yes, this was the *new class* at work, growing stronger before our eyes—numerically, substantively, and financially.

By 2013, Russia took first place in Europe and third place in the world as a venture capital market, lagging behind only the United States and Israel. That year's volume of high-tech venture capital deals exceeded $1 billion.

This was a remarkable achievement.

In the USSR, economic and other indicators were compared with the level of 1913, the highest point in the economic development of the empire. A full century later, 2013 became the highest point of innovation and the best time for markets in Russia.

However, in 2014, the value of achieving these accomplishments was wiped away.

Why?

Because of the war with Ukraine.

Soon, all the Russian innovators—members of the *new class*—were fleeing from the country as fast as they could.

And that was just the beginning of the problems.

Because in the West, Rusnano and other institutions we created were beginning to be perceived as spy centers.

Things went from bad to worse when the Russian Venture Company began to "finance" fictitious venture funds; presumably, they were doing so because there were almost no actual companies to invest in since so many Russian founders had left the country.

Meanwhile, the downward spiral continued as the heads of many start-up companies funded within the Yaroslavl Plan were using their government funding to escape to the States while leaving only small research offices behind for reporting purposes. So, of course, Skolkovo took a hit.

Almost all the jobs, people, and business activities produced by the approach laid out in the Yaroslavl Plan left the country and went abroad. The irony is not lost on me, since the Plan was created to give founders and their companies (again, the *new class*) lots of reasons to stay!

Members of the *new class* did not approve of the 2014 war in Ukraine. So they left. Because they could. And they could leave because they were members of the globalized *new class* we had been trying so hard to keep and nurture in Russia.

CHAPTER SIXTEEN

Putin Screws the Pooch Again

One

Meanwhile, after Bolotnaya and the Skolkovo pushback and the war in Ukraine, the authorities conducted an operation to nationalize and impose control over the largest Russian high-tech companies. Mail.Ru went to Alisher Usmanov. VKontakte, the Russian Facebook, went to Usmanov and Igor Sechin. Rambler went to Alexander Mamut, Vladimir Potanin, and others.

At this point, even more companies left. Yandex held on the longest, but in 2019, they gave up too.

Believe it or not, this was a conscious policy of the authorities, starting with the security forces.

Security forces (except foreign intelligence) operate within national borders. And they see a threat in any cross-border businesses, because they can't control them completely.

At the same time, their psychology tells them to keep control of everything as if in a fist.

However, the *new class* is, by definition, transboundary. Its members are cosmopolitans. In many cases, their businesses are designed to reach customers worldwide. So they can be run from anyplace on this planet. (And maybe even beyond.)

Now, the Kremlin is pressing them with a choice: Are you here, or are you there?

When offered a choice, they chose the world in all its diversity. East or West, home is best—but home can be anywhere—so they left.

Two

The few who stay are offered a different choice.

In the 2000s, the Russian special services (primarily the GRU and the FSB) actively recruited hackers.

For instance, those hackers who in 2016 "brilliantly" hacked the servers of the U.S. Democratic Party, providing a high-profile diplomatic scandal.

Then, in 2017, General Sergei Mikhailov, the head of the Second Directorate of the FSB Information Security Center, was arrested.

In the style of Stalin's times, the special forces put a bag over his head at the general assembly of FSB with some thousand astonished and scared eyes watching, and took him out for interrogation.

His crime was that he told the States who had broken their servers: These were the people of the GRU, competitors of the FSB. Their mutual hatred was more important for Mikhailov than the state's interests. And that's the case currently for most Russian bureaucrats.

Mikhailov's crime was state treason, but the national IT industry was hit with the consequences.

Many Russian computer firms have been kicked out of international markets as potentially working in the interests of the Russian security services. One example is Kaspersky Lab, which is a global leader when it comes to making antivirus software. Many who did not previously work for the state now do just to survive and compensate for their losses.

And the result for the *new class* is another new push for emigration.

Three

I always despised how oppositionists like Navalny were fighting the few initiatives we have managed to push through the state to support the development of the *new class*. They criticized Skolkovo. They also didn't like urban development projects supported by the authorities in Moscow and other cities, which created the most modern and enjoyable environment there.

It is a paradoxical situation: Opposition leaders quite understandably criticize the authorities simply because they are in power. However, their supporters—many of whom directly or indirectly benefit from these initiatives—undercut what has been designed to help them and benefit their well-being.

Political logic is clear—it is a competition for their hearts between the Kremlin and the opposition. But besides short-term politics, we should think about long-term benefits.

The innovation support programs and the creation of a "modernization" program by the Russian state led to the rapid and large-scale growth of the *new class* until the beginning of the second Putin regime in 2012.

Criticism of these efforts is also the result of a false narrative generated by neoliberal dogmatists; they say that innovations grow themselves from the grassroots, without the state's participation.

But this is not true.

Silicon Valley, Bangalore, Finland, South Korea, Taiwan, Boston, Israel, and other places like them were kick-started by the state.

For instance, Silicon Valley—as a technology, business, and cultural ecosystem—has gone through a number of stages, all of which were connected with demand from the military-industrial complex.

The military-industrial complex needs a lot of electronic devices, from navigation to communication. Also, during World War II, there was a threat of a Japanese invasion. So money poured into California, and they built an electronics and, later, semiconductor industry. Then venture funds were also created with state funding within Small Business Investment Company (SBIC) and Small Business Innovation Research (SBIR) programs to invest in semiconductor production. Then they created the Internet as a Defense Advanced Research Projects Agency (DARPA) project. Today, the state is the key player and investor in the green energy and space industries and is standing, for instance, behind Elon Musk's many successes.

In other words, Silicon Valley was originally a government project. Now it is developing independently and with private initiatives at the helm. However, contrary to popular belief, it was initially built by the state, and government orders still play an essential role.

The American bureaucracy is still inspired by Benjamin Franklin and Thomas Jefferson's leadership on science and technology and understands the need for research. Otherwise, the potential enemy will get ahead and become even more dangerous.

Meanwhile, it is also clear that it is impossible to provide the growth and innovation necessary using only internal resources and based solely on domestic sales. In many cases, these businesses must be cross-border to become financially successful.

That's why, in Silicon Valley (which initially considered companies outside Santa Clara and San Mateo counties and even in nearby San Francisco as foreign and "far, far away"), they were eager to invest in overseas projects by the time we started Skolkovo, including Russian and Chinese high-tech companies. And companies around the world also welcomed highly qualified tech specialists from Russia to join their teams.

Or so it was, until the 2012 return of Putin. Then things screeched to a complete halt after the 2022 invasion.

Four

Suddenly, the security forces in Russia understand they can't do their jobs effectively without the development of new technology, but there are fewer and fewer people capable of building it.

So they introduce a policy of "import substitution," or creating copycat products—and they promise money to those who create analogues of Western products.

This standard business logic is offered: You will earn good money if you give us what we need.

And they nod at Pavel Durov, who, copying Facebook, made his VKontakte. And at Yandex, which is a copycat of Google. And so on.

Of course, Russian security needs copies of these popular Western platforms to prevent Russians from using the actual Facebook, Google, and Gmail; if Russians use these original Western platforms, then Russian security cannot control their usage and data and spy on them.

But what they do not take into account is that the same Pavel Durov who makes a Russian copy of Facebook will also create yet another copy, called Telegram, that is designed for a global audience and works like an improved WhatsApp, because he still wants to feel like he is changing the world.

For him, this is psychologically important. He knows that if he does not change the world but simply takes what already exists to copy it in Russia for loot, he will have lots of money but no meaning in his life.

And now you know how and why four-fifths of high-tech people in Russia have chosen to live in the West.

Five

Meanwhile, Putin is getting old. After all, believe it or not, he is just another human being. At least physically.

But the system is built on him personally. He destroyed all the institutions of power.

There are no regions. There are no courts. There is no parliament. Not even a president, as Dmitry Medvedev demonstrated.

There is just Vladimir Vladimirovich Putin.

So State Duma speaker Vyacheslav Volodin is right when he says, *"There is no Russia without Putin."*

I agree—99 percent. One clarification: there is no Russian Federation without Putin.

Putin created all the prerequisites for his disappearance to lead to the disappearance of the Russian Federation as we now know it.

And God forbid that Putin's disappearance would collapse the country. But, unfortunately, there is such a possibility. Even if there wasn't, we should put a stop to the Russian Federation, which committed an act of aggression and stands behind the atrocities of that war.

We will bring to life a new Russian Republic in its place.

No one in Russia has enough authority and connections to replace Putin. As a result, when he disappears, his current subordinates will inevitably fight and divide their spheres of influence, their feeding grounds: vertical (when a potential successor exercises control, for example, over the military-industrial complex or construction) and horizontal (when he controls particular regions—the Center, Urals, Siberia, etc.).

Right now, vertical connections are the most important. But most likely, horizontal ones will become critical at the moment of truth.

Without a unifying figure in the center, the elites will begin to squabble among themselves, not for life but death. The losers will escalate the confrontation in order to win back some influence. All players have already accumulated both vast financial and political resources for themselves.

Will the center manage to keep the country within its modern borders in such a situation?

It is a big question mark.

At the same time, a successful transfer of power from Putin to a designated successor is unlikely.

Why? Because a genuine transfer of power will require a strong frontman, with a group of influential figures behind him. But Putin always eliminates such people or builds complex, contentious relationships between them.

So if Putin decides to transfer power during his lifetime, his successor can only be a weak, compromised figure controlled by Putin himself. Medvedev, for example, could be tapped once again. Or Kirienko. Or somebody else. But as long as Putin is alive, this successor will have to rely on his authority. So what's the point of such a replacement?

There is no doubt that the country needs a strong government rooted in the power of institutions, not someone's personal power.

Personal power erodes institutions. Putin has shown us that.

Putin is neither a dictator nor a great leader.

He is the spider at the center of the web. When the spider dies, the web dies with it.

Trouble awaits Russia.
And this is Putin's main crime.
He endangers the very existence of the country,
concentrating all the power.

Do we or don't we want to survive?

Part Four: The Ponomarev Plan: How Russia Gets from Here to Democracy

CHAPTER SEVENTEEN

It Starts with a Russian Invasion

One

On February 24, 2022, my wife woke me up at 7 a.m. at our house in the peaceful Kyiv suburbs. Her alarm had just gone off, and she read the latest news.

"Get up! They have started a war on us!"

Her voice trembled noticeably along with the mobile phone in her hand.

"Which war?" I muttered, half asleep.

I don't know about you, but I do not like it when someone wakes me up in the morning for all sorts of trifles.

Only lazy people have not discussed the impending Russian invasion of Ukraine in the past six months. I am not so lazy, and I was never tired of repeating on numerous television broadcasts that there would be no Russian offensive in the near future, that Putin is a bastard, but not crazy, that his army is unable to conquer Ukraine. Therefore all the maneuvers of his troops are a banal intimidation of the West that began after losing the presidential election with Trump.

His successor, Joe Biden, was seen in the Kremlin as a weakling diplomat who needed a little scare in a big war, and it was assumed he would agree to any demands.

Maybe Poland will not be expelled from NATO, but it will definitely stop meetings with Zelensky.

I had no illusions about Putin's desire to subjugate Ukraine, but from all points of view it would be much easier first to absorb Belarus, get new footholds and new soldiers, proclaim a new Union of Sovereign Slavic Republics, and only then attach to it an enormously strengthened military plan for Ukraine.

My friends and partners, on the contrary, unanimously tried to persuade me to leave Ukraine. I usually answered that my parents taught me to defend my land and my family and to fight fascism.

On February 23, I was at a business negotiation in Dubai about investing in a wonderful Ukrainian company. The deal went exactly as planned, we shook hands, and I was in a great mood on my way to the airport. I was scheduled to return to Kyiv for two days, and then fly to the States to close the deal.

All morning, different people sent me messages like, "In Ukraine, it's about to begin." However, I'd heard this "about to begin" for the tenth time already, so I answered everyone with a grin and the response that my machine gun was already locked and loaded, and my guards were prepared with loads of ammunition. This, by the way, was the truth. Or so I thought.

The last in this line of messages was from my partner Vadim, who, escorting me to the airport in Dubai, also once again asked me if I wanted to fly directly to the States, just in case, without stopping by Kyiv. Of course, I didn't want to. Miss a chance to spend a few nights back in the beautiful, exciting, and vibrant Ukrainian capital? Never!

But an unexpected problem awaited me at the airport. For the first time in my life, an airline rescheduled a flight for half an hour *earlier* than its scheduled departure time. I understand now that they knew they had to arrive in Kyiv before midnight because of the invasion, but I was furious when I found out about the early departure only when I arrived at the closed check-in counter. I then called my aide Anastasia for help securing a ticket for me to Kyiv, even if it meant buying a ticket on a flying carpet.

"Listen, judging by CNN reports, this is a sign from above for you," she said. "Fly to the States, instead!"

I balked.

And then Anastasia's very logical argument for heading to the States lost out when I heard an announcement that there was one ticket left for Kyiv on the Dubai low-cost airline. This was indeed a sign from heaven—and I did not miss it.

At 11:40 p.m. on February 23, my plane landed in Kyiv.

And then, at 5 a.m., without declaring war, armored armadas crossed the border of a peacefully sleeping country, and rockets flew over peacefully sleeping cities. The soldiers of the "Center" group, again, as in 1941, marched across Ukraine.

Alas, I was wrong in my predictions. Yet I ended up where I was supposed to be.

Two

Anyway, an invasion has a way of waking you up.

My wife rushed to her hospital, where she worked as the deputy chief surgeon, to prepare it for treating the wounded, and I was left alone. After an hour of studying the situation with a phone in my hands and a computer in front of me, I went to the center of Kyiv to look around. A dense stream of cars was moving toward me—people hastily leaving the city as I was headed in.

Judging by the messages I saw on social media, the critical battle of the day was to be the airfield in Gostomel, a small town to the west of Kyiv. There, the Russian army landed airborne rangers from the Kostroma. They were apparently supposed to create a bridgehead for the entry of the main forces into the heart of Ukraine's capital.

If this plan had been implemented, Kyiv could have fallen on the first night.

Fortunately, this did not happen because the Russian command organized everything in its typical idiotic and incompetent style.

The rangers (according to my information, they were members of Russia's 331st Guards Regiment of the 98th Airborne Division) encountered unexpected resistance from a unit of the National Guard of Ukraine during the landing.

The Russian helicopter group, which was supposed to support the landing, flew away in a panic, after losing several machines during the first five minutes of the fight.

As a result, the Russian soldiers on the airfield found themselves without support, and were now being shot at from all sides. This was surely quite a surprise, since they'd been told they were liberators and heroes, and therefore had expected no resistance.

The primary loss of the Ukrainians at the end of that day was a unique aircraft standing in the hangar at this airfield—it was the largest airplane in the world—AN-225 "Mriya." Since the beginning of the month, it has been undergoing maintenance repairs there, and therefore, unlike all other military aircraft that were hidden even before the start of the Russian offensive, it could not be moved before the invasion began.

But I didn't know all this at the time. I knew the troops had landed, and it was not difficult to understand that the coming night could be decisive. Therefore, I closed my house, wrote a note to possible invaders suggesting that they should behave decently, and went to the recruiting office to sign up for the territorial defense.

In Ukraine, of course, this was a day of infamy.

There was no panic on the streets, but there was also no hope for the effectiveness of the authorities' actions. Everyone understood that their future was in their own hands, and they and wanted their hands to be as armed as possible.

In general, one thing that helped Ukrainians prepare for this day was the endless television discussions about a possible war broadcast daily in Ukraine for the past two or three months. So your average Ukrainian responded to all these discussions (which usually stated there would be no war) by acquiring as many weapons as possible. I, in principle, was no exception, especially since my name is on all sorts of "Putin kill lists," so I am one of those whom the invaders were supposed to eliminate in the first place.

The only problem was that the chief of my security, who kept a robust cache of weapons, several days before the war while I was still on my business trip to Dubai, left for another city, where his official residence was, to help them build their defense. And when he left, he took his entire arsenal, including the machine gun I had told all my friends about.

So on the morning of February 24, I headed to the closest military enlistment office because it was the only place I could go to get a weapon.

It was located on the outskirts of the city in an inconspicuous building adjacent to an industrial park. There was a crowd of people around, clearly hinting that it was already too late for everyone who wanted to sign up to fight to get to see the officers before nightfall. However, many in line recognized me, so it became impossible for me to leave.

"Wow, that Russian, Ponomarev! Great people are with us! Thank you for the support!"

I thought my shoulders might fall off even before the fight from the number of hands that clapped them.

"What weapons are being given out?" I quietly asked the others in the queue.

"Patience, patience! We have to wait and see."

I regretted that I neglected to accept a bulletproof vest that friends had recently offered me.

Unfortunately, the line did not move. But we were in Ukraine, meaning some creative way out of the impasse would be found.

Three

That's when Volodymyr Omelyan, the former Minister of Infrastructure in the government of previous Ukrainian president Petro Poroshenko, arrived. He was known throughout the country for negotiations with Elon Musk to construct Hyperloop high-speed transport between Kyiv and Lviv.

"Oh, Ilya! Hi! What are you doing here?"

"What do you mean? Like everyone else: I came for weapons!"

"Ahh, that's good," he said while he tried to squeeze past the crowd to the entrance to the recruiting office along with a few lads with him in camouflage.

I realized that I should not miss my chance to get him to help me get into the territorial defense before he was gone. Many in the West do not know this, but so many Ukrainians were immediately rushing to join that in the first days after the invasion, in many places of the country, you actually needed an influential and connected friend to help you get in.

"Volodya, you can't get through this line today!"

Omelyan thoughtfully looked at me, and at the crowd.

"Okay. We actually need some assistance here. Could you please help to load all the hardware for us into trucks? And then we will help you enlist."

Four hours later, at the location of the unit where Omelyan was enlisted, I am finally filling out an application to join the territorial defense. Then I had a brand new RPK-7 light machine gun in my hands, and for that, I felt lucky because the last of the standard Kalashnikov automatic rifles had just been taken. The guys that already got them were looking at my new baby and me with envy!

"Do you have combat experience?" the mustachioed colonel asks.

"No," I confess. "But I have the experience of street fighting in 1993, and the preparation of the Left Front. . . . In general, I have held weapons in my hands, but . . ."

"So, let's consider the basic level. You will go to the second platoon. The first one is for beginners. The third one is for professionals. Your military rank?"

This is a surprisingly tricky question.

"Well, I have military training from the Physics Department of Moscow State University—I'm a lieutenant, an operator of the S-300 antiaircraft complex. But, as a deputy, I have the rank of major general."

The colonel perked up when he heard the word "general" in my rank.

"What kind of army was this?" he asked with undisguised irony.

I blushed.

"The, uh, Russian Army."

"Hmmm," he said. "So write 'private,' please, and go to the post. The first platoon goes for orientation. The second's task is to prepare positions for the defense of the center of the city. The third goes to Gostomel, to clean up the territory from enemy landings.

"And just remember this: the machine gunner is the first target for the sniper, so as soon as the shooting starts, change position after two or three bursts, do not sit in one place, okay? Any questions?"

Thus began my first army duty in Kyiv, on a freezing cold night.

Four

I did not serve long, however, in territorial defense. On February 25, just after the end of my night shift, my phone rang.

"Where are you?" asks the country's former prime minister Alexei Goncharuk. "We urgently need you here."

I was already committed to a unit assigned to guard the center of Kyiv, a very honorable assignment, but a call and a summons from the former prime minister was even more important. So I made my way through the traffic jams at the exit from the city and the country roads that were not yet blocked, and then stood before a secret bunker. In front of me was Goncharuk, covered with weapons all over his body like a commando.

"Territorial defense is, of course, good, but it is not effective for you."
Alexei really likes everything to be effective.

"Think about where you are most needed, and what you can do to deliver the greatest value at this time."

Alexei knows me well. Of course, I had already come up with what I might be able to do during my first long night of the war, during my long embrace with my new machine gun: the idea of a "Russian-speaking Al Jazeera," or, an even more fitting analogy, a "Russian NEXTA."

NEXTA is a Belarusian mass media channel that is distributed through Telegram, YouTube, and other social media and instant messengers. The name NEXTA is pronounced "nekhta." The title uses a play on words: Generation Next (from English—"next") and the Belarusian word *nekhta* (from Belor.—"someone"), which hints at anonymity. NEXTA was the key factor in the anti-Lukashenka protests of 2020, coordinating them and cutting through the censorship.

It was clear that traditional liberal journalism in Russia would end in the next few days, and it was important that someone, or something, should replace it. Otherwise, it would be very difficult for most Russians to access information about the invasion that was not being fabricated and then pumped out by Russia's propaganda machine.

In full disclosure, it should be noted that what I had in mind, like the Belarusian NEXTA, would not be some textbook journalism. As Lenin, who is quoted many times in this book, would say, our media had to become "not only a collective propagandist and agitator, but also an organizer." And what I had in mind was a media channel that was also a new anti-war organization.

In general, I set an impossible goal for myself: in three days, in wartime conditions, to create a TV studio and a TV channel, and fully staff a news agency that could tell the Russians, in Russia and in Russian, the truth about everything related to the war.

The next day, February 26, through Ukrainian Public TV, I was given the use of an unused premises for a studio near Kyiv, a space that was unlit on the outside so as to provide us with safety from Russian sabotage groups. The latter factor was extremely important, as the Kremlin also knew what NEXTA was, and the chances they would try to quite literally kill it was very high. And we were very grateful for another former prime minister of Ukraine, Volodymir Groysman, who provided us with the necessary security.

Five

On February 29, there was a test broadcast of the channel, which we called "February Morning." (The name was chosen in connection with the beginning of the invasion, and also because February 1917 was when the revolution in Russia began.)

Initially, there were many misadventures: our Internet was cut off, and we were saved with the help of Starlink satellite communications, urgently delivered on behalf of Elon Musk. Then we were blocked by YouTube because of complaints by the Russian special services, and we had to reach out to fellow Russian Sergey Brin, the cofounder and former CEO of Google, in order to protect us from these complaints. One way or another, by the end of March we had half a million viewers, of which almost three-quarters were in Russia. A month later, we deployed twenty-seven correspondents from the Far East to Kaliningrad, and from St. Petersburg to the Caucasus. Yes, you read that right—we are not only broadcasting live from Kyiv, but also from our secret studio inside of Russia. In fact, "February Morning" has become the only Russian-language media that works and speaks to Russians directly from the center of events in Ukraine and Russia.

Often the conversations are very difficult.

At one point, we included in our broadcast a very revealing story from the United States.

We talked to a good friend of mine, originally from Kharkov, who lives in Silicon Valley. He relayed a conversation he had with his aunt, who has lived for twenty years in Silicon Valley, the capital of American innovation. My friend showed his aunt footage taken by their mutual relatives in Ukrainian Bucha, with all the horrors of the war: people killed on the streets, houses burned down, neighbors subjected to rape and violence. The woman just shook her head:

"We Russians are not like that! This cannot be. I know for sure, we are not like that! And because of that it is obvious it is all fake, take it off!"

She does not watch Russian TV, she is a U.S. citizen, a Republican, she works in a high-tech company, her own relatives from Ukraine sent her pictures taken with their own hands—and yet she refuses to believe in them.

For her, accepting this photographic evidence as real is equivalent to admitting that she herself is a fascist.

The Russian authorities, in Freudian fashion, made it so that the parallels between the Russian invasion of 2022 and the German invasion in 1941 are now through the roof for Ukrainians. They hear from Russian TV about the brave soldiers of the "Center" group (Z—Zentrum, the Z symbol was also actively used by the SS), and wake up from the bombing of Kyiv at dawn (dozens of songs were written about this in USSR), and see Russian soldiers breaking into small Ukrainian cottages and raiding supermarkets, asking for milk, eggs and chicken. The annexations of Crimea and the Anschluss of Austria, the Sudeten Germans and the Russians in the Donbas, the rhetoric about "national traitors," and, above all, the denial of the very existence of the Ukrainian nation. As a cherry on the cake, the invasion began on February 24—exactly on this day in 1920, the Nazi National Socialist German Workers' Party (NSDAP) was created in the Munich beer house *Hofbräuhaus*. The Russians, of course, prefer not to notice these striking parallels. But they exist, and they cause fear at the subconscious level and inflate the hatred.

Six

At the end of March 2022, I met in a café in Vinnitsa, two hundred kilometers from Kyiv, with my relatives, who had just gotten out of the small village of Berezovka, on the Zhytomyr highway going west from Kyiv. I felt a deep sense of guilt while I talked to them, because right up to the very last moment I told them to stay at home, that there would be no war, and that even if something happens, that Russians were not fascists, they would not fight civilians. As a result, they—husband, wife, their schoolgirl daughter and ninety-year-old grandmother—stayed at home.

First, a full-fledged battle broke out right around their house, with tank attacks and counterattacks, with downed planes and helicopters, the advance and retreat of either Russian or Ukrainian troops.

And then a miracle.

A missile with cluster munitions struck their house. After it hit, it scattered its deadly contents throughout the house and across the backyard.

But it did not explode. Instead, the unexploded ordnance saved their lives—and not because they were sitting in the basement at that time.

The Russian soldiers came the next day. Seeing a protruding rocket and ammunition scattered everywhere, they did not go inside to check their house for occupants, because they got scared. But they checked the houses of all the neighbors—those who remained were taken out into their yards and shot.

The only person in the house who kept absolutely calm during all these events was the grandmother.

"I saw it once before," she said. "In 1941. And I know how it will end."

Seven

After the story of my relatives, what happened in Bucha and Irpin did not come as a surprise to me.

Then I went by myself, and talked to friends there about what they had seen. They said that many Russian soldiers who entered these small towns northwest of Kyiv went wild before their eyes.

Not because they were told to behave that way, but for a completely different reason.

They entered Ukraine having been told they were liberators. Only after they arrived did they find out that they were invaders.

They expected to be greeted with flowers. But they were greeted with bursts of automatic gunfire, instead.

They thought that they were there to fight Nazis. It turned out that they were opposed by a whole nation who considered them to be fascists.

And death was waiting around every corner.

Bucha and Irpen are prosperous suburbs, which even the suburbs of New York can envy in terms of living standards; Russian soldiers from a remote province have never seen anything like this.

Those who lived there were mostly relocated people from the Donbas, who were just waiting for the right moment to avenge their lost home in the east of the country.

It turns out that the Russians were first psychologically oppressed by Russian TV, then by their fathers-commanders, and then by the entire resisting Ukrainian nation.

They really lost all human appearance, hiding from the fighters of the defense in the captured apartments of the innocent civilians. Everybody was trying to kill them: men, women, kids, and even pets, it seemed. They poured out anger on those weak enough who could not answer back, by raping and murdering women and even children.

Don't think I'm justifying them. Not at all, each one of those who committed atrocities is a war criminal.

But I want to say that behind each of them, in their every action, stood a menacing and ugly ghost of their military leadership and their main leader, Putin. And never will those Russian military men who behaved like human beings in different parts of the country, and even sometimes told the Ukrainians "I'm sorry that we are here," (and we have quite a lot of such evidence of this on our "February Morning" channel) make amends for those who acted completely differently, turning all of my beloved Russian nation into a nation of evil.

Which now will be washed only with blood.

Eight

After all this, it is not at all surprising that literally every day since February 24, 2022, I have to answer the same question:

"Are there any 'good' Russians?"

Maybe this question is the one which Ukrainians have been asking for much longer; maybe since the invasion of Crimea.

After all, to the point I made earlier in the book, while this war for the West started on February 24, 2022, for Ukrainians it started in 2014.

Still, it seems like a stupid question. But it's a question that many people keep asking me.

So who are *we*? Are *we* bad?

"No, of course not!" we Russians think to ourselves. "Obviously, some exceptions do exist. Each family has its black sheep! Those crooks and thieves that temporarily captured the Kremlin and Okhotny Ryad. Well, some military went maybe too far. And yeah, in particular regions there are some places and people . . . but, still, they are just an exception, and you should not judge *us* by *them*, that's racism!"

"Krymnashists"—those who eagerly supported the annexation of Crimea at the end of the day by shouting "Crimea is ours!"—being approximately 80% of the population, slightly spoiled the blissful picture of nice and peaceful Russians. Well, okay, a few years have passed, and these percentages somehow slowly vanished. By 2022, it seemed the situation was actually not so bad.

True, all these eight years between 2014 and 2022, somehow it was impossible to explain to "good" and "not-so-good" Russians that the war has been going on since the annexation of Crimea—the real one, in which people were dying every day. Yes, one can blame the omnipotent, brainwashing Kremlin propaganda organized by definitely very bad people. Meanwhile, now those Kremlin warmongers who call themselves "media" and denied the war started to talk about "what were we doing during these eight years" (meaning the Russian Army) should have destroyed Ukraine eight years ago, during which "people of Donbas suffered so much."

And that every Russian (to stay good) should have supported that "noble mission" of rescuing our brothers and sisters.

Before the invasion, one could assume that my fellow Russians simply couldn't prove to others how good they were; it was just inconvenient, not timely, and a bit scary. We could promise to ourselves this was all temporary, and everything would definitely work out eventually, we had recovered from Covid, we would recover from this, too! Even the Ukrainians, for the most part, showed their empathy.

However, now it's a post–February 24 world. And Bucha and Mariupol have happened—events that shocked even those who once did not want to admit military atrocities in Chechnya. Somehow, the question about "good Russians" from the conversation of frostbitten outcasts suddenly became the mainstream discussion not only in Ukraine, but throughout the world.

It's not about ethnicity, of course. We should never forget that several thousand Russians are fighting on behalf of Ukraine against Russia's aggression—and no one is talking about them in terms of how "good" or "bad" they are. The certificate of their quality as human beings is provided by what they are doing with the weapons in their hands, and by their deeds, not words.

And what about the other 115 million adults in Russia? Are they all "bad Russians" because they have not grabbed a gun and fought to defend Ukraine?

Well, we do know that very biased, controversial polls that are allowed to be taken in Russia suggest that 25–30% of Russians, even in the darkest hours, were not afraid to admit to sociologists that they were against the war.

On the other hand, what did they do to stop this war?

When it comes to this question about if there are really any "good" Russians, there are two different approaches to this matter.

Nine

The first approach is based on the statement that although passive resistance is better than nothing, it is still not enough in the face of conditions of nonstop bloodshed on the fields of war in Ukraine.

In other words, Russians have done terribly little, given the scale of the tragedy. And I agree with this.

But on the other hand, it is worth noting that if 30% (and maybe even 50%) of Russian adults oppose the war, albeit passively and quietly, that still means there are more people in Russia against the war than all of Ukrainians!

Think about how many Germans during World War II were against Hitler.

There were no opinion polls then, but something tells me that there are many more Russians against Putin.

Does it make all Germans bad? Or at least inferior to Russians, who are inferior to Ukrainians, who are... wait! Stop here!

One should never make a whole nation a pariah, despite the atrocities that could be committed by its representatives. Neither should the responsibility be put exclusively on Putin's shoulders. Still our main problem is that Putinism has done everything to ensure that Russians are politically castrated, made impotent, feel powerless, and that they do not have any political will and might behind them, and no different point of view is ever heard.

And also so that in Russia itself, there would be nobody left who is ready to lead our people to fight. It turns out cunningly—it seems like all these ordinary Russians had indeed no voice in deciding whether to start the war, and even most people in the government hadn't, so they all were not to blame, at least directly, for what happened, but the responsibility still falls on all Russians.

So, are there a significant number of Russians who can make a difference?

With the start of the "special operation" in February 2022, two social groups emerged clearly in Russia who did not approve of the authorities.

The first is the liberal urban intelligentsia and the globalized youth. Largely they belong to the *new class*. These are people who Putin is trying to squeeze out of the country.

He does not physically destroy them, as they would have done in 1937, but as we've discussed previously, he creates conditions for them to leave on their own—with the same effect as NKVD executions, so that they disappear from Russian society, making it easier for the Kremlin to carry on its dirty work. They now complain a lot about how miserable they turn out to be in emigration in the West, and I sympathize with them; but damn it, I worry about the future of Russians in Russia much more, and am calling to get them organized into an effective resistance and mutual solidarity!

The second group of anti-Putinists, on the contrary to the first, is anti-liberal.

These are the poorest and most socially unsettled layers of the population.

It is in this core that anti-war sentiment is strongest. They are opposed to Putin's government, first of all, because today they live worse than in Soviet times, and they see Putin not only as the leader of the bureaucracy, but also as a benefactor of large corporations; more precisely, oligarchs, who squeeze all the juice out of the ordinary people.

At the same time, they see enemies in the liberal opposition, not unreasonably suspecting them of wanting to return the country to the failed approaches of the Yeltsin era. When they care to vote (most usually don't), they usually choose national populists from the Liberal Democratic Party, and the leftists from the Communist Party of the Russian Federation, although they do not see them as their trusted representatives. All of the systemic opposition allowed by the Kremlin looks corrupt and fake to them. The ghost of a future Russian rebellion wanders among them, but has not yet found its spellcaster. I don't think they now have long to wait.

After February 2022, most Russian liberals, both systemic and foreign, just resigned to their fate and started to wait for the regime to fall by itself under the pressure of internal contradictions and the hits of the Ukrainian army. Everyone just hopes for changes "from above" when certain members of the elite would get tired of drowning and decide to save themselves.

Worse, in this emigrated opposition cluster, one influential group is especially timid and spreads doubts about success. Another is very cynical and expects that the ordinary people, that same youth for example, will break through the Kremlin wall, and then those ambushing manipulators will enter through this pass and rule on the ruins of the Putin regime.

I can guarantee that it won't work that way.

You can sit on the shore of your favorite Russian river for as long as you like, waiting for Putin's corpse to float by (and his body really will float by pretty soon), but this will not get you closer to getting your hands on power.

I think that the change in Russia is possible only as a result of a combination of two factors. It should be a simultaneous action both from below and from above. A top-down coup will be inevitable when an uprising starts from below, when the elites would feel a real threat to their security. And the task of those who want to go down in history as "good Russians" is to create such uprising and very tangible threats.

Ten

The second approach to the question of "good Russians" is quite a bit more optimistic. Its supporters say "definitely yes, there are some 145 million people there, some should be perfectly good by all means!"

And many Russian oppositionists agree. At first, they went to peaceful protests, just to show their opposition without any hope for a possible positive outcome in the foreseeable future, knowing that they would be detained and, in many cases, beaten. But still they went. From February 2022, the form of resistance began to move into the category of guerrilla confrontation, and the resistance also became violent. Arson and attacks on pro-war officials and activists became common in Russia.

"Thanks" to Putin, there are now quite successful Russians who are dissatisfied with the authorities and scattered all over the world.

These are the "good Russians" who left the country and are now weighed down by a sense of guilt. They flood streets all over the world and also overload social media with their pleas for help to Ukraine: they collect donations, help refugees, send humanitarian aid, and some even send military aid.

This is all wonderful, but unfortunately, it is not what Ukraine really needs *from us*.

The key to peace in Ukraine is not only on the battlefield. What Ukraine needs from "good Russians" is to stop counting on the fact that Ukrainians will pay for the freedom of Russia with their blood.

We, as Russians (and others as members of the global family, including you), need to help the resistance inside of Russia as vigorously as we are helping the Ukrainian resistance. Ukrainians will protect their Motherland from the invasion, and they are helped in this by all of the world's support.

But who will help Russia to get rid of this cancerous Putinism?

In other words:

**It is the good Russians, and others like them,
who must lead the battle to finish off Putinism.**

In the end, much of the hard work will be done by ordinary people inside and outside Russia; young people, idealists who sacrifice themselves and risk everything for the sake of a common victory, and people like you.

Inside Russia, these are the people who are burning down Putin's military registration and enlistment offices, piercing the wheels of cars with Z-symbols, resisting military aggression, and even building—and then using—drones to blow up refineries.

This is scary shit.

Yet, they do it every day.

Now, how about you?

What can you do today to become a "good" Russian, whether you are actually Russian or not?

CHAPTER EIGHTEEN

"Be Brave Like Ukraine."

One

Thirty years ago, there was a very famous ad campaign called "Be Like Mike."

"Mike," as you may know, was Michael Jordan.

And Michael Jordan, of course, is a role model for people worldwide as an example of one of the most talented, hard-working and beloved athletes of all time.

In 2022, a spin-off of this campaign took root worldwide:

"Be Brave Like Ukraine."

Across most of the world, this grassroots campaign inspired people to support Ukraine with donations, with social media posts, with letters to their own country's leaders encouraging them to support Ukraine with money, and weapons, and diplomacy.

Two

Militarily, Ukraine's success in the face of Russia's invasion is more *MacGyver* than General MacArthur.

By this I mean Ukrainian soldiers are largely self-organized and self-regulated in small self-formed groups.

This makes soldiers and their small groups very nimble, creative, relentless, and effective. Like MacGyver with a knife against guns. We

Mykhailo Fedorov ✔ @FedorovMykhailo · May 31   •••
🏴 Ukraine government official
Ukraine has meaningful and up-to-date branding @brave_ua. Due to the efforts of Banda agency this campaign became world-scale. 19 countries; 140 cities; 100,000+ screens. Ukrainian bravery is shown everywhere; from Times Square in NYC to floating screen in Stockholm. 🟦=Bravery

Photo via brave.ua/Creative Commons

have all seen the videos and the photos and the social media posts on the Internet that glorify the manifestation of this Ukrainian fighting spirit.

I have said before that Ukrainians are anarchic, meaning they are at their best when they have a clear mission and are left to figure out things on their own, when they are not governed by a lot of rules or commands from above.

Three

When Russia first invaded Ukraine, millions and millions of people around the world (and my guess is, this included you) responded like it was a personal call to arms.

You didn't know what you could do, but you figured it out. You went online, you talked to your friends, maybe you called your member of Congress or Parliament, you sent money, you posted online.

Ukraine's war became your war, dammit.

You became another MacGyver in Ukraine's defense against Putin's invasion.

Four

Now, it's time for you to begin a new phase of fighting.

Yes, Ukraine still needs to drive Putin's army out of their country.

But it's also time for all of us to begin thinking about the future—not just Ukraine's future, but also Russia's future.

Because let's be realistic about this:

The day after the Russian Army has been completely removed from Ukraine, the threat from Putin and Putinism will still be there for Ukrainians, and therefore for all of us.

CHAPTER NINETEEN

What I Am Doing,
and What You Can Do

One

I will go first, because it's finally time for me to show my cards.

Then it will be time for us to talk about what you can do.

Two

Throughout this book, there has been discussion of a new social vision that I call the Big Project, the purpose of which is to create a new model for life and development in Russia, a democratic and free country of the twenty-first century.

Yes, we will have to work hard to put to rest the specter of the Empire of the past hovering over us forever. To end the generations of suffering, so that the old Russian ladies we talked about at the beginning of this book would never again attack a Polish priest for failing to see suffering as both inevitable and virtuous. Instead, it's time to build a country of the future that offers all members of the Russian family equal opportunity in the name of common prosperity.

This cannot be done in one fell swoop.

I am a very practical and entrepreneurial person, and I know that by having exact plans and strategies, we can carry out many transformations not according to some abstract theories, but in real work on the ground, in concrete deeds. Responsibly and without populism.

Responsibility should become the main feature of those who will replace the degrading elites. Responsibility and commitment to the vision that Russian constituents have supported.

It was well said by Nobel prize laureate Hermann Hesse in one of my favorite books, *The Glass Bead Game*, which was written in the darkest hours of World War II about the imaginary country of Castalia: "Our Castalia [or Russia, in our case] is not supposed to be merely an elite; it ought above all to be a hierarchy, a structure in which every brick derives its meaning only from its place in the whole. There is no path leading out of this whole, and one who climbs higher and is assigned to greater and greater tasks does not acquire more freedom, only more and more responsibilities."

I will list some important features of people who would come with me to replace these failed Russian leaders:

- The ability to innovate socially, culturally, economically, and politically—produce radical ideas, quick decisions and coherent actions.
- Talent and, I'm not afraid of the word, giftedness in the areas of their expertise.
- Willingness and ability to work in teams and cooperate for the public good. Rejection of private interests.
- High level of competitiveness, competence, education and practical work experience.
- And also, of course, loyalty to the grand vision of the Big Project.

In the classic and most philosophical Russian science fiction novel by the brothers Arkady Natanovich Strugatsky and Boris Natanovich Strugatsky, *Roadside Picnic*, the protagonist, Stalker Redrick "Red" Schuhart, has discovered a magic machine which could fulfill just one wish—the one which was the most intimate, most wanted, and usually the most unspoken. Nobody who acquired the machine knew beforehand which wish would actually be recognized as the dearest, as no one could influence the very core of his own soul. Red was very much afraid that his dream would be about money or some dirty and shameful desires. Instead, he appeared to be the new Messiah: "Happiness, for free, for everybody, and let no one be left behind!"

Red, who had lived all his life from one odd job to another, risking everything for the sake of an extra dollar, *did not* wish for the health of his crippled daughter and did not ask for wealth for *himself*, but desired with his very core everyone else's happiness. The thing that would change the world in the most profound way.

And nothing for himself.

This is what he works and lives for. Metaphorically, he is the role model for the *new class*. Joyously and selflessly giving of himself so as to provide justice and unlimited and harmless progress for all mankind. A world without violence and borders.

Ironically, I often think that a politician who tries to follow this same formula is not worthy of power because of it. How can one desire the most powerful thing on the planet and then be trusted to give it all away? The desire is the problem. The more one desires the power, the less worthy one is of having it. Isn't this the ultimate test of the main sacrifice in your life: to come to the very height of power, only to make sure this power is immediately given right back to the people?

This is why I believe the profession of being a politician is eventually doomed. Why the *new class,* with their drive to solve problems and democratize the world around them, makes a change to remove the politicians and replace them with direct democracy.

This is why, for now, I continue to function as one who does politics, but I very much want to stop being a politician as soon as possible, after this mission is accomplished!

Three

Here is a complex ethical question that was once put before me by a very smart political strategist. He said:

> **"Imagine—you have a critical choice:**
> **either to become the best ruler in the history of mankind,**
> **or to give eternal happiness to everyone else for free,**
> **to everyone but yourself.**
> **Which will you choose?"**

My answer was quick and unequivocal: "Happiness for all. The dream should be above one's career."

Yet, ironically, I am about to share with you a plan for the future of

Russia that may at first make me appear to be power hungry. However, I am also confident that you will also see that it is the opposite that is true. I am not hungry for power. I am hungry for my vision that will make my fellow Russians free, prosperous, and happy, and not at the expense of somebody else.

A dream is more important than a career. Political experience suggests this ironic and unfortunate irony: only those for whom a career is a bigger priority than a quiet comfortable life usually achieve power. The one for whom their career is everything will always trail the one for whom the dream is even more important.

Many politicians justify their compromises, dirty tricks, and walking on the heads of their rivals by saying, "Let me come to power first, by all means, and then I will implement my dream." I think we all need to understand the importance of rejecting such an approach—and people who embody it every time a choice could be made.

I am convinced:

**Power is worthy only of those
who can give it up in the name of their dreams.**

In the famous 1978 Soviet film, *Ordinary Miracle* by Mark Zakharov, based on the play by Evgeny Schwartz, whom I've quoted already, the question was asked:

"What have you done in the name of your love?"

The answer was: "I gave it up!"

I will not give up on my dream of a great democratic future for Russia and Russians. I believe that I have the best plan—the Big Idea—for leading post-Putin Russians to that great future. I would be honored to lead Russia to that future. But it is the dream of the future which drives me, not any kind of dream of being a leader or having power.

Of course, I know that when I say all this, some will suspect me of insincerity.

That is why I am writing here:

**The only ones can be trusted with power are those
who proved they can sacrifice their personal interests and themselves in the name of their dreams.**

But these same people are the most dangerous ones. Try to see through their personal appeal, dedication and charisma to what their dreams are. Ask to talk about ideas and vision, and not some short-term problems. Ask to talk about their future after their dreams for the nation have been achieved: Are they willing to commit now to an interim role with a hard deadline, and the requirement that they step aside once the deadline arrives, and/or their stated mission has been accomplished?

Yes. That's why I am writing this.

And yes, sometimes I, too, doubt that I will be able to resist such temptation. But I believe that I can, because it is also my dream to do this, and only this, and no more. I have no dream to amass and then hold on to power for power's sake. I have no personal greed or hunger for power, only for the accomplishment of my dream of a great democratic future for Russia and Russians. And for our neighbors. And for the rest of the world.

Four

I believe this has to be true about leadership and power:

> **Leaders must always doubt themselves.**
> **They should not seek power at any cost.**
> **They must strive at all costs to implement their own *dreams*.**

Like the Pope should question his faith every single day, the true leader should every single day question his or her commitment to the great vision promised to the people. So if, by serving again as a leader in Russia I can help usher in a new age of freedom and democracy, that for me would be the fulfillment of the dream I have tried to outline in this book.

In the same play by Schwartz, it says: "Once in a lifetime there is a day when those in love succeed in everything they do."

Every dream has such a crescendo.

For dreamers, there is the period in which everyone just ridicules you for your dream, and then, suddenly your dream is seen and heard and embraced by the majority.

This is what determines my attitude toward a person: Can they, being alone with their hands on the wish-fulfillment machine, wish "happiness for everyone, and no one left behind?" What is more valuable for them— their dream, or themselves implementing and benefiting from the dream?

Some say that this is a very elitist position.

I disagree, and I repeat, responsibility is a key feature of people building a new order. They cannot indulge in the lust for power and wealth. They must work for the country, for others, following their ideals. These people are the true elite, not those who now call themselves such. I believe they will lead the *new class* as well as the rest of the nation.

Only such people have the right to do so.

Five

Before we go any further, it's important that you understand what typical Russians today think about democracy, because this also helps us to understand how Putin and Putinism have been able to gain so much power.

For many Russians, unfortunately, the concept of democracy is still very much associated with the chaos of the 1990s and the Yeltsin years, along with lots of corruption, humiliation, and poverty.

As you can imagine, after that disastrous period it would be easier for someone like Putin to take and amass more and more power, as long as he didn't try to pull a "Yeltsin" on us.

So, it's not enough to just have a plan for instituting democracy within the government and legal system; there will also be an incredible amount of promotion of the vision required to ensure the people understand what is real and possible, agree with the basic ideas and trust the new leaders at the front, and also for the people to understand what will be required of them and what it will cost them; for instance, success may require a trade of one's false sense of promised (but so highly compromised) Putinesque security for the promise of freedom and democracy instead.

Six

When we look closely at present time and at the lessons of previous years, it becomes clear: the choice between the revolutionary and evolutionary path is false. The revolution does not start in the Kremlin or even in Moscow. It starts in our families, in our homes, in our yards, in our neighborhoods.

**A bloody revolution is in the interests of
greedy and deceitful politicians.
A peaceful revolution is in the interests of our children.**

Nobody sane ever wants bloodshed. That's why the Kremlin, firstly, works so hard to send a message that there are never bloodless revolutions (which is absolutely not true). They are programming the very inability to make a peaceful revolution, so that we ourselves would feel we must call people to arms and violence. Indeed—what else can we do when all the peaceful ways of protest are no longer there?

However, they do not count on two things:

- First, by starting the invasion in Ukraine, they themselves started an event involving major bloodshed and violence, so our calls for resistance are no longer as foreign or frightening,
- Second, they trained and armed thousands to fight in Ukraine. This also means there are now thousands who are ready to use that same training and those same weapons to fight for freedom at home. Typically, Russia is a country where citizens have limited access to guns. Now, the elite must worry about a large number of trained soldiers who are armed, dangerous, and in many cases primed and ready to join a revolution.

So once again, we are returning to the issue of what we are calling for and how to send our message to the masses, to the people. With the current state of the media in Russia being so controlled, so many oppositionists just give up and say, "Being against Putin is good enough." But this is a mistake.

Anyone who says, "We will win, and then we will figure out where to go and what to do," does not have vision. They just want power for themself and actually have nothing to say or offer.

Anyone who says, "It doesn't matter who comes to replace the current corrupt leaders, the very fact of the change of power is important," also does not understand the complexity of the situation and how the system works. He or she is more dangerous than the first, as such an attitude paves the way for irresponsible populists who would eventually compromise the revolution, and restore revanchism within Russian society.

The one who says, "You are my team," is often just a demagogue. He or she just wants to be alone at the top, and does not need a team—just a herd to lead. Team players never speak about teams, they just build them naturally.

Whoever says, "Trust me and don't ask questions, my critics are my enemies and the Kremlin's agents," is most certainly lying to you. This individual wants to be a dictator, as a true leader will debate and not accuse.

Whoever asks you to choose with your heart is lacking one themselves. This person wants to replace your thinking with their manipulation.

It is necessary to choose as a future leader a person who is transparent, and whose steps after the victory are predictable, understandable, and beneficial to the citizens who cast the votes or fight at his or her side. It is necessary to choose the one who brings peace and development, and not conflict and revenge.

My dream is to be that leader for the Big Project, for a great democratic future for Russia and Russians. My dream also has a beginning, a middle and an end. At the end of the interim period as leader, my dream is to step aside for other leaders to take charge. I hope this book makes this clear in every regard.

Seven

My friend, the Russian novelist Yuli Dubov, once confronted me with this puzzle:

"Imagine you have an irregularly shaped cake, and you need to fairly divide it into two parts. How would you do it?"

True to my technical education in physics, I answered in a simple way:

"Roll it into a ball and cut it in half!"

He laughed, but suggested another solution—not a physics solution, but a lyrical one that I've heard many of you in the West also learned from your mothers:

"Let one cut, and let the other choose."

This is right. After all, then you can't divide "for yourself," like the "reformers" of the 1990s and the Putinites of the 2000s.

The most stable political system in the world—the American system—is created that way.

Inspired by our American friends, and the success of their "American Experiment," we, *the new class*, will write a new Russian Constitution that will once and for all prohibit the monopolization of power by just one person or party.

It will be a constitution that guarantees both the succession of power and the separation of powers.

It will be a constitution that replaces the power of politicians with the power of justice and the power of the people in the *state of truth.*

**Russia needs a stable political system
that none of its members can change to fit their needs.**

Impossible in modern-day Russia?

Not at all.

In fact, it's every bit as possible as a ragtag bunch of New World colonists successfully declaring their independence from the British Empire in 1776.

Eight

It will be possible if we are very clear about three fundamental things:

1. The process by which this new Constitution will be written, which we will discuss at length in the next chapter.
2. This new Constitution must adhere to these five simple and fundamental rules:
   » First. There is no single governing center in the System that can impose its will on the rest of its participants. Although it is likely that such a center will have to exist temporarily and with broad multi-partisan support, during a not-so-long transitional period predetermined in time, while the main institutions of the system are being formed. [In the next chapter, you will learn about Roza Otunbayeva, who in 2010 became the president of Kyrgyzstan for a predetermined interim period of two years and then stepped down, for just this reason.]
   » Second. None of the existing political forces in society can grab control over the basic elements of the System.
   » Third. All branches of power are equal, independent, control each other and cannot acquire the role of the primary branch in the System. The Judiciary is the guardian of the System, its representatives cannot participate in economic and political life.
   » Fourth. The main economic and power centers are concentrated at the level of local authorities, and their influence and capabilities decrease moving from regions to the center. The regions delegate the center certain rights and responsibilities and finances,

the System does not grant the center authority to revoke certain rights from the regions.

» Fifth. The System is protected from attempts to change it, meaning the process of amending the Constitution should be carried out only in the conditions of consensus in society.

3. We must create a new Russian Court, one truly independent of the influence of the Executive Branch, one with judges being delegated and elected by the citizens, not from the professional lawyers community. These would be judges with defined term limits and accountability within a judicial system we design to ensure that Russia is always guided by the rule of law. I firmly believe that the current judicial system was designed to ensure that it is unreformable from the inside, so new people should come and do it.

I do not want to participate in the future races of my fellow politicians for power; but I do want to make sure no one can seize all of the power for themselves at any point in future.

As you read this, you may guess all the other oppositionists "love" me—but I say that with the greatest amount of sarcasm possible. The truth is, they hate me because they want to grab power and design the laws to stay there forever. And my intention is to make the legislation neutral, so that nobody can ever do that again.

Nine

Remember, I told you that I originally studied to be a physicist?

There I was taught how it would be within a system when everything settles down. This is one story, but how to get there quickly and with minimum losses, is quite another.

We all know the story of Moses, who told the Israelites that they must wander the wilderness for forty years because they were not worthy of inheriting the land. Of course, in our case, we don't have forty years to spare, so we'd better learn from the Israelites' mistakes—and Yeltsin's mistakes—and show that we see all the promise that Russia offers all of the Russian people when we work together to maximize the value and promise of this vast land.

This story of Moses is particularly relevant for those Russians who lived in the 1990s, when they were told every day that all difficulties were just temporary and will be over soon. Unfortunately, it turned out in the end that all the torment under Yeltsin was just to get from the USSR into Putinism. So:

The transition period is a key stage of any transformation.

Moreover, after the start of the 2022 war between Russia and Ukraine, we began to hear more and more about what had previously seemed impossible: the possibility of the collapse of the Russian Federation. I think there is no smoke without fire, and if we want to save the nation, then:

The question of the reestablishment of a free Russian Republic will stand in front of us loud and clear.

Much of what I am describing here will take time to accomplish.

Again, I believe direct democracy should be our goal. Most likely, however, in the conditions of postwar revolutionary chaos, it will not be possible to introduce it overnight (although I would still try to do my best for this).

Most likely, a Russia liberated from Putinism will first become a parliamentary republic, with a government accountable to a bicameral parliament (the upper house is directly elected by the territories in two-mandate constituencies, as in U.S. Senate; the lower is elected by party lists, as in most of Europe) and with a technical president in charge of foreign relations and the military.

The desire to move to direct democracy (and we will talk more about it in chapter 20) will be expressed from the very first day, with proof of intent being that the maximum number of decisions should be put to referendums at the national and local levels.

An immediate reform—without which the probability of the territorial disintegration of the country will increase sharply—is decentralization (in Ukraine, a similar reform has become almost the most successful of recent changes in the country) with the redistribution of income to the localities.

Self-governing, armed communities are our ideal (let's call it Ukrainian-style), and transferring power and money to the localities will be the first step toward achieving it.

Economic issues, even during the transitional period, cannot be left "for later" when a new government is formed. This is particularly true in Russia, because we as a nation already lived through the disastrous Yeltsin years.

Russians should feel from the very first day of change that they, and not just another fat cat, have become a priority for the state.

On the one hand, it will be necessary to resolutely dissociate ourselves from the embezzlers of the past: Review the results of privatization, and nationalize businesses built on the proximity of their owners to power (and, if they support Putin, also confiscate assets without hesitation).

Meanwhile, let's also acknowledge something that will be of utmost importance to most Russians: A poor man cannot be free.

For this reason, we will have to declare the development of healthcare, education, and technologies as the top priority, and prove this with decisive, practical actions.

Finally, a free person should be able to maximize his or her creative potential.

For this, a tax reform is needed that would enable small entrepreneurs to grow and prosper as quickly and easily as possible, without looking back at the greedy hands of officials and security forces. It would be a priority of the reform of the tax system.

Transformation of fiscal policies of the state should be made, shifting the burden from production to consumption as much as possible. The taxes should be maximized when money leaves the economy and goes into luxury goods and expensive real estate, and minimized when they are invested. Again, this reform should not be postponed for some point in the future, but should be enabled right after the revolutionary changes.

Ten

This transitional period, I believe, can really be passed in two years. This is exactly the period that should be given to de-Putinization and the restart of normal life in a now liberated country.

The sequence of steps I see is as follows:

- Immediately after taking power—the formation of a paramilitary Revolutionary government headed by the Chairman, a Supreme

Court of twelve people, the People's Militia to protect public order, and the National Republican Army. (If you've been following news of the invasion closely, you know the National Republican Army already exists as the partisan movement, and I am certain it will grow into something more by the time Putin is gone.) There will no longer be a FSB/KGB: those from there who are in actual crime prevention should join the Militia, while a new FBI-like central investigations service would be created.

- Second. Within sixty days—preparation of the initial draft of the new Constitution, as well as transitional electoral legislation (including the rules for creating parties, election commissions, and uniform election rules for the country from the local to the national level). All of this must be done using tools that provide the greatest amount of efficiency, transparency, and citizen engagement as possible.

- Third. Over the next sixty-day period—the formation of parties and election commissions, the preparation of elections.

- Fourth. The next sixty days are for election campaigning.

- Fifth. During the first 150 days—in tandem with steps two to four—a working group uses crowdsourcing technology to prepare the draft of the new Constitution (see chapter 20), and a special task force group with the representatives of interested Russian regions is also working on the text.

- Sixth. On the 180th day, final elections are held at three levels (with two-year terms); the election also includes a referendum on the adoption of the crowdsourced Constitution, and the election of delegates to the Constituent Assembly.

- Seventh. The Constituent Assembly and Parliament start working on the two hundredth day. The Constitution must be ready and adopted by the Constituent Assembly by the end of the first year. Parliament has partial powers (controls the budget, but does not form the Revolutionary Government and the Judiciary)—its task is to prepare basic laws that are consistent with the new Constitution.

- Eighth. According to the new Constitution, the second year after the change of power is given to the nations that live inside Russia to make decisions about their future status inside or outside Russia. The decision is made on regional referendums after a yearlong period of discussion and free campaigning, in the presence of international observers.

- Ninth. Elections to permanent ruling bodies are held after two years from the date of the first elections (two and a half years from the moment of the revolution). From that date, all the powers of all branches provided for by the new Constitution are exercised in full. The transition period is over.

As you know, I am diligently working right now, day and night, to make this Revolutionary Government happen.

Eleven

Now, all nations should decide on their future by themselves. However, very often, they cannot overcome their problems by themselves, and ask for outside help.

Would the American Revolution have been successful, if not for the French? Would Ukraine now stand against the invasion, if not for Western assistance? The answer could be yes, and it could be no. One thing is certain: In the 1990s, hopeful to become one with the rest of the world, Russia was betrayed by that world when it fell into the hands of neoliberal dogmatists and outright crooks, who discredited the West and very much assisted Putin's accession to power.

It is time to fix that mistake—that is my mission, together with you.

Do you remember how wound up and energized you were to help Ukraine, right after Putin invaded?

I hope you see now that there are millions of "good Russians" in Russia and around the world who got just as wound up as you did. Meanwhile, they feel helpless and disarmed before the face of the powerful machine of suppression led by Putin. They try to embrace everyone—the Western aid to Ukraine, the Ukrainian army fighting the invaders—just to overcome that feeling of total impotence.

In most cases, they are just being rejected by Ukrainians. President Zelensky even called once to the world's leaders to stop giving Russians tourists visas—let them stay home and get themselves busy fighting Putin. While this is a rightful approach to a large degree, as for me, they should do something about their Motherland, and leave the rest to those already engaged.

Their depression and dejection are not their fault, they are their illness. An illness which needs to be cured.

I am doing my best from Ukraine to restart the popular movement in Russia and ignite the feeling of strength, flipping the idea of "resistance" with the idea of "offensive." Ukrainian leadership understands the importance of it; the rest of the world still lags behind.

Will you join me?

Yes, this time it's harder than it could have been back in 1992.

After all, for years you've been told that it is just Russian leadership, and the Russian government are rotten to the core. Then, just a few months ago, you began to be told—and perhaps, also believed—that the Russians themselves are all evil, and the enemy.

If you believed some or all of this, you should not blame yourself. Instead, take a minute to appreciate that both "good" and "bad" Russians have been subjected to this kind of manipulation every day of their lives, even when there is no war.

It sucks, doesn't it? To feel manipulated like that?

And that's my point: for Russians, it sucks like that every day.

So let's help throw out the system and the people that suck, for a future for Russians where they live the kind of life that you and I get to take for granted.

Twelve

So, what can you do?

Let yourself be a MacGyver again and figure it out.

Meanwhile, I think I can offer you some things to consider as you start this next phase of your journey.

First: Do some homework.

This is important because, at first, it may be hard for you to feel right about supporting Russians and Russia.

If you're like most people, Putin's invasion has poisoned your mind.

And if you grew up in the West, and you are of a certain age, your mind might have already been poisoned.

Maybe it's time to find out how much of what you know about Russia and Russians is true, and how much of what you think you know is really a lot of hype and old stereotypes.

I believe that if you do a little homework, what you will find is that there are a lot of "good Russians" who think like you do, and want the freedom to live like you do.

At the risk of stating the obvious, I am one of them.

Do you know how many "good Russians" live right there in your city or town?

I'll bet there are a lot more of us than you know.

Get to know us. Ask us what we are doing. Ask us what you can do to help.

Then do it.

It will take a global movement to transform Russia into a democracy, and we need you to be part of the movement.

So release your inner MacGyver again and figure out what you can do starting today, and how you can do your best to help.

Third: Consider helping me.

Since I was kicked out of my own country in 2014, I have dedicated myself to returning to Russia—and doing whatever I can to take freedom and democracy back with me.

You can help me directly by doing several things:

1. Obviously, you can help by sharing this book with your friends and family.

2. You can follow me on Twitter or Facebook at @iponomarev (or any other social media you use—I have accounts virtually everywhere). And don't stop there—please find others from around the world who share our goal of bringing democracy to Russia.

3. If you really want to get crazy, you can open a free VKontakte account. (This is Russia's version of Facebook, which we've discussed earlier in the book.) Once you have opened your account, go to my "February Morning" YouTube channel, and post the stories from there onto VKontakte to make sure more Russians see them and have access to news about the war every day that is true. Going forward, this will also become a news source about our shared vision and movement toward democracy in Russia.

4. Find out more about my Bravery Foundation, and consider helping us. As you know from earlier discussion in this book, the Bravery Foundation offers financial support to reformed "bad Russians" who have decided to switch to the side of truth—and by making that switch are suffering from punishment or oppression by Putin's regime. We are offering legal support, and sometimes even literally saving lives by exfiltrating someone from the country, so they are out of reach

of Russian security forces. You can find out more about the Bravery
Foundation at www.beamz.live/bravery.

5.   Talk to people. Your friends. Your family. People you start meeting
     online. Write to your Congresspersons and Senators, explaining how
     important it is not just to attend to symptoms of the disease—the war
     in Ukraine—but to cure the illness of Putinism. Mention this book.
     Encourage decision-makers to learn more and undertake action ASAP.

Thirteen

Take a moment to reflect on all the ways Putin's invasion of Ukraine has
impacted the rest of the world: politically, economically, culturally, strategically, ecologically, psychologically, militarily. New relationships have
been formed, existing relationships have been strengthened, leaders and
assumptions have been tested, truths have been proven while myths and
lies have crumbled. People and nations all over the world have seen how
quickly they can be robbed of their own security, comfort, well-being;
and they've also seen how powerful they can be as allies when driven by
a cause greater than themselves.

Now, take a moment to reflect on the impact that a Russia transformed into a nation of people who enjoy the same kind of democracy
and freedom that you do, would have on the rest of the world; politically, economically, culturally, strategically, ecologically, psychologically,
militarily.

Clearly this is not just a dream for the people of Russia, but a dream
for the benefit of all citizens of the world.

Often when I am thinking, planning, and dreaming about the work
that lies ahead, I remember the words my grandfather said to me when I
was just four years old, on the day he sent his letter to Brezhnev, the day
he stopped a war from starting between the Soviets and Poland, the same
day he killed he own career by doing so:

"Never be afraid of anyone," he said, as I was falling asleep and he
ruffled my hair.

"Don't go with the flow, serve the country, believe in your cause and
act according to your conscience, no matter what people say."

That's the legacy my grandfather left me. That's what I am doing
now, and what I have been trying hard to do my entire adult life.

Of course, it will be even better if we do this together. The work
starts today. Will you join me?

CHAPTER TWENTY

New Laws, New Constitution, Direct Democracy

One

In Russia, the State Duma at each meeting (which happens three times a week eight months a year!) adopts from thirty to sixty laws and resolutions. That is an order of magnitude of more bills than the U.S. Congress, which passes less than a hundred laws a year.

I think I am not mistaken in saying that the American quality of legislative work is higher.

The U.S. Congress is one of those American institutions that has been stable and unshakable for almost its entire existence.

Americans understand that the three branches of their government (executive, legislative, judicial) are designed to work together to protect them from an excessive concentration of power in any one branch, especially in the executive branch and the presidency.

Even as I write this, Americans are passionately debating recent rulings by their Supreme Court on issues like abortion that many feel indicate the judicial branch has too much power. But the fact that Americans can debate this topic and also have discussions about possible remedies executed by the other two branches validates the checks and balances of their overall system; the very fact of the conflict suggests that the American political system is a real democracy. And, in general, the system meets the expectations and needs of citizens.

I am convinced that a country should be run by people. Not parties. Not the ruling class and not their friends.

This means legislators should only be intermediaries, a mere tool for coordinating laws. And if disputes about laws arise, both citizens and politicians should be given the opportunity to ask each other: "Do we really want this?"

Such a mechanism is necessary.

What's needed is a "safe space" for discussion, debate, and development of effective laws that the Russian people support.

I propose that to make this "safe space" we use a tool that is frequently used in the tech world, called a "sandbox."

A sandbox is a development environment that allows one to isolate and then test code without risk of harming existing code or exposing the existing platform or new code to the dangers of the outside world. So you can experiment and test and experiment with different scenarios and permutations at will, without risk to the status quo.

What I am proposing here is applying the same principle to the process of making laws. We create a judicial sandbox, and we the people get to play together in the sandbox until we are happy together, as a group, that we have developed a new law that is reasonable and acceptable to as many of our fellow citizens as possible, so the law is therefore ready to face a vote.

This is called direct democracy.

After all, the right to produce and vote on laws should not be restricted only to "specially designated people." It's like when laying a path in the park—first look where people have trodden the path, then put asphalt on it. In city planning, this practice of placing the path where the people have already shown they want to go is common; and this "pathway of the people" is called a "desire path." It's giving the people what they really want, what they've proven to themselves and the world that they really desire. In the context of the judicial system, this mindset allows common sense and the will of the people—not the will of some elites—to determine the basis for new laws. No one can arrogate to himself the right to speak on behalf of the people and thereby rise above the law.

Two

I talk often about direct democracy. About power from below. I often talk about the right of so-called "ordinary citizens" to participate in government without encountering barriers. About a real, not a fantastic, opportunity at some point in future to abolish the State Duma and all other parliaments.

And every time I speak of such things there are skeptics among listeners and readers. Some snobbishly brand this "ochlocracy" or mob rule.

Others make technical remarks like:

"How do you imagine it? Have people ever written and adopted laws themselves—without any parliament? Do you think they can write them adequately? And after being written—will they be honored?"

Of course, there are reasons for questions. My proposals require deep and thoughtful, also judicial and technical solutions. But under them there is a practical basis. Both in Russia and outside of it.

Here is an example of how this can work, and in fact did work, in Russia:

I was elected as deputy in Novosibirsk twice: in 2007 and 2011. Novosibirsk is the capital of Siberia and is the third-largest city in Russia.

During the second election campaign, my partner Alena Popova and I created a web tool that later grew into the OpenDuma website, which received the prestigious OSCE Parliamentary Assembly SocialScape international award in 2013 as the best web resource on parliamentary activities.

This was the first site in Russia where you could watch broadcasts of the meetings of the State Duma and make proposals in real time, appealing to particular deputies online. Obviously, Putin's United Russia party usually blocked any initiatives of citizens, but it was a big deal to enable them to speak; and it was met with significant public interest.

But this example, like many examples of special lawmaking applications in other countries, proved that direct democracy really does work.

Of course, most citizens cannot write a proper legal text on their own without the help of professionals, and this model of direct democracy accounts for that.

But we must also acknowledge that today the deputies usually do not write the laws themselves anyway (there are some rare exceptions, but they rather prove the rule). The deputy sets the task, proposing the concept of the law. And then lawyers and their apparatus select the wording and write the bill.

Think about the lawmaking process in your country.

Does it ever frustrate you because it feels like it's inefficient, it's misdirected or misguided, or maybe it's even full of favoritism or corruption, and you never feel as though you actually have any say about it?

Well, you're not alone.

But what if the entire process could be dramatically overhauled in a way that provides unheard of levels of efficiency, transparency, and citizen engagement?

Three

"Oh sure! Sounds great!" you say. "Let me guess? When it comes to lawmaking and even writing a new constitution, there's an app for that?"

Yes.

But let's not allow ourselves to be guilty of oversimplification.

What I am about to describe here is more than just an app for your phone, but like many things today it does all start with an app.

Let's call it "Russian Lawmaker 1.0."

There will be five main modules of our new lawmaking platform:

- Automated, secure collaboration tool with AI for researching, writing, and editing proposed laws
- Secure crowdsourcing tool for allowing citizens to make comments and contributions
- Secure, encrypted voting tool
- Global, encrypted database of laws which have both been passed and failed
- Secure app and website with personalized dashboard for every voter and every lawmaker.

Some of these modules are self-explanatory, but the ability for citizens and lawmakers to collaborate on the preparation of laws and the benefits of creating and maintaining a global database of both successful and failed laws are particularly powerful and disruptive.

When it comes to a global database of successful and failed laws, it's important to first understand that lawmaking is highly technical, and there are already a number of amazing, and incredibly interesting projects for codifying laws in the world.

When we talk about codification; it's not in the technical sense of creating lines of code as a programmer does, but in the sense of digitizing the text and concepts contained in all proposed laws (whether they ultimately pass or fail or are abandoned) to create a database of laws that can be accessed and mined by others, which may include humans as well as innovative new platforms that don't even exist yet, that will bring new tools to lawmaking like blockchain and artificial intelligence.

There are many advantages to codifying the text of all proposed laws; for instance, when you as a citizen want to propose a new law, you can quickly and easily use the platform to research other similar laws that have been written in other parts of your country and even other parts of the world, and then try your hand at creating a first draft of your own law by "copying and pasting" text from the other laws you find. With the addition of AI, the platform can even tell you what to do in order to avoid redundancies or contradictions in the first draft of the legislation you are writing.

Laws can be, and should be, written in the same way as computer software.

It is no coincidence that the pioneer in this area was IBM, with their LegalMation project (which is currently the leading platform for AI-driven litigation). Other start-ups working in this area include Ravel Law, originally funded by the New California Foundation Enterprise Associates and now part of LexisNexis, and Judicata, supported by Facebook cofounder Peter Thiel and Sun cofounder Microsystems Vinod Khosla.

The same platform will eventually be used for the unification of legislation across cities, counties, states, or even internationally. Again using AI, the platform can take an existing law from one place and rewrite it to meet the legal requirements of a new location, for instance, from one U.S. state to another, or from one country to another, by translating both language and legal requirements for the same law into Russian, English, Chinese, Arabic, or Swahili.

This solution also provides a previously unheard-of level of transparency, so everyone knows what everyone else is doing, which makes it much more difficult for anyone to interject favoritism or corruption.

For citizens, this is a way of using technology to give them direct access to, and therefore ownership of, their nation's laws and government.

Four

But this is only part of my plan.

The next step involves "crowdsourcing."

If that term is unfamiliar to you, think about the fundraising platforms GoFundMe and Kickstarter. Both use the power of "the crowd" or a large group of people to achieve a goal.

The goal with Kickstarter is to give anyone the ability to participate in the launch of a new product or service, and the goal with GoFundMe is to give anyone the ability to help raise money for a good cause.

Another great example of crowdsourcing are product reviews on Amazon.com. Members of the crowd buy the product, then review the product; then you as a potential buyer can use the crowdsourced reviews to help you make smarter, better informed purchase decisions.

One last example of crowdsourcing is called "equity crowdfunding" where companies skip traditional fundraising approaches like an IPO or getting money from venture capitalists and go directly to the public (a.k.a. the crowd) to raise capital for their businesses. Many countries around the world now allow businesses to use equity crowdfunding to raise capital. In the United States in 2021, over $1 billion dollars were invested via equity crowdfunding, and that amount is expected to double in 2022.

The same principle of crowdsourcing can also be used to complete tasks such as preparing, discussing, and adopting laws or even drafting and voting to adopt a new constitution.

Meanwhile, it's also important to note that crowdsourcing is a great way to reject a law.

When we developed our system in Novosibirsk, we learned two important lessons:

First, people should definitely be given the opportunity to speak out either in support of or against a law.

Second, sometimes people reject a law because they object to the existing wording even if they agree on the principle of the law itself. So we let people continue to change the wording of the law until it's worded in such a way that a majority votes for it. Or a majority may never vote for it, in which case the law dies unless someone else tries to revive and alter it in a way that it can later get the required votes to become law.

If a citizen, using the Internet, comes up with a legislative initiative, and other citizens, through crowdsourcing, edit it and then discuss it and then vote "for" or "against" the proposal, then I see this as a prototype of the electronic parliament of the future:

- The first step is drafting a bill.
- The second step is the presentation of the bill.
- The third step is mass discussion and collaborative editing.
- The fourth step is citizens voting on the bill.

Everything is like in Parliament. Only the citizens themselves become the legislators.

But it is important to understand: the path to the complete withering away or abolition of Parliament, as an institution that sits in Westminster, the Capitol, or Okhotny Ryad, is not so simple.

It will certainly meet with serious opposition and will take time.

In Russia, in particular, this form of direct democracy will meet lots of resistance.

Why?

Because the elites will push back because it means they lose power. We should also expect both older and less educated groups to initially push back because they are afraid of the technology and/or afraid of another Yeltsin-style disaster.

This is where the *new class* becomes such an important part of our success. Given their comfort with technology and mastery of social media and communications platforms, they can help introduce their fellow citizens to this new form of governance and show others why it's a better path for all of Russia.

Meanwhile, as long as a representative legislature like today's parliament or congress exists, any law proposed to it should first be submitted to the public for online discussion and collaborative editing. Then the parliament, taking into account the public opinions of their constituents, should make a decision.

But as the technological base grows, I am absolutely convinced that parliament will disappear. Everything can be done online with citizens speaking and voting for themselves, instead of having members of parliament (hopefully) voting as citizens wish they would on their behalf.

Five

Perhaps you're now wondering if the ideas of direct democracy and crowdsourcing can be applied to the crucial but daunting process of writing a new constitution?

The answer is yes, and this was proven very successfully by Iceland in 2012.

As you now know, crowdsourcing can be used as a way of collectively writing a text. So, an initiative group of citizens prepares a draft document and places it on the Internet. Then anyone can offer their edits. Other users vote on, approve or reject these changes, and so—in the course of crowdsourcing—they together can create the final text of a constitution.

I really like this method. But most importantly, the example of Iceland's 2012 crowdsourced constitution shows that this is not a fantasy. It's been done. It works. And the whole process was very successful; and at the same time, truly democratic.

Such a working group writing a country's constitution should be absolutely open. We should not trust the writing to some "specialists" appointed "from above" and fulfilling the will of the boss (who is yet another elite).

But who decides who gets to participate?

That's the beauty of it; everyone should be able to participate.

A thousand people? Ten thousand? A million? Yes, as many as want to be part of it.

As far as crowdsourcing goes, it doesn't matter how many people are involved. What's important is that the mechanism for editing and accounting for the amendments is open and accessible and works for everyone who wants to participate.

Thank you again, Iceland, for proving it can work.

Six

But how does it work?

First, you start with a constitutional drafting group that is formed by the political group that took power at the time of the establishment of the new state.

Choosing the members of this constitutional drafting group is critically important; because each member must be sufficiently competent to evaluate proposals according to the degree of their literacy and relevance, but mature and self-aware enough not to impose their own rigid point of view. This will also be a very compact team, whose work is extremely transparent.

And each team member must be able to coherently explain why some proposals can be accepted, while others cannot, based on criteria that's been previously agreed upon.

The group constitutional drafting group has two main tasks:

- First, it draws up the original—the very first—version of the text, so the people have something to discuss and rewrite, supplement and develop in the process of crowdsourcing. It should be expected that the group will change this starting version beyond recognition. But this first draft is very important, as it will set the general tone of the discussion.
- Next, the group sums up all contributions which are made via crowdsourcing, and the group also moderates the discussion among all contributors and observers.

The work of this group is difficult. It conducts an open analysis of the proposals received, edits their language, combines similar thoughts into single formulations and explains why it rejects certain ideas.

Indeed, in the course of the discussion, proposals may be received that are absolutely unacceptable from a legal point of view, which means that they will have to be deleted. But such a filter should be used only in extreme cases.

If the constitution is written by the people, then it will be respected and can be enforced. And the voice of the people is not "advisory," it is mandatory.

Once the text of the new constitution has been discussed, voted on by the people and accepted by them, it cannot be rewritten.

Of course, the new constitution can be amended, via the same crowdsourcing process by which this new constitution was created.

And the end result is a new constitution that is the product of unlimited, free creativity and input of all interested citizens.

Seven

You may have noticed in the previous section that we quickly glossed over something very important: campaigning for and voting on a new law or the new constitution.

Let's take a more in-depth look at that part of the process:

Earlier in this chapter, we used Kickstarter and GoFundMe as examples of crowdfunding.

If you've ever used either of these crowdfunding platforms to raise money, you know that your ultimate success will depend on your ability to drive people to your Kickstarter or GoFundMe page so they can vote for you with their hard-earned cash.

Crowdsourcing a bill or law or constitution works much the same way.

Like a Kickstarter or GoFundMe campaign, a bill or law or new constitution can only be successfully adopted if all political and public groups work hard to educate the public about their side and win the public's approval and votes.

If the votes are split more than 80 to 20, or a minimum threshold of votes for approval is not met, a bill or law or new constitution fails.

In this way, the last word remains with the people.

Eight

Let's say the new constitution has been adopted . . . hurray!

The next thing to happen are free and fair elections based on the rules of the brand-new document.

But wait a minute!

We already witnessed how Boris Yeltsin's supporters drafted a constitution for themselves in 1993. They committed the coup, fully supported by the West, monopolized the power, disabled the parliament and the courts, and delivered all the levers of power to Mr. Putin in 1999—who did not hesitate to use them to his maximum personal benefit.

Looking at some of my colleagues in the Russian opposition, I have zero doubts that this story could be repeated. It has to be a figure of George Washington's integrity and stature to restrain from drafting the new legislation to the benefit of his or her political force. The competition between politicians at the time of the launch of the constitution will be at its maximum, and their feuds can bury the best ideas. So what should we do?

The answer can be given by the Republic of Central Asia—Kyrgyzstan.

In 2010, a small and fragile lady by the name of Roza Otunbayeva became the president of the already independent Kyrgyzstan. But she knew that her country, which had recently survived two coups, needed to form a new, honest, and open political system. She was a compromise between competing and powerful clans.

That's why she agreed to take office for only two years as interim president, with a promise to successfully reset the Kyrgyz statehood, and retire from politics after the end of her term.

And that's what she did.

I think a similar scenario should be implemented in Russia.

Nine

Other figures do not want to let go of control over the discussion of the constitution. "I'm the smartest!"—think those who are dumber. "I have to show who is the leader!"—think those who are afraid that they will not be able to insist on their own. It is necessary that everyone who wants to participate in the discussion is on an equal footing. I am going to make proposals to the draft of the new constitution based on the ideas presented in various chapters of this book. And if people agree with me, they will become part of the new rules of our life. But I cannot and should not insist on them, whatever my position would be after the change of power in Russia.

But the main thing is that we will write our Basic Law together - without any political intermediaries. This is my absolute priority. And also—the maximum delegation of power to the localities, the full empowerment of ordinary people, and the weakening of the political class—the class of professional "representatives of citizens."

Of course, the Basic Law does not need the provisions introduced at Putin's proposal in the current Constitution—promises of the minimum wages, their regular indexations, and all that. They cannot become a universal rule. It's like writing in the constitution that from now on we no longer have the right to tighten our belts, but are obliged to grow richer every new day in comparison with the previous one. Nice, but these are empty promises that undermine the very idea of the Basic Law.

Putin included them as a populist. But he did not dare to include what should be there: the right of citizens of the country to decide on such things. People, if necessary, have the right and should be given the opportunity in each case to vote, for example, whether to lower or raise the retirement age, the minimum wage, index payments, provide benefits to some category of the population, enter into an international conflict or participate in peacekeeping forces, conclude an alliance agreement with another country or join one or another coalition. The constitution should have mechanisms for this participation, and not pre-written answers to all questions.

The tasks of any government should be fixed in the constitution. All its priorities. And the main priority: the person and his or her well-being. The right of every person to a decent life, the inadmissibility of the prosperity of some at the expense of others.

Ten

I want to especially emphasize that I do not think that we will be able to build a free and fair society if we do not guarantee the right of self-determination of the nations who live on the territory of Russia. As well as if those nations that will decide to stay will not form a single political nation.

This is an inevitable stage of development that precedes the departure of nation-states into oblivion. We don't need to jump over it. We remember quite well from the experience of 1917 what happens when one attempts to make such a shortcut. Therefore, I consider it important to repeat:

> **The new system will be free, fair, stable, and safe**
> **only if Russia recognizes itself as a single nation.**

Although this may be contrary to popular belief by some in the West, the nation of Russians is not a vast collection of communities of migrant-hating blond and steely blue-eyed Slavic boys and girls. And it's not just a nation of "Russians" who live within randomly drawn borders and are united only by the fact that they speak Russian and some of them read Dostoevsky.

Instead, I see a nation-family, where "one for all, and all for one."

But there was one day back in 1999 when Yeltsin's family invited just another family to rule Russians. And they forced their will on us, using threats, violence and corruption, and making an honorable life almost impossible without giving into a system of lies and theft. That other family, which intruded, is like the Italian mafia family, the Cosa Nostra, with its godfather—Vladimir Putin. Only for Russians it wasn't a family of mobsters who trapped us into their dark underworld, it was (and still is) mobsters at the head of our own government.

CHAPTER TWENTY-ONE

The Ponomarev Plan—FAQ

1. In this book you call for an interim president to lead the charge to create a new democratic government for Russia once Putin is gone. Who will choose this interim president? And what is the process by which this interim president will be chosen?

If the changes happen from the top, the revolting elites will select the next leader. If they are smart, they will select someone neutral and truly interim, but capable of being the guarantor of changes and normalization of relations with the outside world. The danger, of course, is that they might (and probably will) choose a next leader who is just another Putin. Or worse. Because that will be the best leader for them to choose to protect themselves and their own selfish, autocratic interests. It would be very much like Malenkov who succeeded Stalin (if you remember this name, I really appreciate your command of history, but if you don't—it would just prove my point: nothing changed) or Brezhnev who succeeded Khrushchev.

But after February 2022, my bet is on an uprising by the people, which will bring a new leader and revolutionary government to power. To understand how this is likely to happen, one must abandon one's Western ideas about the transfer of power. This will not be a large, formal ceremony that's planned in advance to take place in front of a large audience of seated dignitaries and lots of TV cameras. The new interim government will take power (preferably peacefully, but most likely not) during the course of this uprising. In that sense, the people will have chosen their new leader and the new government by giving their support for the populist uprising.

Sometimes, the words of the past help us understand and then pave the road to the future:

There are decades when nothing happens;
and there are weeks when decades happen.
—Lenin

Sometimes you have to pick the gun up to put the gun down.
—Malcom X

What country before ever existed a century and half without a rebellion? And what country can preserve its liberties if their rulers are not warned from time to time that their people preserve the spirit of resistance? Let them take arms. The remedy is to set them right as to facts, pardon and pacify them. What signifies a few lives lost in a century or two? The tree of liberty must be refreshed from time to time with the blood of patriots and tyrants.
—Thomas Jefferson

2. Just to be clear, you are calling for a revolution in Russia?
Yes, what we are talking about here is a revolution. The people revolt, and they push new leadership and a new form of government into power, while pushing the old elites out.

And as I have said many times in this book, I am at work day and night to make this revolution and Revolutionary Government happen.

3. For how long have you been thinking that a revolution would be necessary in Russia? And at what point did you realize you could and should be the leader of this revolution?
I've always dreamt of positive change. Revolution, as romantic it sounds for certain people and as scary for others, is just an instrument of change. Before 1991, we were experiencing evolutionary changes of the Soviet Union and hoped for a better life. By 1991, many expectations proved futile, and many illusions were lost. But the energy in society was so high that it blew the USSR apart—and it was the first revolution I witnessed, almost without blood. Just three men died during the August coup. In

1993, there was an unsuccessful attempt of a counterrevolution, which was way more violent—nobody knows its death toll, but for sure it is counted in hundreds of souls. After that, for a decade, I firmly believed that "the limit for the revolutions is over," as the leader of Russian pseu-do-communists suggested. And when I came to politics, when my younger comrades were calling for a revolution, I usually smiled, know-ing there would be none, and that we would need to use parliamentary methods to change the system.

In 2004, Ukraine's Orange Revolution was a true wake-up call for me. It appeared that revolution a) was possible and b) could be peace-ful. In 2005 we almost got to the same point during protests against the monetization of privileges. But in 2008 there was a new president, Medvedev, and many of us decided there could be positive evolution-ary changes. But in 2011, when Medvedev and Putin announced they were going to swap positions, and that they actually fooled the whole nation about their arrangement, my last hopes for peaceful resolution were gone. It became clear that it would take a revolution to bring about the necessary changes. But I never saw anyone who could actually lead the organizational efforts to make that happen, so I am working in this direction myself.

4. Do the people of Russia want a revolution? Are they ready for a revolution?

Usually, nobody but a very limited circle of people want revolutions, wars, or violence. Most people prefer a stable and peaceful life. Unfortunately, there are times when one has to fight for the ability to maintain that stable and peaceful life, and Russia is at this moment in its history now; so the question is when this recognition becomes common knowledge in the country. I believe it will happen at the very moment Russians see a clear and realistic alternative to Putin. You, as the reader, have a role to play in this too; you can add fuel to the fire by using tools like social media and also protesting in your own country to make sure Russians see that the world is with them as they take whatever steps are necessary to fight against Putin.

5. What happens to the current Parliament once Putin is gone and there is a new interim president?

There is no Parliament in Russia at this moment, it is just a decoration.

The Constitution will be suspended, and during the transition period the transitional government will be the only legitimate source of power. It will reset and re-create the political system, as described here in this book.

As an example of how this will work, look to the successful revolutionary changes of governments in other nations:

a. Poland was transformed via a peaceful "velvet" revolution driven by the Polish Round Table Talks that created a transitional government that existed for two years and prepared free and fair elections.

b. The April 25th [1974] Revolution in Portugal, or *Revolução dos Cravos*—an example of a successful antifascist military coup that was supported by the majority of people and which eventually led to democratic elections after a two-year transitional period.

c. The twenty-one-year reign of Ferdinando Marcos in Philippines was ended with an unsuccessful military coup that was superseded by a popular uprising, which we now know as Yellow Revolution.

6. What happens to the current court system and all the existing judges once Putin is gone and there is a new interim president?

The Russian opposition currently has an explicit list of judges that were involved in political repressions. They, as well as the management of the courts where they worked, are the subject of lustrations. The rest may reapply to the positions of the judge; and if they are elected, they can continue.

7. What are "lustrations"?

For readers in the West, the idea of lustrations may be foreign, so let me explain it this way:

History does not know examples of successful revolutions and even peaceful transformations that are done *only by* people who are not connected with the current elites.

At some point, "specialists" from the toppling regime appear who want to come to the side of the winners. I don't want to call them rats, but they are the first to escape from a sinking ship and look for a new vessel for travel. And that's good—if they really help us to make the change, it should be appreciated.

But victory usually has a lot of fathers. Most of them—just pretending. And also, there is a problem of numerous people who just by being on certain government jobs under Putin supported and facilitated crimes against Ukrainians (and Russians as well!) that simply cannot be forgotten.

Lustrations, therefore, are legislative restrictions for the political elite of the previous government, for the exercise of active and passive suffrage, as well as the right to participate in the management of state affairs. They are introduced after the change of power. More precisely, after the revolution.

The authorities, possessing political will and inspired by the idea, must be aware that old people who have appropriated the status of "elite," especially in a situation like in Russia, where arbitrariness and decay have reached enormous proportions, cannot and should not occupy positions in the state.

But lustration is not a punishment. It is, on the contrary, in conditions when there are too many potential and accomplished violators, the refusal of punishment, which risks developing into a "witch hunt," in exchange for an end to sabotage. Cleaning up the reputation of the authorities from the dirty stains of the past. In this sense, lustration is an act of both justice and also mercy.

Postwar Germany and the countries of Eastern Europe went through this experience after the collapse of their totalitarian regimes, deciding: how to close the path to power for those who were involved in atrocities? What to do with the designers, ideologists, and propagandists of the regime? And what about those who ordered the dispersal of popular demonstrations, orders for torture and unjust sentences? How to deal with perpetrators—those who beat protesters; kidnapped oppositionists; searched, arrested, and interrogated; lied to the court? With those who passed unlawful sentences? And with those who secretly helped the special services? Should we dissolve the services themselves? Should we open their archives? Should ruling parties be banned? What about regime symbols? How to change a compromised control apparatus? How about making the new one efficient? And at the same time, do not turn restrictions into an instrument of political struggle and settling scores.

The first lustration law in Eastern Europe was adopted in Czechoslovakia in 1991: it was called "A law prescribing certain additional necessary prerequisites for taking certain elected and appointed positions in state bodies and organizations." In the same year, Latvia and Lithuania did it. Bulgaria in 1992. Hungary in 1994. A year later, Albania and Estonia. Poland in 1997. Serbia in 2003. And in each of these revolutions, the lustrations were all noticeably different. For example, in the Czech Republic, lustration affected not only about a third of judges who "violated the principle of impartiality and fairness" and 63% of prosecutors or employees of law enforcement agencies, but also media workers, and, in Bulgaria, university professors.

It is believed that in Eastern Europe lustration laws worked successfully where the nomenklatura was completely deprived of influence. I am also a supporter of this approach. For those who were members of Putin's "United Russia" party, for instance, and did not leave it before the start of changes? For those who were members of the executive branch that violated the rights of citizens, and did not repent? Didn't resign before the change of power? Sorry, you already chose which side you're on.

There are also examples of completely unsuccessful lustration. For example, in Iraq, after the fall of Saddam Hussein's regime, the lustration of members of the Ba'ath Party led to the creation of a powerful armed opposition to the new government, which even the occupying American troops could not defeat. This did not bring closer the settlement and normalization of life in the country, but greatly pushed them back. But I do not think that it is possible to compare the party of timid bureaucrats of Putin's "United Russia" party and the paramilitary and mass party of the Arab socialists, who went through the crucible of many wars and revolutions.

There are many people who should be given a chance to go over to the side of good. There are a lot of people who justify themselves with the best of intentions. I am categorically against forgiveness, but national-party defamation is unacceptable. It shouldn't be. Let everyone decide who they are with: do they support this new system, are they for this new power, power without corruption?

I repeat: I am not advocating for the idea of total forgiveness. The lesson of 1991 is before our eyes: people wanted to get rid of the rotten and deceitful elite, hiding behind communist ideals, and save a great country. As a result, the USSR was destroyed, but the elite remained in power, abandoned ethical constraints, and collaborated to produce a self-serving system of privatization of national wealth.

And let me emphasize: this does not mean indiscriminate plantings and "witch hunts." Lustration is a compromise, an agreement: you are no longer trying to manage us, and we are not interested in the affairs that you were involved in when you were at the helm. It cannot be selective, but must cover all people of a certain status voluntarily obtained by them: say, in 1991 it could be members and employees of the apparatus of the CPSU or Communist Party of the Soviet Union committees at all levels.

The level of confrontation and mutual distrust in society has now exceeded all reasonable limits. It is impossible to restore citizens' trust in bureaucrats without lustration. But everything must be done so that as many officials, functionaries, and other servants of power as possible come to their senses and come over to the side of good. They need to lend a hand, not hide behind false principles.

8. What happens to the existing military once Putin is gone and there is a new interim president?
Those who committed atrocities in Ukraine, in Syria, in Georgia, and in Chechnya should be given to the international court for a fair trial. As for the rest—I see the Russian military reformed to the standards of NATO and becoming part of the organization.

9. What happens to all the oligarchs and all of Putin's supporters once he is gone and there is a new interim president?
Supporters—it is not an official position or title. The same is true for the oligarchs. Members of United Russia and Putin's government structures should be lustrated—not punished, but restricted from getting any government jobs or government financing in the future. As for large businesses—if they made money by themselves, we will praise and encourage them. If they made money by illegal privatization and/or other benefits and gifts from the state—such deals will be reversed. And we will definitely be watching to ensure that no large business can become oligarchic, by restricting their control over media and political parties and restricting their access to actual government influence.

10. The foreword of this book is a stunning reminder of how far Putin has fallen from his own ideals and vision for the future of Russia. How can the Russian people be sure that you, as the interim

president, won't turn out to be another Putin? Or another Yeltsin? Or someone who will decide you should be "president" for life?

The interim president (or the leader of the revolutionary government) must agree to remain president only for a short, clearly defined period of time. And also agree at the same time to never participate in the political system again as a player in the future political system, or leading any political party or taking part in any elections. These agreements will be bound by contract and law. As you know from reading this far, I propose that the interim president serve in that capacity for a period of two years. When the transition period is over, the interim president will follow the law and automatically step down. This ensures the new Constitution and new laws will not be drafted to support the interim president's personal ambitions and plans, like Yeltsin and Putin did.

11. How can the Russian people be sure this "new plan" won't just be another failure like the plans they got from Gorbachev, Yeltsin, and Putin?

Gorbachev and Yeltsin were party apparatchiks. Putin was a KGB officer selected by party apparatchik. How could we expect they would deliver on democratic reforms? I am proposing that democracy should be built by people themselves represented by individuals of a strong freedom fighter background.

12. Logistically, how does this work . . . what happens on the day Putin is gone? And what happens the day after that? And the day after that?

It is tempting to say, "Oh, it will happen like this, and this, and this. Then this will happen and then this will happen and then this will happen."

But that's not how a revolution works. Yes, there is a plan. Will I tell you the plan? Of course not.

And will the plan be executed exactly as written? Of course not.

Broadly speaking, what will happen is that the Russian people themselves will take to the streets and take to the internet and demand change and new leadership. Their efforts will be passionately supported by others around the world; and they will also take to the streets and the internet to show their support. The leadership of the Russian peoples' chosen Revolutionary Government will assume the collective leadership of the country. They will appoint the new ministers and the new governors of the regions. On the very first day important decrees on lustration and key reforms of the political system will be announced. The war in Ukraine will stop and the army will retreat to positions of February 2014. Then the process of resetting the country that is outlined in this book will continue to be initiated.

13. Is it possible this transition from Putin and Putinism to democracy can be done without violence and bloodshed?
Theoretically yes. Practically, I am afraid the process has gone too far. But I will do my best to minimize the violence. The lustration act could be the key for that.

14. Besides you and your team, are there others who are also preparing for this?
Yes, many Russians both inside and outside of Russia are getting ready. Many Russians who have left the country are preparing to return. Leaders of other nations are also getting ready. And of course, as we have all seen, people worldwide who are supporting Ukraine are also signaling that they are prepared to support a new Russia that is democratic and follows the rule of law. Meanwhile, most Russians, both in the opposition and in the government and ordinary people are waiting and watching, not yet understanding how they can influence the outcome. Others, including myself, are actively fighting; and an immensely important part of our job is to show the people what we must do next together.

15. How do we know this isn't yet another "regime change" program being supported by another world superpower?
It is not. Firstly, other countries are quite afraid of Putin and Russian nukes so they are afraid to support regime change just as they have been afraid to cross a red line with Russia in their support of Ukraine. These dramatic changes in Russia are for Russians to make. We were never anyone's puppets and will never be. Period.

16. Successful revolutions all have names like the February Revolution, the Velvet Revolution, the Mexican Revolution. Ukraine has had two successful revolutions in just the last twenty years; the Orange Revolution and the Maidan Revolution. When a revolution

has a name, it adds legitimacy and gravitas. Often the name helps explain the cause. The name of a revolution often becomes a rallying cry for supporters. Does the Russian revolution we are discussing here have a name?

Yes. It is the New Russian Revolution.

17. And you are the leader of the New Russian Revolution?

Yes.

CONCLUSION

Does Putin Have to Die?

One

Now that we've traveled through these pages of history, and the current state of Russia, and Putin and Putinism together, it's time to answer the question that's been hanging around like an eight-hundred-pound gorilla in the room:

"Does Putin have to die?"

Obviously, this question is one designed for speculation and debate. It is for each of us to answer for ourselves, given our new knowledge and understanding.

For me, the answer is a qualified, "No."

I'd like to say that I don't wish that anyone should have to die. But as I write this, U.S. President Joe Biden has just announced that al-Qaeda leader Ayman al-Zawahiri has been killed in a U.S. drone strike in Kabul.

In response, the *Washington Post* reported:

News that Ayman al-Zawahiri, the leader of al-Qaeda, was killed in Kabul in a CIA drone operation over the weekend drew celebration from Democrats and Republicans in the United States as well as from some foreign governments.

In his remarks, President Biden said: "Justice has been delivered."

This, of course, opens the debate: Is Putin as bad or worse than Ayman al-Zawahiri?

This is a worthy debate, but since we're at the end of this book let's save it for another day—or perhaps even for another book.

But it does make me suggest that we reframe the question like this: "Does Putin have to go?"

Then the answer can only be "Yes. Putin has to go."

Does he have to die?

Truthfully, I think that is up to him.

There is no doubt in my mind that Putin will be gone very soon. I have said it many times and in the most public of places; over and over again, for instance, on U.S. and European TV.

Will he be gone by his own hand, or the hand of another?

That I cannot say.

If he leaves very soon, and peacefully, and extracts himself fully from all Russian affairs and Russian life (which I assume would include successfully negotiating freedom for himself and pardons for all of his crimes), then maybe he can escape with his life.

As the recipient of countless riches from many Russian oligarchs, he has many places he can go and hide around the world with more money than he could ever spend in his, his children's, or even his grandchildren's lifetimes, and buy all the comfort and security he could ever want or need until the end of time.

However, if he chooses *not* to go, then I think that yes, he must die.

But this is not my decision or your decision to make for him. It is his decision to make for himself.

I think there are many inside Russia, and even inside his own inner circle, who are prepared to execute this task at the first opportunity to do so.

Of course, it would also be fair of you to ask, "Would you, Ponomarev, pull the trigger, given the chance?"

Truthfully, I doubt that Putin's people would actually allow for such a moment to come. Not that they will defend him—rather, when the situation starts to fall apart around them, they will pull the trigger themselves. Putin knows too much about too many for him to live without endangering everyone else who was once around him.

Two

The first chapter of this book begins with these words:

Imagine Putin's death.

It doesn't matter from what: coronavirus, a brick falls on his head, or now, during his unsuccessful war in Ukraine, he takes a bullet in the head from an insider. Perhaps there's even a rope involved.

Now, as we approach the end of this book, let's imagine that Putin's death is upon us.

So, what's next?

Three

At the beginning of the twentieth century, Vladimir Gilyarovsky wrote the famous couplet:

> **There is no law in Russia.**
> **There is a pole.**
> **And on its top sits a crown.**

It was a bitter mockery of the arbitrariness of the courts, which often carried out the instructions of the executive authorities in the autocratic empire, where until 1905 there was no parliament, and those who demanded its creation and called for separation of powers, the state considered its enemies.

Meanwhile, now the courts are even worse and even more controlled by the autocratic authorities.

By that time, the principle of separation of powers had not only been known to the world for a long time, but also lay at the basis of the organization of many states.

This concept was developed in the seventeenth and eighteenth centuries by the Enlightenment philosophers John Locke and Charles Montesquieu.

Within it, the power in the state is divided into three branches—legislative, executive, and judicial—independent of each other. And the violation of their independence, for example, the independence of the court, is among the abuses.

The principle of separation of powers is not absolute.

Most likely, it will lose its relevance in the transition to direct democracy.

Then all power institutions vertically, and all regions and municipalities horizontally, will receive full autonomy from each other within the framework of their functional duties.

Of course, in modern representative democracy, it is mandatory, and guaranteed that the government (executive branch) cannot dictate to people's representatives (deputies) and judges.

John Locke offers this approach back in the seventeenth century, because those in power will always use their status "not for the good of those who are under it, but for his own private, separate advantage. When the governor, however entitled, makes not the law, but his will, the rule, and his commands and actions are not directed to the preservation of the properties of his people, but the satisfaction of his own ambition, revenge, covetousness, or any other irregular passion."

He also states that "force, or a declared design of force upon the person of another, where there is no common superior on earth to appeal to for relief, is the state of war; and it is the want of such an appeal gives a man the right of war even against an aggressor, though he be in society and a fellow-subject. Thus, a thief whom I cannot harm, but by appeal to the law, for having stolen all that I am worth, I may kill when he sets on me to rob me, because the law, which was made for my preservation, where it cannot interpose to secure my life from present force, permits me my own defense and a liberty to kill the aggressor."

That is not the ideologue of Bolshevism, Lenin, but the creator of the theory of bourgeois liberalism, Locke, who for the first time speaks of a civil war, i.e., war of unjustly offended people against those in power.

As a pretext for it, he speaks of unjust judges.

Without going far into history and without going into details, let me remind you of the essence of the matter:

In democratic societies, parliament sets the rules (laws) for society as a whole and develops plans for the executive branch.

The executive (government) implements them.

And the interests of citizens are protected by the court; and the court also controls that everyone lives by the rules.

The independence of the judiciary as well as the rule of law are two key principles of a society based on law.

Montesquieu writes that "no tyranny is more cruel than that which is practiced in the shadow of the law and with the trappings of justice:

that is, one would drown the unfortunate by the very plank by which he would hope to be saved."

There are many examples of laws that are far from justice. One of the classic examples is the Holocaust, most of which was justified with German thoroughness by the laws of the Third Reich.

For far too long, Russia has been too far on the wrong side of the continuum from democracy to dictatorship. It's time for this to end.

Accomplishing this will require heroic strength and fortitude from many; from those who lead on a national down to a local level, to the typical Russian family who joins the movement because they, too, believe there must be something better than the status quo; that even when the struggles of a life of one's own self-determination are their greatest, it's still better than living under the boot of a cruel, corrupt, autocratic ruler.

But this transition can be done. And I am here for it.

Four

There are examples. Including very recent ones.

Although not a perfect analogy, South Africa's transition away from apartheid in the past is worthy of consideration despite of all problems that the country walked into after the first years of euphoria.

Apartheid was, at its core, forty-six years of the policy of officially dividing the country's population into a privileged white community and a discriminated black majority. In reality, racism was brought to that land by the Europeans and was over 100 years old.

During this time the society was deeply divided. The wall of mutual fear, distrust, and hatred between blacks and whites was strong, high, and almost impenetrable. Black rights communist activist Nelson Mandela had to deal with this situation after his release in 1990 from prison, where he spent twenty-seven years out of his life sentence. Four years later, in 1994, he was elected president. And in this post, he immediately ran into an ocean of problems.

Along with the fight against crime and poverty, he sought the reconciliation of the people and races living in the country. His goal was their transformation into a single nation of South Africans, although relations between whites and blacks were at risk of coming close to civil war.

Even his bodyguards—white professionals from the special forces and black bodyguards from the African National Congress party—did not trust each other.

Meanwhile, Mandela began to unify the country by calling on white and black administration officials to work together: "If we unite, our country will become a beacon of light in this world."

But South Africa was not only caught in a whirlwind of change. Life went on as usual, and the country participated in international rugby championships. Mandela noticed that during the match between his country and England, whites supported the national team, and blacks supported the English. As he did himself by the time he went to prison many years before. Because almost all the players on the South African team were white.

And now South Africa was losing the match. With a high margin.

But Mandela believed the next World Cup should take place there. So he told the sports committee that had decided to disband the South African national team, "Now is not the time for petty revenge," and urged them to cancel the decision.

And then he invited the captain of the national team, the blond Afrikaner François Pinaar, for tea.

Mandela told him: "We need inspiration, François, to build our nation." And he convinced the team's captain that for the good of the country, they needed to win.

The national team began training, although no one was sure that the game could ever unite a people split by years of racial prejudice.

But François believed the president. And in the opening match, he led his team mates to victory over the world champions, Australia, and then over Samoa. Almost the whole country was already rooting for the team, whom Mandela introduced, saying, "This is my family." His white and black guards became one team—they played rugby together. And South Africa defeated France and advanced to the final, where they played the undefeated New Zealand.

The team faced the final match in front of a billion viewers. On the way to the match, Mandela said, "Our country yearns for greatness," and François thought about how noble it was—after thirty years in a tiny cell, Mandela had forgiven those who put him there.

This most intense match ended with a powerful drop goal from Afrikaner Joel Stransky a few seconds before the end. The victory of South Africa with a score of 15:12 delighted both blacks and whites. And although this was not a complete victory on the path to building a nation, it was an important step on the way to it.

Each nation has its own path to unity. Before history makes a new turn, we will walk along ours.

Five

On this very difficult path, the first thing to do is to restore the management of the country.

In Russia, it was effectively destroyed by Putin's "vertical of power," which actually deprived the leaders of regions and cities of the ability to manage resources and make independent decisions. They no longer know how to do it.

So, we will take the next step—we'll create a limited set of rules based on values that are shared by most of the people, and that are actually enforced on everyone.

Then we can gradually upgrade the system, moving toward maximum decentralization, internationalization, direct democracy and the transfer of the maximum possible power to non-profit, non-state, extra-territorial, self-regulatory organizations and communities, along the lines that I have described in this book.

Our new Russia will be especially supportive of the emerging *new class*, the objectives of scientific and technological progress, and the goals of economic prosperity. We will build a country that will reward the commitment and creativity of a person, regardless of his or her origin, religion, or wealth.

Maintenance of order plays a huge role during this period.

I have always been skeptical about the ideas of forgiveness, nonviolence, and the like.

I remember how the Inquisition operated under the flags of Christian forgiveness, and the Conquistadors slaughtered entire nations of the New World.

As a result of the Indian policy of nonviolence, a huge country fell apart, and hundreds of millions of people shed each other's blood.

**During a political struggle,
turning to violence is a sign of a system's failure.
It is the job of the state to preserve the integrity of the country,
prevent great bloodshed and injustice,
protect the weak, and uphold common values.**

To protect the nation should be the duty of every citizen in the new Russia. Every officer of the state should be ready to use violence to enforce the Constitution and uphold people's rights. But if a politician is not doing it for the "happiness for everyone," then for me he or she is unworthy of power.

To be candid, I have changed my own attitude about violence several times over the course of my life.

Once upon a time, Nelson Mandela was also influenced by the powerful personality of Mahatma Gandhi. However, after the unexpected shooting of a peaceful black protest in Sharpeville in 1960, he switched to guerrilla tactics against the government.

In 1961, he led the armed wing of the black party, the African National Congress.

The acts of sabotage organized by him were aimed at reducing the investment attractiveness of South Africa, and were aimed at reducing the efficiency of the national economy.

Mandela was captured, spent twenty-seven years behind bars, and was released only in 1990.

After that, he did not come to power immediately, but only after four years, which he spent in tense negotiations with the white president of South Africa, Frederick de Klerk.

Despite tense personal relationships and a contested election, which Mandela won by a landslide 62%, he offered de Klerk the vice presidency.

It was an eloquent gesture of reconciliation toward the white minority.

That is, Mandela, a militant who spent many years in prison, the head of an organization recognized by the Western world as terrorist (because of this, the Nobel laureate and holder of orders from around the world for eighteen years after his release, until 2008, was allowed to travel to the United States only on personal invitation of the Secretary of State), who received life sentences along with his associates, suddenly showed mercy to those who hunted, tortured, and tried to kill him and his comrades.

How is this possible? What prompted him to do this?

State wisdom, leaving no room for fanaticism.

Political foresight that helps to avoid adventures.

And the ability to think strategically, removing insignificant things from the agenda.

And vision informed by a dream.

Six

In 2012, parliamentary elections were held in Georgia. To the surprise of many, the ruling party of President Mikheil Saakashvili lost in a tough competition.

Despite numerous predictions of his haters, the "Caucasian dictator" recognized the results of the elections, and did not try to "twist" a few extra percentage points, which could have decided the outcome of the whole battle.

For the first time in the history of this country, there was a peaceful change of power.

And what was the first thing the new government did?

It opened criminal cases against most of the prominent figures from among his predecessors.

The crowd went on to cheer the repression: "Crucify them! Rogues! There are no honest people in power!"

Saakashvili's rating went down sharply, and the winners' went up.. And what is the result?

The conclusion that other politicians will make is obvious—under no circumstance should anyone ever give up power, because those who come to replace you will hang all the sins on you.

Will there be a peaceful change of power in Georgia after this?

I hope so, but I doubt it.

Mandela, after all those years in prison, sensed and understood this very well.

He was not a megalomaniac. He wanted to build a stable political system in the present, and for the future, in the interest of the majority.

This was his majority—the black population of South Africa.

However, he understood that without reconciliation with the white minority, chaos would ensue in the country. Despite all the crimes the whites committed against blacks.

And he acted wisely in choosing a difficult but necessary reconciliation.

Seven

Although South Africa continues to experience tremendous political and economic difficulties, at the same time it sets an example for the whole world.

Meanwhile, in Russia, things are much more complicated.

In South Africa, where belonging to political camps was almost unequivocally determined by the color of one's skin, which cannot be changed even by dozens of plastic surgeries, we have a whole caste of people who were hard-core "communists" until 1991, became ardent "democrats" in the 1990s, and turned into staunch "conservatives" in the 2000s.

This speaks of a very high degree of "political flexibility," and in simple terms unscrupulousness, cynicism, and hypocrisy of a huge part of the so-called "political class."

Therefore, without unleashing repression and without starting a witch hunt, after the victory and the beginning of the construction of the state of truth, we, nevertheless, will have to carry out lustration.

That is, to limit the active and passive suffrage of figures, officials and officers of law enforcement agencies of the former regime, who stained themselves with theft, corruption, participation in lawlessness, torture, persecution of oppositionists, making unjust decisions and custom-made sentences.

We should also deprive them of the right to ever participate in the management of state affairs. But there should be no direct repression. It would be a great deal of national reconciliation: no more meddling with the state for the forgiveness of the past.

Otherwise, our project will be forced, with much greater difficulty, and perhaps with sacrifices, to overcome secret but powerful resistance, which will seriously slow down the change in the life of the people for the better.

Thieves, embezzlers of public funds and crooks, who have stuck around the pole of the power vertical today, must be excommunicated from the feeder once and for all. Those who commited war crimes, officers from the "centers for combating extremism" and other headsmen will be jailed. But the desire for revenge should not dominate our hearts.

As well as a sense of personal hostility to certain individuals.

Yes, there is *a political* calculation, but there is also a *human one.*

I am a politician and should be driven by the emotions of my constituents; but rational calculation still always comes first for me.

And this does not allow me to be guided by prejudices and myths. Only by considerations of public interest, and the upbringing that my parents gave me.

The actions of the new power of the *new class* will be dictated not by emotions, but by ideas of justice and our common good.

We must go forward.

We must think about the future.

We must rely on the examples of the heroes of the past, such as Nelson Mandela.

Reading about this great man, I often wondered: "How does he have so much stamina? Such immense confidence in the final victory?"

Mandela himself answered this question that both in the most difficult moments and in moments of happiness, he was given new strength by a poem by the English poet William Henley: "Invictus" in Latin, and "Unconquered" in English.

He once shared this poem with the rugby player Pinaar, along with the task of defeating and uniting the South African nation.

So this is how I end this book:

> *Out of the night that covers me,*
> *Black as the pit from pole to pole,*
> *I thank whatever gods may be*
> *For my unconquerable soul.*
>
> *In the fell clutch of circumstance*
> *I have not winced nor cried aloud.*
> *Under the bludgeonings of chance*
> *My head is bloody, but unbowed.*
>
> *Beyond this place of wrath and tears*
> *Looms but the Horror of the shade,*
> *And yet the menace of the years*
> *Finds and shall find me unafraid.*
>
> *It matters not how strait the gate,*
> *How charged with punishments the scroll,*
> *I am the master of my fate,*
> *I am the captain of my soul.*

Novosibirsk, Moscow, Riga, Barnaul, Boston, Washington, Kyiv